Cornell Studies in Civil Liberty

Double Jeopardy

THE DEVELOPMENT OF A LEGAL

AND SOCIAL POLICY

Double Jeopardy

THE DEVELOPMENT OF A LEGAL AND SOCIAL POLICY

Jay A. Sigler

Cornell University Press » « *Ithaca, New York*

First published 1969

Library of Congress Catalog Card Number: 69-15673

Printed in the United States of America
by Vail-Ballou Press, Inc., Binghamton, N.Y.

»«

Preface

The principle that no one shall be put twice in jeopardy for the same offense has been declared by many jurists to be a part of the universal law of reason, justice, and conscience.[1] Blackstone, Coke, Chitty, and innumerable other commentators have expressed the view. It has been said that the right not to be put in jeopardy a second time is as essential as the right to a trial by jury, if not more important.[2] Whatever the higher source of the doctrine, it is very much a part of the law of American constitutions, enshrined, together with more familiar rights, in the fifth amendment to the federal constitution. Few provisions of the Bill of Rights have been more frequently litigated, but the mere volume of activity has not cast much light upon the meaning of the concept of double jeopardy.

The American Bar Association has recently joined the growing chorus of critics who call for a re-examination "to see just where we should go, just whether these ingrained principles that are in the common law ought to be thrown out of consideration, or whether or not we should do something either administratively or otherwise to give some solace to the poor criminal."[3] Doubt has been cast upon the fundamental character of the doctrine by the language of some

[1] *United States* v. *Keen,* 27 F. Cas. 510, 686 (No. 15) (1839), and *United States* v. *Parcon,* 6 Phil. 632 (1906), among others.

[2] *State* v. *Panchuck,* 53 N.D. 669, 207 N.W. 991 (1926).

[3] American Bar Association, Section of Criminal Law, *Proceedings,* ed. Hickman (Chicago: American Bar Center, 1959), pp. 52–53. This report was spurred by the unfavorable reaction to the *Bartkus* and *Abbate* cases, mentioned below.

v

recent Supreme Court opinions. A time to take stock may be at hand.

It may be that the doctrine of double jeopardy is not even a rule of law which is capable of delineation by hard and fast rules without causing injustice to the defendant or creating obstacles for those branches of government charged with the enforcement of the criminal law. If one or the other conclusion is justified by the observations to be made in this volume, then the usefulness of the doctrine may be said to have diminished with the years and double jeopardy could be decently ignored henceforth.

But since this treatise rests upon the belief that "the doctrine is nothing more than the declaration of an ancient and well-established public policy,"[4] the history and development of double jeopardy as a legal and social policy as well as its present application in the fifty-one jurisdictions in the United States must be traced. To gain perspective, the study compares the policy with the practice in other nations; to discern the operative effect of the policy, it emphasizes the role of the prosecutor who shapes the criminal indictment, since it is he who is circumscribed by double jeopardy. The changing dimensions of the problem in its modern context require, also, a consideration of the possibilities of doctrinal reform.

The approach of this study will be to stress the policy formulation of double jeopardy as well as the social purposes served by it. Such a technique is not new,[5] but it has rarely been applied to constitutional concepts, even though as a subsidiary concern many writers have touched upon some of the policy issues underlying those concepts. The approach is potentially useful for the examination of other constitutional clauses, and may prove of some value in such studies. Its advantage is that it provides a research method which is a keen critical tool and suggests, as well, the avenues of possible reform. It seems to follow the precepts of sociological jurisprudence, the currently dominant and most productive contemporary legal philosophy.

[4] "Double Jeopardy," 24 *Minn. L. Rev.* 561 (1940), ed. n.

[5] See McDougal, "Law as a Process of Decision: A Policy-Oriented Approach to Legal Study," 1 *Natural L.F.* 53 (1956).

Certain consistent features of double jeopardy appear when a policy analysis is employed. Such an analysis reveals that double jeopardy arose as a common law doctrine only after the criminal law had developed to a sophisticated stage and after the prosecution of criminal offenses had become a matter of public responsibility. A policy approach to the American formulation of double jeopardy demonstrates that policy-making has been left to the courts because the legislatures have neglected to consider the effect of increasing the number of punishable acts. In response to the burden placed upon them, American courts created formulas which could restrict the prosecutor's discretion through the use of the double jeopardy clause. The experiences of other nations suggest that many of the problems of double jeopardy could be solved by legislative codification of substantive criminal law. One persistent thread runs through the entire analysis: the observation that double jeopardy issues precede all matters of substantive criminal law when possibilities of multiple incrimination are presented and that the purpose of double jeopardy policy is to restrict the prosecution by applying judicial standards of interpretation of legislative intent, even in the absence of any actual intent.

In the construction of this project, many research designs have been considered and rejected for reasons to be indicated below. Perhaps the best approach would be an empirical study under controlled conditions, but no legal laboratory is, as yet, available.[6] The best that can be done is to make crude comparisons between states with differing views of the doctrine. But criminal statistics are not so trustworthy as to permit many assumptions to be derived from them. Perhaps consulting the popular will would help clarify the problem. Such sociological studies as have been undertaken, however, show sharp divergencies in public expectations of legal results, especially in the punishment of crime.[7] There is an observable dis-

---

[6] Such a study, of bad check law, was made along limited lines by Beutel in *Some Potentialities of Experimental Jurisprudence as a New Branch of Social Science* (Lincoln, Neb., 1957).

[7] Rose and Prell, "Does the Punishment Fit the Crime?" 61 *Am. J. Soc.* 259 (1955).

crepancy in the law itself, the application of the law, and popular judgment as to how the law should be applied. The first two factors being more constant, the concentration here will be upon them.

Another alternative approach is concerned "with the socio-psychological dimension of the formal decision-making behavior" of the judges, of "the *motivations* which lead individual members of this small group to choose, in their conjoint voting behavior, to select certain alternatives." [8] Since this study is not concerned so much with judicial motivations, or even with predicting judicial behavior, as much as it is with describing the paths the law has followed as operative public policy, this approach is not too helpful. It may provide aid in discerning the behavior of the public prosecutor, but scalograms and mathematical tables are not useful in this regard. For the same reason, the utilization of factor analysis and voting behavior has been slight.[9]

Similarly, this work is not a study of bloc voting in the Supreme Court, nor are supreme courts emphasized. Voting cohesiveness as revealed by bloc-voting studies does not advance the study of double jeopardy policy appreciably.[10] Terms employed by bloc analysts, such as "civil libertarian," are not of much significance in the double jeopardy area.

The emphasis here will be upon "a study of law in action as well as law in the books, an insistence upon justice through rules in contrast to abstractly just rules," [11] as proposed by Dean Pound over thirty years ago in calling for a unification of the social sciences to clarify problems of the criminal law. Jerome Hall, leading jurisprudent and criminologist, has insisted, too, that integration of the social disciplines to solve a social problem is needed to permit "the

[8] Schubert, *Qualitative Analysis of Judicial Behavior* (Glencoe, Ill., 1959), p. 11.

[9] See Thurstone and Degan, *A Factorial Study of the Supreme Court* (Psychometric Laboratory Report No. 64) (Chicago, 1951), pp. 1–7.

[10] See Pritchett, *The Roosevelt Court: A Study in Judicial Politics and Values* (New York, 1948), which uses this approach with great perception, as do others of his studies.

[11] Pound, *Criminal Justice in America* (New York, 1930), p. 211.

viii

specific perceptions [to] cumulate and fuse into an integrated perception of the object." [12] Materials from history, law, comparative law, political science, and criminology have been utilized here with the intention of shedding light upon a constitutional liberty that is threatened with becoming an antique.

The bulk of data which had to be sifted in order to employ this approach required some selective scheme to prune away repetitious detail. Accordingly, long lists of citations of cases and statutes have been kept to a minimum. Well-settled areas of double jeopardy law are omitted, in large part, since they present no problem. The legal encyclopedias, which provide a brief, uncritical overview of double jeopardy, are adequate for the use of the practicing lawyer, but are of slight value to the more critical jurist or scholar. This, then, is not an encyclopedia of double jeopardy law.

The original meaning of the term "jeopardy" was that of a divided game, uncertain chance, or a general uncertainty, and the phrase was used to describe the playing of chess or similar games.[13] The word may have stemmed from the French *perdre*, to lose, which may have become considerably altered when anglicized. The notion of a risk of loss, of harm or of death, of an undecided state of affairs, became attached to the early connotation of the word. This negative significance still clings to the legal concept of double jeopardy so far as its effective implementation as a social policy is concerned. Its limits are vague. The chance element, despite centuries of legal commentary, plays a considerable role. Since "jeopardy" still involves a risk of harm, even of death, it seems desirable to reduce the risk aspect by a reconsideration of the contours of double jeopardy.

In any serious research the effort to remain objective and aloof from personal preferences is a necessary ingredient. Whenever conflicts arise, the various alternatives should be presented in some detail. This aim has been pursued throughout, with as few lapses as

[12] Hall, *Theft, Law and Society* (2d ed.; Indianapolis, 1952), p. 15.
[13] Murray (ed.), *A New English Dictionary on Historical Principles* (Oxford, 1901), V, 568.

seemed possible. Nevertheless, the author's preferences are indicated, since personal conclusions based on adequate evidence are also indispensable to critical writing.

The use of foreign legal materials in documenting this study calls for special explanation. Translations made by other authors from the original documents are so acknowledged, the materials being treated as secondary sources, even where no paraphrasing has taken place. This device is employed because the translations have not the force of the original law, not being capable of use as evidence in the court of law of the nation in which the legal provision originated. The well-known scarcity of foreign legal materials has required the use of differing and duplicating sources. Generally, only those sources have been cited which actually have been used and are available.

In preparing any such study, the help of many individuals is indispensable. Some people have supplied the names of cases, others have helped with translation difficulties, still others have supplied stimulating ideas, a few have lent a patient ear. It is impossible to assign to each his specific contribution; it may be sufficient to reassure those who have aided me that they are not responsible for the treatment given their contributions, but that without them the work would have been virtually impossible. Nevertheless, I would like to thank Miss Melva Sanzon, my research assistant, and my wife, Margaret, who provided their critical technical talents.

J. A. S.

Camden, New Jersey
August 1968

» «

Contents

Double Jeopardy

THE DEVELOPMENT OF A LEGAL
AND SOCIAL POLICY

»1«

The History of
Double Jeopardy*

Historical study has long been a part of the legitimate concern of political science. Political institutions do not arise in a day, and the course of their development helps explain their present signficance as well as their future potentialities. In constitutional law research, the study of history is even more pertinent, since the American fundamental law is largely case-built interpretative law. The Constitution itself is framed in the language of two centuries past, its drafters looking toward still earlier legal developments in England. The phraseology of the Bill of Rights is evidence itself of the antiquity of the American Constitution. Accordingly, the examination of the double jeopardy clause must begin on another continent with another legal system of an earlier period.

In considering the contemporary meaning of double jeopardy, many courts have claimed that changing times cannot affect the original protection against double jeopardy, "whose contours are the product of history." [1] Others have said that it is impossible to trace the doctrine to any distinct origin, one court blithely announcing that "it seems to have been always embedded in the common law of

---

* This chapter originally appeared in *The American Journal of Legal History*, Vol. 7 (Oct., 1963), and is reprinted with the permission of the *Journal*.

[1] *Green* v. *United States*, 355 U.S. 184, 215 (1957), dissent.

England, as well as in the Roman law, and doubtless in every other system of jurisprudence, and instead of having a specific origin, it simply always existed." [2] Judges sometimes resort to the common law in order to ascertain the true meaning of the double jeopardy clause.[3] More adequate historical research is needed, however, to buttress historical assertions made in judicial opinions.

The principle of double jeopardy was not entirely unknown to the Greeks and Romans, although the legal environment was quite different. The principle found final expression in the *Digest of Justinian* as the precept that "the governor should not permit the same person to be again accused of a crime of which he had been acquitted." [4] Criminal procedure was quite unlike modern state-directed prosecutions, since, according to the Roman jurist Paulus,[5] "after a public acquittal a defendant could again be prosecuted by his informer within thirty days, but after that time this cannot be done."

The phrase *nemo debit bis puniri pro uno delicto*, beloved of later English legal writers, was probably a part of Roman law, but one cannot assume that the maxims carried the same legal force and

---

[2] *Stout* v. *State*, 36 Okla. 744, 756, 78 P. 207, 219 (1913).

[3] Justice Story argued on the basis of old English precedents, with success, in *United States* v. *Gilbert*, 25 F. Cas. 1287 (No. 15,204) (C.C.D. Mass. 1834).

[4] *Digest of Justinian*, Bk. 48, Title 2, n. 7, trans. S. P. Scott (Cincinnati, 1932), Vol. XVII: *The Civil Law*. This precept is not to be confused with the civil maxim *res judicata pro veritate accipitur* (the familiar *res judicata* concept of Anglo-American law) which is mentioned in the *Digest* at Bk. 50, Title 17, n. 207. The best description of ancient procedure is to be found in Bonner, *Lawyers and Litigants in Ancient Athens* Chicago, 1927); see also A. F. Berner, 2 *Archiv für Preussisches Strafrecht*, 202–30 (1855), for more specific criminal matters. Another important maxim of civil procedure noted by Cicero and Gaius is the principle *bis de eadem re agere res non licere*— that the same thing (*eadem res*) could not again be brought into court. "It was of the utmost importance for *praetor* and *iudex* to determine when a subject was the same; but no complete definition of the identity of a claim appears in juristic writing" (Greenidge, *The Legal Procedure of Cicero's Time* [Oxford, 1901], p. 247).

[5] *The Opinions of Paulus*, Title XVII, translated in S. P. Scott, *op. cit.*, I, 323.

2

significance among the ancients that they bear today. Notions of constitutionalism or of bills of rights were still primitive. More importantly, the criminal procedure pattern was not as formal as our own nor as that found much later in England. The significance and weight accorded the double jeopardy maxim is conditioned by the state of criminal procedure which it affects.

The canon law, which began its development at the close of the Roman Empire, opposed placing a man twice in jeopardy. This position was based upon a reading given by St. Jerome in 391 A.D., to I Nahum 9 (as set forth in the Douay version): "There shall not rise up a double affliction." The King James version reads: "Affliction shall not rise up a second time." In modern canon law, a crime may give rise to both a penal and a criminal action in an ecclesiastical court, and a crime may violate the laws of both civil and ecclesiastical society, resulting in a punishment by both or either power.[6] In early church law, however, there arose the principle that God does not punish twice for the same transgression.[7] It is possible that Thomas Becket's disagreement with Henry II, when Becket maintained that clerks should be tried once and then only in courts established under church law, may have foreshadowed the current legal doctrine. On the other hand, the principle of double jeopardy may have been derived from the Continent through the canon law, rather than being native to England.[8] Speculation on this point is difficult to resolve since much of Western law derives from a common fund of shared judicial concepts.

[6] Bouscaren and E. Ellis, *Canon Law* (Milwaukee, 1955), pp. 859, 864 (cc. 2198, 2210). No reference to double jeopardy is to be found in the Babylonian Code of Hammurabi, while the concept is briefly mentioned in the Hebrew Law (*Makkot*, 136, as quoted in 35 *Ind. L.J.* 445 [1960], n.). Talmudic law does not describe the principle. The alleged universality of the double jeopardy principle is not apparent from a study of early law.

[7] Pollock and Maitland, *A History of English Law* (2d ed.; Cambridge, 1899), pp. 448–49.

[8] 35 *Ind. L.J.* 446–47 (1960), n.

The Genesis of English Double Jeopardy

No statement of the double jeopardy clause appears in Magna Charta, nor can it be discovered by implication. Despite this fact, out of reverence for the concept, one court declared:

We are mindful of the fact that this rule was deemed of such importance that it was given a place in Magna Charta, and that it was regarded so vital to the maintenance of the Anglo-Saxon concept of individual liberty that it was made a part of the Constitution of the United States.[9]

Beyond its historical invalidity, such a statement is unfortunate because it leads to dubious interpretations. As will be seen, the sources and meanings of double jeopardy are far more varied and more subtle than such assertions intimate.

Other parts of the Bill of Rights show a clearer historical development than does the double jeopardy clause. Trial by jury was mentioned in the Assize of Clarendon of 1166, and, according to an eighteenth-century commentator, "this great Jewel of Liberty . . . [had] no less than fifty-eight times since the Norman Conquest, been established and confirmed by the legislative power." [10] Bail and habeas corpus were mentioned specifically in early statutes, most notably in the Bill of Rights of 1689. Yet double jeopardy is not mentioned in English statute law before its adoption into the American Constitution. Probably double jeopardy was not so fundamental a privilege, or perhaps it was obvious and well-established before the great writs of English history. Both propositions are tenable, but the former is much more probable than the latter in view of the development of English criminal law itself.

The need for a protection against double jeopardy was especially marked in early Britain. The law during the reign of Henry I provided that the punishment upon a second conviction was death or mutilation for almost any offense. Similar provisions are to be found as far back as the laws of Cnut and Ethelred. Only a few crimes

[9] *State* v. *Felch*, 92 Vt. 477, 482, 105 A. 23, 28 (1918).
[10] Care, *English Liberties, or the Free-Born Subject's Inheritance* (Boston, 1721), p. 203).

were punishable by death or mutilation on the conviction of the first offense. All such crimes were punishable, instead, by the devices of wer, bot, and wite, systems of compensation to be made to victims' relations or to the king or local lord.[11]

The phrase "life or limb" contained in the fifth amendment has a literal meaning in English history. Ethelred's laws directed that upon a second conviction the accused "be smitten so that his neck break." [12] The laws of Cnut describe the maiming of various extremities and other forms of mutilation, especially of hands, noses, and ears.[13] But by the eighteenth century it was well settled that a distinction was to be drawn between capital and other offenses, double jeopardy applying largely to the former. One's "life and limb" were not in danger in a trial for a misdemeanor.[14]

Some legal writers, attacking the basic premises of double jeopardy, have claimed that double jeopardy may have outworn its usefulness. Thus one scholar concluded that "the conception that a new trial after acquittal would subject the defendant to double jeopardy arose at a time when the death penalty was imposed for over a hundred crimes and persons accused of having committed a crime were at a decided disadvantage." [15] The accuracy of this criticism may be disputed, since even in 1688, despite the exceptionally rigorous Tudor and Stuart laws, no more than fifty offenses carried the death penalty. A spectacular increase in the creation of capital offenses occurred in the eighteenth century, reaching a high point during the reign of George III.[16] At common law only a few serious

---

[11] Stephen, *A History of the Criminal Law of England* (London, 1883), I, 58–59, 57.

[12] Ethel., vi. i, in *ibid.*, p. 58.

[13] Cnut, ii. 66, in *ibid.*, p. 60. See also Stubbs, *The Constitutional History of England* (Oxford, 1880), I, 227, which limits Danish influence on English law.

[14] *King* v. *Mawbey*, 6 Term R. 619, 638, 101 Eng. Rep. 736, 746 (K.B. 1796).

[15] Slovenko, "The Law on Double Jeopardy," 30 *Tul. L. Rev.* 428–29 (1955).

[16] Radzinowicz, *A History of English Criminal Law and Its Administration from 1750* (New York, 1948), I, 4.

offenses such as treason, murder, rape, and burning a dwelling house
entailed the punishment of death on the commission of the first
offense. Thus, there appears little parallel between the increased
harshness of punishment and the rise of double jeopardy. At any
rate, such a criticism rests upon the assumption that since the
doctrine was intended to solve a problem of another period, it can
have little relevance today, which is not a necessary inference.

There is some evidence that the earliest English rulers after the
Norman Conquest had little regard for questions of double jeopardy. In one situation, William Rufus tried fifty Englishmen by the
ordeal of hot iron. Since they escaped unhurt, they were, of course,
acquitted; thereupon the monarch "declared he would try them
again by the judgment of his court, and would not abide by the
pretended judgment of God." [17] The use of trial by ordeal had been
an important part of the criminal law of the Anglo-Saxon monarchs,
but Henry II would not allow an acquittal awarded on the basis of
trial by ordeal to prevent the possibility of a second trial.[18] In these
situations, at least, double jeopardy was simply ignored.

In order to separate these marginal cases from the more typical
legal solutions one must examine, however briefly, the early English
substantive criminal law. The endeavor itself involves a considerable
degree of conjecture and surmise, for as one authority testifies:

[17] Finlason (ed.), *Reeve's History of the English Law* (London, 1869),
I, 234.

[18] See *The Laws of King Ethelred III*, c. 6, as translated in Commissioners
of the Public Records of the Kingdom, *Ancient Laws and Institutes of
England* (London, 1840). Even at this early date, the accuser could elect
the penalty: "And let every accuser have the power of whichever he will,
whether water or iron; and let every vouching to warranty and every ordeal,
be in the king's 'borh'; and if he flee from the ordeal, let the 'borh' pay for
him according to his 'wer.' " Trial by ordeal had been replaced by other procedural devices by the reign of Henry III. Major felonies were not to be
tried by ordeal. A party accused, could, in some cases, choose to defend himself upon appeal by participating in a duel with his accuser. If the duel
failed or if the appellee had otherwise won, he was acquitted as against all
others who had appealed him of the same fact. Often, jury trial was an alternative. Those charged with inferior offenses were to abjure the realm (Finlason, *op. cit.*, I, 474–77, drawing from Bracton, in some degree).

6

It is a matter of great difficulty, indeed I think it would be impossible, to given a full and systematic account of the criminal law which prevailed in England in early times. . . . Both the laws of the early kings and our own statute book presuppose knowledge of an unwritten law. Our own unwritten law can still be ascertained, but such parts of the earlier law as were not written have absolutely disappeared.[19]

Yet some understanding of the relationship between substantive criminal law and the state of criminal procedure is indispensable, since double jeopardy operates between the two and is dependent upon the stages of their development.

Briefly, the separation between the areas of criminal law and civil law developed very slowly, the beginnings being discernible during the reigns of Edward II and Edward III in the early fourteenth century. The familiar doctrines of criminal liability were evolving out of more primitive substantive rules. Murder became the worst kind of homicide, to be distinguished from that homicide which is accidental or justifiable.[20] A crucial point was reached when Edward III's statute of treason clearly distinguished treason from felony and high treason from petty treason, thus establishing degrees of crime.[21]

The relationship between substantive criminal law and criminal procedure, so vital for an understanding of double jeopardy, is beclouded by uncertain distinctions between criminal and civil liberty. Although only the king could charge generally during the period of the rise of substantive law, a private person could still sue if he showed a special harm or grievance.[22] A suit by a private person usually yielded damages, while the king's suit could result in a harsher punishment.[23] Besides this, the distinctions between crime, tort, and contract were still hopelessly confused, the frequent overlapping being due in part to the lack of an organized police force or

19 Stephen, op. cit., p. 51. Radzinowicz, in op. cit., has carried on Stephen's monumental work, taking it up at the point where he left off.

20 Finlason, op. cit., II, 416–17; 14 Edw. III, st. 1, c. 4 (1348).

21 25 Edw. III, st. 5, c. 2 (1350).

22 Maitland (ed.), Yearbook of Edward II (London, 1904), II, 120.

23 Maitland (ed.), Yearbook of Edward III (London, 1904), IV, 64.

inspectorate.[24] In this context, familiar concepts of crime and punishment are hard to find.

Since double jeopardy involves a limitation upon the power of the state to bring suit, by the time of its formulation criminal procedure must have developed to a point where the state had the power to conduct criminal actions at its discretion. This state of affairs did not obtain in England until quite late in its legal history. The operation of Anglo-Saxon criminal procedure was wholly dependent upon the initiation of suits by private persons. Limitation upon repeated prosecution was secured to some degree by a fine of 120 shillings for failure to appear to substantiate a charge.[25] Obviously, this restriction is only dimly related to the idea of a double jeopardy protection.

The appeal by private accuser still held an important place in criminal law as late as the early thirteenth century. It was "the bridge between the earlier law, when the appeal was the substitute for the blood feud, and the later law, when criminal proceedings are taken by the state." [26] Later, the action of trespass became an efficient substitute for the appeal, which was under attack by the newer procedure of indictment.[27] A statute of Henry VII [28] (1485-1509) provided that indictments would be proceeded on immediately, at the king's suit, for a man's death, without waiting for the bringing of an appeal, and also provided that the plea of *autrefoit acquit* (a type of double jeopardy plea) to an indictment, should be no bar to the prosecution of an appeal. The statute, passed to escape the usual common law rule which made an acquittal on an indictment a good bar to an appeal, marks the beginning of a recognizable double jeopardy statement, even if it is a negative one. The right of appeal

[24] Holdsworth, A *History of English Law* (London, 1903), II, 376-77. Of course, centralized enforcement of law occurred quite late in England, so this cannot be accepted as a complete explanation.

[25] This probably existed as early as 930, during the reign of Aethelstan (2 Aethelstan I).

[26] Holdsworth, *op. cit.*, I, 156.

[27] Finlason, *op. cit.*, II, 421-23, III, 38-39.   [28] 3 Hen. VII, c. 1 (1491).

fell into decay.[29] Criminal law enforcement became a state prerogative, and double jeopardy became a meaningful possibility.

The institutionalization of justice under the king seemed, at first, to signify a lessening of the severity of criminal punishment. Trial by ordeal having been abolished in 1219, Henry III directed that those accused and suspected of great crimes be imprisoned, but not so as to endanger life or limb, although much was left to the discretion of the judges.[30] The king's pardon, another mollifying instrument, had been employed since Anglo-Saxon times.[31] However, the tendency to create more severe criminal punishments seems to have moved popular assemblies. One observer, commenting on this development in 1772, noted that the great severity of penal laws "has been in some degree owing to their having been made *flagrante ira,* on some sudden occasion, when a combination of atrocious circumstances attending some particular offense inflamed the legislature." [32] The problem of multiple criminal accusations, as an aspect of double jeopardy, is more one of our own day, when assemblies, not monarchs, are in power. The state's gathering of the power to institute suit is a prerequisite to a true double jeopardy situation, but that step is not of sole importance in the emergence of the doctrine. Protection of the accused became even more significant

[29] In 1818, appeal which was used in a murder case after a previous trial on an indictment resulted in an acquittal. The brother of the dead girl brought the appeal. The statute of Henry VII barred a double jeopardy plea (*Ashford v. Thornton,* 1 B. and Ald. 405, 106 Eng. Rep. 149. [1818]).

[30] Holdsworth, *op. cit.,* I, 143, 153.

[31] 2 Edw. III, c. 2 (1328), put this custom in a statutory form.

[32] Dagge, *Considerations on Criminal Law* (London, 1772), p. 24. The tendency to incriminate more and more aspects of criminal behavior serves to increase the prosecution's opportunities to select alternative formulas in proceeding against the accused, presenting the opportunity for repeated prosecution for one action which may be violative of different statutory provisions. This aspect of double jeopardy, which will be described in other chapters, is a more modern dilemma which created the need for a stretching of double jeopardy to protect the accused against the legislature as well as the executive. The change in the environment of the double jeopardy precept will be noted again and again.

when the number of crimes and the severity of the punishments were increased.

There is some evidence of a plea somewhat similar to double jeopardy as early as the fourteenth century. The context in which the need arose was in the transition from the older procedure to the indictment. It was settled that an acquittal on an appeal after a trial by jury was a bar to prosecution for the same offense by subsequent indictment.[33] Conversely, an acquittal on an indictment was held a bar to the suit of the injured party seeking an appeal,[34] but this was altered by the Statute of 1487. After the Statute, neither a conviction nor an acquittal on an indictment acted as a bar to a prosecution by way of appeal, for the same offense, if the appeal was brought within a year and a day.[35] As late as 1709 Chief Justice Holt ordered an appeal on the same offense for which a man had been acquitted, against the evidence, on a prior indictment for murder.[36] The Statute of 1487 was also employed by the king in Star Chamber.[37] This plea was statutory and controlled by the king as a matter of royal policy and was not a protection against the authority of the state, unlike those rights usually considered to be fundamental, such as the plea of double jeopardy as presently conceived.[38]

Other evidence of the existence of a plea barring subsequent suits can be discovered. The common law courts established in the twelfth century heard criminal cases and kept records permitting the

[33] 9 Hen. V, f. 2, pl. 7 (1421); 34 Hen. VI, f. 9, pl. 19, (1455).

[34] Trin. 21 Edw. III, f. 23, pl. 16 (1346); Mich. 44 Edw. III, f. 38, pl. 35 (1369).

[35] 9 Hen. VII, c. 1.

[36] *Young* v. *Slaughterford*, 1 Queen Anne's Cases 217, 228, 88 Eng. Rep. 999 (1709).

[37] The Statute of 1487 was entitled "Authority of Court of Star Chamber." Cases are collected for the period 1593 to 1609 in Balldon (ed.), *Les reportes del cases in camera stellata* (London, 1894). These cases show the pleading of a pardon as an acquittal (*Blage* v. *Allen*, p. 118), but no other plea in the nature of double jeopardy. The procedure of the Star Chamber was not according to the common law, dispensing with juries, proceeding on rumor and employing torture. Most Star Chamber cases are not reported in other English legal collections.

[38] See *United States* v. *Aurandt*, 15 N.M. 292, 107 P. 1064 (1909).

development of legal precedent.[39] Scattered among the early cases are some which display the use of a protective plea against repeated suits. For example, in one case decided in 1203 appears the following:

Jordan, son of Warin, appealed Reiner Read, for that he in the king's peace and wickedly assaulted him and cut off his fingers, so that he is maimed. . . . And Reiner comes and defends the assault and the felony and the mayhem, and says that on a former occasion this appeal came before Sir Geoffrey Fitz Peter, Earl of Essex, and by his leave a concord was made between them, so that [Jordan] remitted him and he offers the king two marks for an inquest by the county and lawful men of the town of Shrewsbury [to wit, the jurors] record that a concord was thus made by the license of Sir Geoffrey Fitz Peter in consideration of the ten marks paid by [Reiner] to [Jordan].[40]

Although it may be tempting to declare this a double jeopardy plea, the context is not even a criminal case. The state merely provided a forum for what is essentially a civil suit with criminal overtones, resolved as a claim in contract by the doctrine of accord and satisfaction. By 1266, an agreement between the criminal and the relatives of a slain man would not serve to protect a murderer from a subsequent indictment and a sentence of death.[41] Still, another 1203 case does show the use of a principle of prior acquittal by the accessories to a murder.[42] These cases are not strictly criminal matters, and do not involve the double jeopardy concept.

Thus far, then, the existence of a double jeopardy concept rooted deeply in English history cannot be demonstrated. Perhaps the most logical step would be to proceed to an examination of the legal treatises for some indication as to its sources. As we shall see, the origin of the plea is indicated there.

The earliest treatise on the common law is Glanville's *Treatise*, which is a record of the proceedings of the Curia Regis, although

[39] Pollock and Maitland, *op. cit.*, I, 165.
[40] Maitland (ed.), *Select Pleas of the Crown* (London, 1888), I, 35.
[41] Pollock and Maitland, *op. cit.*, I, 165.   [42] Maitland, *Select Pleas*, p. 37.

the authorship of the text has been questioned.[43] It was finished around 1187 and remained in use for at least one hundred years. Glanville describes in some detail the procedure of appeal and trial by ordeal. He also employs the familiar phrase "life or limb" in its older usage.[44] But this "first treatise on the subject of jurisprudence to compile the then current state of law since the fall of Rome" [45] omits mention of double jeopardy. Considering the state of criminal law and procedure, the concept was probably nonexistent in Glanville's day.

Bracton, writing a few years later than Glanville, also fails to mention a double jeopardy principle, although there is a hint of the concept as applied to church courts.[46] Sir Edward Coke, a later oracle of the common law, discovered some double jeopardy principles in his perusal of Bracton's works,[47] a highly personal interpretation. Legal critics have declared that "the influence of Roman upon English law was exercised through the founders of the English common law long after the Norman Conquest through Glanville and Bracton, but especially Bracton," who "had little or no assignable influence on the modes of procedure." [48] This observation certainly is true of double jeopardy.

Britton, another important legal commentator, wrote his works during the reign of Edward I, at the king's command, as part of

[43] Holdsworth, op. cit., I, 147–48; also p. 1.

[44] Glanville, A Treatise on the Laws and Customs of the Kingdom of England Composed in the Time of King Henry the Second, trans. Beames (Washington, 1900), pp. 278–80; also p. 2. At this time the distinction between felony and misdemeanor often determined whether the guilty person was to be in the king's mercy of life and limb. Mere petty offenses might result in imprisonment or amercement. Minor crimes below a felony could result in a punishment of mutilation. Outlawry was reserved as a final resort as punishment for contumacy toward the king or his courts. For outlawry, see Bigelow, History of Procedure in England (Boston, 1880), pp. 346–47.

[45] Finlason, op. cit., I, 223.

[46] Maitland (ed.), Bracton's Note Book (London, 1887), II, 320, case 391 (1230).

[47] Coke, The Third Part of the Institutes of the Laws of England (4th ed.; London, 1669), pp. 212–13.

[48] Stephen, op. cit., I, 49.

Edward's design to codify the laws. Less than a century after the time of Glanville, a former judgment barrier is perceptible, even though it does not amount to a double jeopardy protection. There is a lack of a full protection for the accused. He may be subjected to repeated prosecutions at the instance of several different people for substantially the same offense. Thus:

Though it happen that the appellees are thus acquitted as against the plaintiff, it does not therefore follow that they are not guilty of what is laid to their charge; wherefore in such case let it be immediately demanded of them on our behalf, how they will acquit themselves of such slander.

And in the reverse situation, "although he acquit himself as to our suit, yet the suit of any other, who will prosecute within the year and day, is not thereby taken away." [49]

The apparent weakness of criminal protection was offset, Britton indicates, by a type of former acquittal plea:

The defendant may also answer by exception to the action in several ways; for he may say that at another time there was an appeal in our Court between the same persons for the same felony, and that he was acquitted therof before such Justices; and if he avouches this by warrant of record, and the record passes in his favor, he shall be awarded quit, and the plaintiff to prison. [50]

The apparent inconsistency of this statement with the preceding may be resolved by examining the word "our" in the previous quotations. Obviously, the word refers to the monarch, signifying that protection is not available against the king's indictment, although it is available to a defendant against whom an appeal is lodged. The principle of former judgment was not available for use against the state. The attempt to restrain the appellor from employing repeated prosecution was codified in the Statute of Westminster, under which it was held that the fact that "the life of the defendant was in jeopardy" in a previous case resulting in the defendant's acquittal

49 Britton, *De legibus anglicanes,* trans. Nichols (Oxford, 1865), I, 104, 112.
50 *Ibid.,* pp. 112–13.

was the basis for a suit of malicious prosecution against the appellors.[51]

Further indication of the unsettled nature of the maxim of double jeopardy is Justice Ascue's assertion in 1477 that "in several cases a man shall put his life twice in jeopardy," although if an appeal was pending, the effect was always to bar a second prosecution.[52] The word "jeopardy" itself appears in the *Yearbooks* only eleven times in criminal cases down to the year 1535.[53] Three of these cases use "jeopardy" in the statement that a man's life should not be "put in jeopardy" twice for the same offense.[54] These three cases, appearing late in the fifteenth century, are the first intimation of a near-modern double jeopardy protection. They occur at the same time that modern criminal procedure is developing.

Previously, whatever protection was afforded by the concept of former jeopardy before the fifteenth century was applicable to appeals, not to indictments, as noted in Fleta, a commentator of the previous century:

If, however, it is not possible to avoid the appeal on the ground of insufficient suit or an omission or variance, the appellee may still except against the appeal and say that he was appealed on another occasion of the same deed and was acquitted thereof by judgment of the court.[55]

Since the criminal appeal was not abolished until 1819,[56] the history of double jeopardy is clouded by the existence of two alternative means of criminal procedure. Nonetheless, since no cases or commentators through the fifteenth century apply the precept to

---

[51] 13 Edw. I, c. 12 (1281).   [52] Hil. 16 Edw. IV, f. 11, pls. 6, 7 (1477).

[53] Trin. 9 Hen. V, f. 7, pl. 21 (1421); Hil. 21 Hen. VI, f. 28, pl. 12 (1443); Hil. 33 Hen. VI, f. 1, pl. 6 (1455); Mich. 34 Hen. VI, f. 9, pl. 19 (1455); Hil. 8 Edw. IV, ff. 24, 25, pl. 7 (1469); Hil. 16 Edw. IV, fl. 11, pl. 6 (1477); Hil. 16 Edw. IV, f. 11, pl. 7 (1477); Mich. 21 Edw. IV, ff. 73, 74, pl. 57 (1481); Trin. 22 Edw. IV, f. 19, pl. 46 (1482); Hil. 9 Hen. VII, f. 19, pl. 14 (1494); Mich. 20 Hen. VII, f. 11, pl. 21 (1504).

[54] Hil. 21 Hen. VI, f. 28, pl. 12 (1443); Hil. 16 Edw. IV, f. 11. pl. 6 (1477); Hil. 9 Hen. VII, f. 19, pl. 14 (1494).

[55] *Fleta*, trans. Richardson (London, 1955), p. 82.

[56] 59 Geo. III, c. 46 (1819).

indictments alone, whatever protection against repeated prosecution may have been available before the fifteenth century seems to have been a bar against the repeated abuse of private prosecution, rather than a protection against the state.

This conclusion is reinforced by an examination of *The Mirror of Justices,* an anonymous work written at the close of the thirteenth century, which is held to be of dubious repute, but which makes the following assertions:

> It is an abuse to adjudge a man to several punishments for one trespass, e.g. to both corporal punishment and ransom, for ransom is but a redemption of a corporal punishment by a money fine.

> It is an abuse that a man is accused of matters touching life or limb ex officio without suit and without indictment.

These clauses demonstrate the weakness of the king's criminal law powers, but do not involve double jeopardy at all.[57] The first clause merely deals with the problem of overlapping punishments, which is no more than ancillary to the double jeopardy protection.

If, as has been claimed, the original purpose of the concept of double jeopardy was to diminish "the danger of governmental tyranny"[58] through repeated prosecutions for the same crime, such a purpose was not attained, historically, until the fifteenth century at the earliest. The existence of an earlier policy to limit the institution of private criminal actions is not necessarily related. The antiquity of the doctrine is probably not as great as is usually declared.

The fifteenth-century double jeopardy concept was still not the same as that found in later English or American law. For example, attachment of jeopardy occurs, according to the American rule, at the time of the opening of the prosecution's case. The English rule requires a final verdict before jeopardy can be said to begin.[59]

[57] Whittaker (ed.), *The Mirror of Justices* (London, 1895), pp. 175, 172, 90. See the introduction by Maitland, which underscores the work's reliability.

[58] 57 *Yale L.J.* 133 (1947), n., stresses this aspect as the historical basis of double jeopardy, the most common interpretation.

[59] *Reg.* v. *Charlesworth,* 1 B. and S. 460, 507, 121 Eng. Rep. 786 (1861), and *Winsor* v. *Queen,* L.R. 1 Q.B. 289, 303, 390, 122 Eng. Rep. 1150 (1866).

Originally, in 1482 at least, English double jeopardy attached at the time of the plea of not guilty, since, as Justice Fairfax explained, "the defendant has pleaded a plea 'not guilty' by which he has put his life in jeopardy." [60] On the other hand, discharge of a jury did not amount to a putting in jeopardy, as exampled in 1406 by a case in which the jurors previously sworn were "later sworn anew as if they had never appeared before." [61] By 1676, the rule required an acquittal or conviction to constitute a prior jeopardy,[62] the modern English rule. The period of the development of double jeopardy paralleled the rise of the modern state.

A transitional stage in the evolution of the double jeopardy doctrine is illustrated in the work of Sir Matthew Hale, a seventeenth-century commentator. The defenses of *auterfoits acquit, auterfoits convict,* and *auterfoits attaint* are set forth in modern detail. However, very few of Hale's statements are accepted today. The reason is that many of his observations are studded with legal anachronisms, including the defense of benefit of clergy and acquittal by victory in battle as adjuncts to the plea of double jeopardy. The importance of a plea of not guilty in the first trial and the use of an acquittal for the purpose of pleading *auterfoits acquit* in the second trial is stressed,[63] although such procedural technicalities have disappeared long since from double jeopardy law.

The Emergence of Modern Double Jeopardy Law

The most important individuals in the history of double jeopardy are undoubtedly Coke and Blackstone. These two writers clarified the concept and first gave it the importance which it subsequently attained in the United States. To colonial lawyers, Coke and Blackstone were names which had become synonymous with the common law itself. In 1779, John Rutledge of South Carolina wrote his brother, who was then studying at the Inns of Court: "In regard to particular law books—Coke's *Institutes* seems to be almost the foun-

---

[60] Trin. 22 Edw. IV, f. 19, pl. 46 (1482).   [61] Hil. 7 Hen. IV, f. 39, pl. 2.
[62] *Turner's Case,* 89 Eng. Rep. 158 (1676).
[63] Hale, *The History of the Pleas of the Crown* (Philadelphia, 1847), II, 240–50.

dation of our law. . . . Blackstone I think useful." [64] As Holdsworth has said, "What Shakespeare has been to literature, what Bacon has been to philosophy, what the translators of the authorized version of the Bible have been in religion, Coke has been to the public and private law of England." [65] Although Coke has his detractors, he is a fountainhead of double jeopardy law.

Coke completed his *Institutes* in 1642, setting forth the full expanse of English common law garnered from the cases and earlier commentators, adding to this the leaven of his own inspiration. In his *Second Institutes* the basis for double jeopardy was described, to be reiterated by Blackstone, who informed generations of English lawyers that in English courts "the plea of autrefois acquit, for a formal acquittal, is grounded on the universal maxim . . . that no man is to be brought into jeopardy of his life more than once for the same offense." [66] But the historical basis of the doctrine he described was quite uncertain and difficult to separate from procedural anachronisms such as the plea of benefit of clergy, which permitted a defendant to be remitted from punishment for the commission of certain offenses. The defense could be employed only once in a lifetime, being a remnant of the fading jurisdiction of the church courts.[67] Coke displays this tangled past:

Before the statutes of 8 Eliz. cap. 4 and 18 Eliz. cap. 6 if a man had committed divers felonies, if he had been indicted of the last, and had benefit of his clergy, he could not have been impeached for any of the former felonies, albeit for the same he could not have had his clergy; by that Act it is provided, that notwithstanding the allowance of such clergy, he may be impeached for any former offence, for which he could not have had his clergy.[68]

Yet even in Coke the protection of double jeopardy is not the same as that provided by the contemporary doctrine. A former ac-

[64] From Bowen, *The Lion and The Throne* (Boston, 1957), p. 514.

[65] Holdsworth, *op. cit.*, V, 132.

[66] Blackstone, *Commentaries on the Laws of England* (Worcester, Mass., 1790), IV, 335.

[67] Holdsworth, *op. cit.*, III, 242, 260, 413.   [68] Coke, *op. cit.*, p. 214.

quittal does not act as a bar to a subsequent prosecution, while a former attainder does:

And albeit at this day in an appeal of death, auterfoitz acquite upon an indictment of the same death is no bar, yet in an indictment of death, auterfoitz attaint de mesme le mort in an Appeal is a good bar [but] in an indictment or Appeal of death, if it be found that he killed him in his own defence, he is acquitted of the felony forever.[69]

The double jeopardy protection described here is still not an absolute protection but seems to be conditional, depending upon the quality of the prior acquittal.

Certain features of Coke's formulation are now discarded. "Auterfoitz attaint," a now defunct plea, was a very significant part of seventeenth-century double jeopardy, as Coke explains that "by the common law auterfoitz attaint, etc. of the same felony was a good plea, as well in an indictment as in Appeal." The attainder could be by way of outlawry, for the two were often intermingled. The rule seems to have had a similar impact to that of double jeopardy, since, "if a man be attainted of manslaughter, it is a good bar to an indictment of murder of the same death, and in the converse." [70]

Coke's conceptualization of "jeopardy" seems to have been modern; unlike the Roman law or any subsequent versions, it was confined to purely criminal matters:

Where a little before it is said, that a felon by his Attainder is *mort in ley,* it is understood of such former offences as require *posnam mortis*: for notwithstanding the Attainder, his body remains subject to arrests and executions for debts . . . [but] if a man be attainted of petit larceny, he may be after attainted of felony, for the which he shall have judgment of death, because it is an higher offence, and is to have another judgment.[71]

The "jeopardy," unlike most modern interpretations, seems to have involved a possible punishment of death. The contemporary categories of double jeopardy are contained in Coke's three pleas of autrefois acquit, auterfois convict, and former pardon. At the time of the adoption of the American Constitution the double jeopardy

[69] *Ibid.*, p. 213.   [70] *Ibid.*, pp. 213, 214.   [71] *Ibid.*, p. 213.

principle was recognized by these three pleas in bar, as well as the plea of autrefois attaint.[72] The nature of those pleas is relevant today, even though their content has changed somewhat.[73] In the United States, the old forms of pleading have been discarded, but they remain in England.

To a considerable degree, Coke improvised the law of double jeopardy. He admitted that in his *Institutes* he had set down his own opinion.[74] His motives may have been the mitigation of the harshness of the criminal punishment of England which caused Christian men and women to be hanged on the gallows tree, "and true it is, that we have found by wofull experience, that it is not frequent and often punishment that doth prevent like offences, for the frequency of the punishment makes it so familiar as it is not feared." [75] Hobbes attacked Coke bitterly for undermining the power of the king by citing centuries-old statutes, long out of use.[76] Combining these two tendencies, Coke may have strengthened the double jeopardy protection in his desire to ameliorate harsh English criminal penalties while weakening the king's power. Whatever the reasons, Coke's hand is present in the formation of the concept for the use of the English-speaking world. By the time the *First Institute* was completed, the double jeopardy doctrine was clearly delineated as a purely criminal concept serving as a protection against the state even for relatively minor offenses. This is the beginning of modern double jeopardy:

Fine, finis, signifieth a pecuniary punishment for an offense or contempt committed against the king, and regularly to it imprisonment appertaineth. And it is called finis, because it is an end for that offense. And in this case a man is said *facere finem de transgressione etc. cum rege,* to make an end or *fine* with the king for such a transgression.[77]

[72] Blackstone, *op. cit.,* IV, 355; Hale, *op. cit.* II, 240.

[73] See *State* v. *Felch,* 92 Vt. 477, 105 A. 23 (1918).

[74] Coke, *op. cit.,* proem.   [75] *Ibid.,* epilogue, p. 204.

[76] T. Hobbes, "Dialogue between a Philosopher and a Student of the Common Laws of England," *The English Works,* VI (London, 1840), 62.

[77] Thomas, *A Systematic Arrangement of Lord Coke's First Institute on the Plan of Sir Matthew Hale's Analysis* (Philadelphia, 1826), III, 605.

Blackstone retained the archaic language of double jeopardy, but began to use the word "jeopardy" with more frequency to describe that doctrine, for *auterfoits convict* was said to stand upon the same principle of common law as *autrefoits acquit*.[78] *Autrefoits attaint* was retained and justified upon the fiction that "the prisoner is dead in law by the first attainder, his blood is already corrupted, and he hath forfeited all he had.[79] Writing one hundred years after Coke, Blackstone describes former jeopardy as applying to state prosecutions alone.[80] But Blackstone's interpretations were not incorporated into the American Constitution without alteration. The contemporary conception is broader and not limited to felony cases, as Blackstone required.[81] The necessity of a prior verdict of guilt or acquittal is accepted in England but not in America.[82]

Viner's *Abridgement*, which was compiled at the time of the writing of the American Constitution, summarizes English legal development up to that point in time. There is evidence that double jeopardy was still entwined with procedural technicalities and was not a clearly fundamental right:

If there are two indictments against H. for the same fact, viz. one found by the coroner's inquest and the other by the grand jury, and H. is acquitted on the one; yet he must be tried on the other to which he may plead the former acquittal; but the usage of the Old Baily is, and indeed, so is the fairest course, to try him on both indictments at once.[83]

Similarly, Viner indicates that the law of autrefois acquit was different for a murder or manslaughter indictment, while in other

[78] S. Tucker, *Blackstone's Commentaries with Notes of Reference to the Constitution and Laws of the Federal Government of the United States, and of the Commonwealth of Virginia* (Philadelphia, 1803), V, 335.

[79] See U.S. Const., Art. III, and L.U.S., 1st Cong., 2d Sess., c. 9, Sec. 24 (1790), which do away with attainder.

[80] Tucker, *op. cit.*, pp. 336–37.

[81] Kirk, "Jeopardy during the Period of the Yearbooks," 82 *U. Pa. L. Rev.* 602 (1934).

[82] Jones, "What Constitutes Double Jeopardy?" 38 *J. Crim. L.C. & P.S.* 380 (1947).

[83] Viner, *A General Abridgement of Law and Equity* (2d ed.; London, 1793), p. 404, citing *Queen v. Gulliford*, S.C. 6 Mod. 19 (1780).

sections he provides more examples of shifting double jeopardy rules in eighteenth-century English practice.[84] Yet the double jeopardy clause adopted by the writers of the American Constitution was supposed to have been "declaratory of the law as it . . . stood" and "to conform to the universal practice in Great Britain and in this country." [85] As will be demonstrated below, this proposition was incorrect.

The state of English law at the time when the American Constitution was written to preserve the rights which Englishmen had traditionally enjoyed does not permit the evaluation of double jeopardy as a clearly established fundamental restriction upon the organized power of the executive. Even in the writings of Coke the immutability of the doctrine was not fixed. It had not attained the significance of certain other rights. The concept had hardened into a maxim: *Nemo debet bis vexari pro una et eadem causa,* that is, "It is a rule of law that a man shall not be twice vexed for one and the same cause." [86] But a maxim may be little more than a slogan, concealing rather than revealing meaning.

American Double Jeopardy before the Fifth Amendment

American formulation of double jeopardy began with the Massachusetts colony. It took a separate tack from English developments and laid the groundwork for the eventual adoption of double jeopardy as a constitutional protection. Massachusetts criminal law was well in advance of that of England with respect to double jeopardy. While in seventeenth-century England the principle meant that no man's life ought twice to be placed in jeopardy for the same offense, the Massachusetts rule extended to all types of criminal prosecutions and to civil trespasses as well.[87] Provision was made that men should not be sentenced twice for the same offense by the civil courts in the *Body of Liberties* of 1641, which was composed by

[84] *Ibid.* (1st ed., 1785), pp. 375, 368–73.

[85] 53 *Nw. U.L. Rev.* 521 (1958), n.

[86] Broom, *A Selection of Legal Maxims* (Philadelphia, 1845), p. 106.

[87] Farrand (ed.), *The Laws and Liberties of Massachusetts* (Cambridge, Mass., 1929), p. 46.

Nathaniel Ward under the direction of Governor Bellingham and the General Court.[88] The *Body of Liberties* was "less a code of existing laws that it was a compilation of constitutional provisions . . . framed in no logical order."[89] This document bears a close resemblance to the bills of rights later to become a stock feature of American constitutions, state and federal. Provisions against cruel punishments, bond slavery, and arbitrary arrest are found together with other provisions guaranteeing equal justice under law to every person within the jurisdiction, "whether inhabitant or forreiner."[90] The *Body of Liberties* went beyond the usual assurances which governments extended to the citizenry.[91] The double jeopardy clause of the instrument read as follows: "No man shall be twice sentenced by civil justice for one and the same crime, offense, or trespass." The policy also extended to the use of habeas corpus.[92]

The Massachusetts Code of 1648 was a comprehensive and relatively complete statement of the laws, privileges, duties, and rights of inhabitants of the colony, and as such "it was the first comprehensive code of laws in the New World."[93] Similar provisions were often adopted directly into the laws of other colonies, especially Connecticut and New Haven. Massachusetts law also spread southward into New York, Pennsylvania, and New Jersey. When it was desired to frame a code of laws for the Province of New York, the New England codes were studied as precedents.[94] Thus, Massachusetts law helped serve as a conveyer of the double jeopardy concept to those other colonies. Perhaps the significance of double jeopardy in Massachusetts law helps explain why the doctrine was elevated to

---

[88] Whitmore (ed.), *The Colonial Laws of Massachusetts* (Boston, 1889), pp. 2, 18.

[89] Haskins, *Law and Authority in Early Massachusetts* (New York, 1960), p. 129.

[90] Whitmore, *op. cit.*, pp. 5–7, 46.   [91] Haskins, *op. cit.*, pp. 70, 75.

[92] Habeas Corpus Act of 1681, Sec. VI.

[93] Haskins, "Codification of the Law in Colonial Massachusetts: A Study in Comparative Law," 30 *Ind. L.J.* 1 (1954).

[94] Ewing and Haskins, "The Spread of Massachusetts Law in the Seventeenth Century," 106 *U. Pa. L. Rev.* 413 (1958).

constitutional dignity, instead of being treated as just another common law concept. The Massachusetts style of double jeopardy law differed considerably from that of contemporary England and undoubtedly was influential in creating the peculiar American type of double jeopardy law. For double jeopardy, the Bay Colony contribution is contained in the statement that "everie Action . . . in criminal Causes shall be . . . entered in the rolls of everie Court . . . that such Actions be not afterwards brought again to the vexation of any man." [95]

The omission of double jeopardy from most post-Revolutionary constitutions is difficult to explain. Provisions concerning bail and cruel and unusual punishments are to be found in eight such constitutions.[96] These rights were borrowed from the English Bill of Rights of 1689, which did not include a double jeopardy provision. The full stature of the double jeopardy concept had not yet been attained.

Whatever the reason, the first bill of rights which expressly adopted a double jeopardy clause was part of the New Hampshire Constitution of 1784, stating: "No subject shall be liable to be tried, after an acquittal, for the same crime or offence." [97] Note that this protection extends merely to former acquittals, only a portion of the protection available in contemporary England or in the Massachusetts of the previous century. This phraseology was not utilized in the Pennsylvania Declaration of Rights of 1790, which declares, in language almost identical to the federal Bill of Rights: "No person shall, for the same offence, be twice put in jeopardy of life or limb." [98] One common feature is found in American double jeop-

[95] Farrand, *op. cit.*, p. 47.

[96] Virginia Bill of Rights, Pennsylvania Constitution of 1776, Maryland Declaration of Rights of 1776, North Carolina Constitution of 1776, Georgia Constitution of 1777, Vermont Constitution of 1777, Massachusetts Constitution of 1780, New Hampshire Constitution of 1784, and United States Constitution, Amendment VIII.

[97] Constitution of New Hampshire of 1784, Art. I, Sec. XVI, as appearing in Perry and Cooper, *Sources of Our Liberties* (New York, 1959), p. 384.

[98] *Ibid.*, p. 327.

23

ardy law of this period, the abandonment of the English requirement that the defendant's life be in jeopardy.[99]

Passing from constitutional provisions to the case law of colonial America permits a more accurate understanding of the roots of double jeopardy. In the law of colonial Virginia, a criminal defendant might make a special plea in bar alleging a former conviction for acquittal for the identical crime charged or a former attainder for any felony, as well as the fact of a pardon, but "not many such pleas appear in the surviving Virginia records." [100] One example of such a case involved the effect of the discharge of an accused for a defect in the indictment. It was ruled that he might be indicted again, "for since he could not have been legally convicted on the original one, he had never been in jeopardy." [101] The Virginia criminal law tended to be closer to English law than that of most colonies, for "the Virginia criminal law was transplanted English law, with modifications due primarily to the different conditions, and not to a tenderness for lawbreakers or a conscious spirit of reform." [102]

Only a few examples of autrefois convict, autrefois acquit, autrefois attaint, and former pardon as defenses are found in colonial New York case reports. In one case Francis Wessells and William Shakerly were presented in New York quarter Sessions on August 4,

[99] The phrase "a man's life shall not be twice put in jeopardy for one and the same offense" appears in *Wetherel* v. *Dary*, 76 Eng. Rep. 982 (K.B. 1588), an English case of the sixteenth century. By the time of the drafting of the American Bill of Rights, a distinction was drawn between capital offenses and other offenses, double jeopardy applying largely to the former. One's life or limb was not in danger in a trial for a misdemeanor (*King* v. *Mawbey*, 6 Term R. 619, 101 Eng. Rep. 736, 746 (K.B. 1796). The borderline between offenses which were serious enough to warrant application of the double jeopardy formula seems to verge toward the capital offenses. See Hawkins, *A Treatise of the Pleas of the Crown*, II (London, 1716), 526, where the formula is stated: "The party ought not to be brought twice into danger of his life for the same crime."

[100] A. Scott, *Criminal Law in Colonial Virginia* (Chicago, 1930), pp. 81–82.

[101] Barton (ed.), *Virginia Colonial Decisions: The Reports by Sir John Randolph and by Edward Barradall of Decisions of the General Court of Virginia 1728–1741* (Boston, 1909), II, 51.

[102] A. Scott, *op. cit.*, p. 323.

1697, and were later presented on February 8, 1699, only to be discharged on the ground that they had been fined before in a case involving the same fact.[103] In 1768, the records show that the plea of autrefois convict was raised by motion.[104] There is no indication of a plea of autrefois acquit having been employed in a New York court. One author attributes this rare use of the plea to "the solicitude of royal officials that there be no double prosecutions." [105] In this situation, the sovereign authority restricted its use of its own powers. Double jeopardy appears in one famous New York case involving many leading citizens accused of outfitting privateers and trading with France, then an enemy of England. One Cunningham pleaded for relief against a double prosecution on the ground that it was "oppressive, contrary to the spirit of government and the dictates of law and reason." [106]

A Connecticut decision in 1783 forbade the second trial of a citizen once he had been acquitted.[107] The rule was reinforced by a similar verdict in 1787 based upon the use of the phrase "double jeopardy." [108] That phrase appears but rarely in the cases.

An eloquent opinion of a 1788 Pennsylvania court declared in clear and ringing terms:

By the law it is declared that no man shall be twice put in jeopardy for the same offense; and yet, it is certain that the enquiry, now proposed by the Grand Jury, would necessarily introduce the oppression of a double trial. Nor is it merely upon the maxims of law, but I think, likewise, upon principles of humanity, that this innovation should be opposed.[109]

Perhaps this decision was derived from an interpretation of Article V of the Pennsylvania Charter of Privileges of 1701, which provided that "all criminals shall have the same Privileges and Council as

---

[103] Ms. Mins. NYCQS 1694–1731/32, 30, 51, 53, appearing in Goebel, *Law Enforcement in Colonial New York* (New York, 1944, pp. 570–71.
[104] Ms. Mins. SCJ 1766–1769 (engr.), 504, 505, appearing in *ibid.*, p. 580.
[105] *Ibid.*, p. 589.   [106] See *ibid.*, p. 244.
[107] *Gilbert* v. *Marcy*, Conn. Rep., 1 Kirby 401, 402.
[108] *Hannaball* v. *Spaulding*, Conn. Rep., 1 Root 86.
[109] *Respublica* v. *Shaffer*, 1 Dall. 137 (Pa. 1788 Oyer and Terminer).

their prosecutors." [110] But more likely, the judge was drawing from the common law, especially from Coke and Blackstone, sources of most of the colonial and Revolutionary double jeopardy decisions.

The common law was the common possession of the colonials. The Maryland "Act for the liberties of the people" of 1639 declared that all Christian inhabitants, except slaves, "shall have and enjoy all such rights, liberties, immunities, priviledges and free customs as any naturall born subject of England hath or ought to have or enjoy," [111] including the common law. Similarly, the Continental Congress of 1774 promulgated a declaration of rights which the colonists retained as Englishmen, including as a fundamental right the right "to the common law of England." [112] Of course, this precious heritage was not, so far as double jeopardy is concerned, anticipatory of later needs of a developing American jurisprudence.[113]

In England one of the policy reasons for the development of double jeopardy was the severity of the provisions of criminal law. In many respects, the basis of the policy continued in the American colonies. The severity of the criminal law was even more apparent in those colonies influenced by the gloomy Puritan view of man. The death penalty was available for crimes ranging from murder to false witness, and even for injury to property in the colony of East Jersey.

[110] Poore (comp.), *The Federal and State Constitutions, Colonial Charters, and Other Organic Laws of the United States* (Washington, 1878), II, 36–40.

[111] Browne *et al.* (eds.), *Archives of Maryland* (Baltimore, 1883), I, 41.

[112] *Extracts from the Proceedings of the Continental Congress* (Philadelphia, 1774), p. 6. The New Jersey constitution drafters of 1776 adopted a constitution which, like the earlier Virginia Declaration of Rights, provided certain fundamental criminal protections. The rights of the criminal accused were protected by the grant of right to counsel, and both common law and statute law "as have been heretofore practiced in this Colony" were to remain in force (Poore, *op. cit.*, II, 1310–14).

[113] As in *Rex* v. *Sugar*, 90 Eng. Rep. 554 (K.B. 1696), where the defendants were acquitted of breaking and entering followed by a theft within. On a subsequent attempt to indict them for larceny of the same articles, an entirely separate offense, the court held that "they could not be indicted a-new for the same fact." This result may be reached under the current doctrines, but certainly not for the same reasons. This is but another example of the uncertain basis for early double jeopardy policy.

Repeated criminal offenses also entailed the use of the death penalty. Whipping posts, stocks, pillories, and gallows were common mechanical devices of punishment, the uses of which were not confined to New England.[114]

The severity of colonial criminal law paralleled the English experience, for, "if one were to mark out the period of greatest severity in modern English law, the sixteenth and seventeenth centuries would undoubtedly form the central area." [115] With this condition extant on both sides of the Atlantic, the need of a countervailing protection must have been evident. That protection was available in the double jeopardy doctrine.

The Fifth Amendment and Double Jeopardy

The need for the fundamental protection of double jeopardy began to be recognized by the drafters of post-Revolutionary constitutions. In 1781 a New Hampshire constitutional convention sent a proposed constitution to the voters.[116] This constitution was prefaced by a bill of rights of some thirty-eight articles. The convention declared that the bill of rights contained the essential principles of the constitution.[117] However the proposed declaration of rights "was a wholesale borrowing of the Massachusetts declaration of 1780, with a few additions." [118] One of these additions was a double

---

[114] H. Weiss and G. Weiss, *An Introduction to Crime and Punishment in Colonial New Jersey* (Trenton, 1960), pp. 10, 11, 91. The privilege to withdraw a charge at any time and of remitting the penalty after conviction was available in West Jersey to the persons making the charge (see *ibid.*, p. 12). West Jersey penalties were usually a severe fine and exclusion from holding any public office upon the first offense and exclusion from any employment in the province for the second offense. Even in cases of treason and murder "the death penalty was not to be inflicted until the case was reviewed by the next session of the assembly" (see *ibid.*). These policies are not only in sharp contrast to those of East Jersey, but differ from those of most nations at that time.

[115] Hall, *Theft, Law and Society* (2d ed.; Indianapolis, 1952), p. 117.

[116] Upton, *Revolutionary New Hampshire* (Hanover, 1936), pp. 132–84.

[117] Bouton (ed.), *Documents and Records Relating to Towns in New Hampshire* (Concord, 1874), p. 851.

[118] Rutland, *The Birth of the Bill of Rights* (Chapel Hill, N.C., 1955), p. 75.

jeopardy provision which prevented a second trial for an offense of which the defendant had been previously acquitted. For the first time in American history, the double jeopardy doctrine (in part) was to be elevated to constitutional dignity. Previous constitutions had ignored it. North Carolina, which had once had a virtual res judicata provision, dropped it in the state's 1776 constitution.[119]

The most significant development in the evolution of double jeopardy was its adoption into the federal constitution. As originally submitted to the states, the federal constitution failed to contain a bill of rights, but an irresistible demand for the incorporation of a bill of rights developed in the states.

Maryland was the seventh state to approve the United States Constitution, completing ratification on April 26, 1788. After ratification, the state appointed a committee to report such amendments to the Constitution as were thought necessary. The committee agreed to thirteen amendments. The second proposed amendment was that there should be "no second trial after acquittal." [120] In this highly attenuated form, the double jeopardy concept was to be proposed for inclusion in the Constitution before the first session of the new Congress of the United States. But it was not to emerge as the officially established double jeopardy policy of the United States in this shrunken version.

On June 8, 1789, the following amendment to the Constitution was proposed in the House of Representatives: "No person shall be subject, except in cases of impeachment, to more than one punishment or trial for the same offense." [121] The subject of amendments to the Constitution was broached in Congress by James Madison "to quiet that anxiety which prevails in the public mind." [122] Madison asserted that certain amendments had occurred to him as "proper to

[119] Fundamental Constitutions of Carolina, Sec. 64 (1669). The clause read: "No cause shall be twice tried in any one court, upon any reason or pretence whatsoever."

[120] Elliot, *The Debates on the Adoption of the Federal Constitution* (2d ed.; Washington, 1881), II, 548–49.

[121] Annals of Cong. 434 (1st Cong.).   [122] *Ibid.*, p. 427.

be recommended by Congress to the State Legislatures," and he led the argument in favor of the necessity of including a bill of rights, placing special emphasis upon free speech, free press and jury trial requirements.[123] Madison moved his own propositions by way of a series of resolutions permitting the House to do what they thought proper. His propositons included the substance of the double jeopardy concept.

Madison's propositions were referred to a committee of the whole, while the proposed amendments emanating from state legislatures were tabled. Elbridge Gerry of Massachusetts was opposed to this treatment, pointing out that "it would be disrespectful to those states which had proposed amendments" not to at least consider the views of their authors, the "wisest and most virtuous men of the community." [124] Nonetheless, the amendments, together with the double jeopardy proposal, went to committee. The views of the states, however, were indirectly reflected in Madison's amendments. While framing his propositions Madison had gone over the amendments proposed by the conventions of Massachusetts, South Carolina, New Hampshire, Virginia, New York, and North Carolina, and by minorities in Pennsylvania and Maryland.[125]

Madison was not completely enchanted by the idea of a bill of rights which could be mere "parchment barriers" or could have the salutary effect of making "the political truths in that solemn manner acquire by degrees the character of fundamental maxims of free government." [126] Although Madison's most comprehensive biogra-

---

[123] *Ibid.*, pp. 433, 440–41.   [124] *Ibid.*, pp. 449–50, 445.

[125] Brant, *James Madison, Father of the Constitution, 1787–1800* (Indianapolis, 1950), p. 264.

[126] Letter to Thomas Jefferson, Oct. 17, 1788, in Padover, *The Complete Madison* (New York, 1953), p. 254. James Wilson was one of the most articulate opponents of a Bill of Rights. He found "from the example of other states, as well as from principle, that a bill of rights is neither an essential nor a necessary instrument in framing a system of government, since liberty may exist and be as well secured without it" see James Wilson, "Debate before the Pennsylvania Convention to ratify the United States Constitution," in McMaster and Stone, *Pennsylvania and the Federal Convention* [Lancaster,

pher, Irving Brant, asserted that not one of Madison's original sheaf of amendments was substantially altered in meaning,[127] this statement does not quite hold true for his double jeopardy clause. Still, to Madison must be credited the idea of including double jeopardy in the federal Bill of Rights.

The House saw no urgency in the proposed amendments. Representative Egbert Benson of New York eventually led the opposition against Madison's double jeopardy proposal. Benson said that the committee could not agree to the statement as it stood because its meaning appeared rather doubtful. In saying that no person should be tried more than once for the same offense, the clause was contrary to the right theretofore established. Benson presumed that there was an intention to establish the principle that no man's life should be more than once put in jeopardy for the same offense. It was well known that a defendant was entitled to more than one trial, to the right of appeal if the first trial should prove unfavorable, which right would be denied with Madison's phraseology. Benson moved to strike out the words "or trial." [128]

Roger Sherman of Connecticut, who had been so prominent at the Constitutional Convention, approved of Benson's motion. Sherman maintained that if a person were acquitted on the first trial, that person ought not to be tried again, but if anything should appear on the record of the first trial, he ought to be able to set aside a conviction. In this, Representative Theodore Sedgwick of Massachusetts concurred, insisting that instead of securing the liberty of the subject, it would be abridging the privileges of those who were prosecuted. Upon being put to a vote, however, Benson's motion lost by a considerable majority. Representative George Partridge moved to insert after the words "same offense" the words "by any law of the United States." This motion, too, was lost,[129] permitting the specu-

---

Pa., 1888], p. 253). Wilson's argument was certainly true of double jeopardy, which had long been a part of the common law and had achieved actual constitutional status only in New Hampshire.

[127] Brant, *op. cit.*, p. 275.   [128] 1 Annals of Cong. 753.
[129] *Ibid.*, pp. 753–54.

lation by negative inference that double jeopardy may have been intended to apply to the states and the federal government alike.[130] On August 20, 1789, the fifth clause of Madison's fourth proposition, the double jeopardy concept as phrased by Madison, was approved by the House. Benson proposed a resolution that the amendments be submitted to the states for the approval of three-fourths of their respective legislatures. Benson was chosen to direct the arrangement of the amendments and, together with Sherman and Sedgwick, to report to the whole House after the completion of their efforts.[131] These three men, although they had opposed the double jeopardy phraseology of Madison, reported their arrangement of the articles of amendment, leaving the clause untouched.

On August 24, 1789, the articles as approved by the House were sent to the Senate for the deliberations of that chamber.[132] As submitted, the double jeopardy phrase still read, "no person shall be subject, except in case of impeachment, to more than one trial, or one punishment for the same offence." [133] This proposition was ultimately adopted by the Senate, with the substitution of "be twice put in jeopardy of life or limb by any public prosecution," for the latter half of Madison's clause. On September 9, the articles were combined and renumbered, the present-day fifth amendment comprising Article VII.[134] With this, the Senate completed its rapid consideration of the double jeopardy concept. The House had disposed of the matter in an even briefer period of time.

A conference committee of Madison, Sherman, and John Vining from the House conferred with the Senate appointees on September 21 to resolve their differences with respect to the proposed amendments. The House had resolved to disagree with the fifth amend-

---

[130] The question raised in the case of *Palko* v. *Connecticut,* 302 U.S. 319 (1937), is fundamental to double jeopardy law—that is, whether the clause of the federal constitution applies to the states. This is some slim evidence that *Palko* may be quite wrong, on historical grounds. Some early cases took this position. See *State* v. *Moor,* 1 Miss. 134 (1823); *Phillips* v. *McCauley,* 92 F. 790 (2d Cir. 1937), discusses the problem.

[131] 1 Annals of Cong. 767, 777.   [132] *Ibid.,* p. 779.

[133] 1 S. Jour. 105 (1789).   [134] *Ibid.,* pp. 119, 130.

ment proposed by the Senate. Somewhere, beyond the ken of the recording secretaries, the words "by any public prosecution" were eliminated from the phrase. At any rate, on Friday, September 25, the Senate concurred in the articles to be proposed to the legislatures of the states, as amended.[135]

It has been noted that the double jeopardy clause was adopted by the First Congress of the United States without much debate or indication of its intended meaning. The clause was intended to be "declaratory of the law as it now stood" and was to conform to the "universal practice in Great Britain and in this country." [136] But there are significant differences between Madison's proposal and the present phraseology of the clause. Madison's proposition may have been taken from the declaration of rights contained in the New York Act of Ratification, or from the Maryland committee's proposition.[137] None of these proposals, or the other American constitutional double jeopardy provision (New Hampshire's) was quite the same as that which was finally adopted. What was the meaning of this hastily adopted clause?

In all probability, the drafters of the clause intended to alter Madison's proposal only with a view to its clarification. Madison's wording called for a single trial for a single offense. The phrase finally adopted uses the much less precise "jeopardy of life or limb," which phrase, though borrowed from reputable common law sources, is not a clear declaration of policy. This antique language only served to open the door to misinterpretation and confusion. It permits the existence of a condition in which a court "without articulating equitable considerations [will] repeat old formulas devised at a time when different historical considerations prevailed." [138] The

---

[135] 1 Annals of Cong. 83, 88.   [136] 53 *Nw. U. L. Rev.* 521 (1958), n.

[137] *Documentary History of the United States* (Washington, 1894), II, 192.

[138] 65 *Yale L.J.* 345 (1936), n. See *United States* v. *Haskell,* 26 F. Cas. 207 (No. 15,321) (C.C.E.D. Pa. 1823), which states, logically enough, that "the jeopardy spoken of in this article can be interpreted to mean nothing short of the acquittal or conviction of the prisoner and the judgment of the court thereupon. This was the meaning affixed to the expression by the common law, notwithstanding some loose expressions to be found in some elementary

drafters of the double jeopardy clause were so steeped in common law that they tended to perpetuate its inadequacies rather than declare a precise protection for a criminal defendant.

The double jeopardy clause, now firmly embedded in the fifth amendment, was ratified by the requisite number of states, though many state legislators were not certain of its meaning. Indeed, it is doubtful that Massachusetts ever ratified the portion of the fifth amendment which affects double jeopardy.[139] No original record of ratification has ever been found. Massachusetts never adopted the protection into any of her own state constitutions, including the present one. The historical irony is striking, since American double jeopardy began in the Bay Colony and there reached its broadest scope as a public policy.

Other states were slow to accept the federal formula for their own. In 1792, New Hampshire included a constitutional provision requiring a prior acquittal: "No subject shall be liable to be tried, after an acquittal, for the same crime or offence." [140] In 1801, in Vermont, the proper defense to be pleaded was *auterfoits acquit*, not double jeopardy,[141] although the federal courts have perceived that the pleas of autrefois convict and autrefois acquit were merged in the one plea of double jeopardy.[142]

The state of Delaware became a convert to the exact words of the federal clause in 1792.[143] At present, the language of thirty-five state constitutions follows that of the fifth amendment rather closely.

---

treatises, or in the opinions of some judges, which would seem to intimate a different opinion." A state court judge concluded that "the clause of the Fifth Amendment . . . being a maxim imbedded in the very elements of the common law . . . is properly interpreted by the authorized exposition established at its adoption" (*Hoffman* v. *State,* 20 Md. 434 [1863]). Both these cases seem to propose adopting the English law of jeopardy. This is not the federal law or the law of most of the states of the union.

[139] Dangel, "Double Jeopardy in Massachusetts," 16 *B.U.L. Rev.* 384 (1936).

[140] New Hampshire Constitution of 1792, Bill of Rights, Art. XVI.

[141] *State* v. *I.S.S.,* Tyler's Reports, Case No. 178 (Vt. 1801).

[142] See *Helvering* v. *Mitchell,* 303 U.S. 391 (1937).

[143] Delaware Constitution of 1792, Art. I, Sec. 8.

Some states have altered the federal requirement. For example, Mississippi stipulates in her constitution that "there must be an actual acquittal or conviction on the merits to bar another prosecution." [144]

Seven states provide a protection against subsequent trials only in cases of prior acquittal.[145] Despite some discrepancies, however, the process of receiving double jeopardy into American constitutions has been fairly complete. In some jurisdictions, the protection is relegated to the common law,[146] but these provide exceptions to a general rule which accords double jeopardy the status of a fundamental right.

In 1816, when Joseph Chitty wrote his *Practical Treatise on the Criminal Law*, the problems and the current conceptualization of double jeopardy seem to have taken form. He gave much attention to the problems of the identity of offenses, of lesser-included offenses, of the attachment of jeopardy, and the like. He cited Blackstone and Coke frequently as authority and usually resorted to the use of the English names for the plea. Chitty, among others, adopted the English law of attachment of jeopardy.[147] But America was not to accept the solutions which England had developed. In time, a distinctive body of American law grew up around the double jeopardy clause.

Summary

The most important event in the development of double jeopardy was the occasion of its incorporation into the federal constitution. This occurrence represents the transformation of a general maxim of

144 Mississippi Constitution, Art. III, Sec. 22.

145 Michigan Constitution, Art. III, Sec. 14; Missouri Constitution, Art. I, Sec. 19; New Hampshire Constitution, P. I, Sec. 16; New Jersey Constitution, Art. I, Sec. 11; Oklahoma Constitution, Art. II, Sec. 21; Rhode Island Constitution, Art. I, Sec. 7; Texas Constitution, Art. I, Sec. 14.

146 See *United States* v. *Benz*, 282 U.S. 304 (1931); *State* v. *Duvall*, 135 La. 710, 165 So. 104 (1914).

147 Chitty, *A Practical Treatise on the Criminal Law* (Philadelphia, 1819), I, 376.

English criminal law into a general rule of public policy. The significance of the event was unappreciated at the time because American criminal law enforcement had not developed an established pattern. Of course, questions of double jeopardy arise only when the potentiality for multiple incrimination arises and that federal criminal law was extremely scant during the early years of the Republic. Double jeopardy pleas were quite rare. At the time of its adoption into the federal constitution, the meaning of the double jeopardy concept was unclear. The latent possibilities presented by the clause could not be encouraged until the dimensions of the criminal law were ascertained. Double jeopardy questions precede questions of substantive criminal law and become more significant as the number of incriminated acts increase, and then only if other methods of restraining the prosecutor's discretion are inadequate.

The moral sentiment which double jeopardy exemplifies is the feeling that no man should suffer twice for a single act. This sentiment is to be found among the Roman jurists, the canon lawyers, and the legal writers of many other traditions. However, a moral sentiment is not a sufficient guide for the formulation of public policy. In its modern environment double jeopardy must deal with the interrelationship between substantive criminal law and the legal powers of the public prosecutor to select the categories of punishment. In order to define that relationship, legislatures could establish the legal pattern. If legislatures fail to act, it is necessary for courts to control the policy by employing the most available instrument, which is the double jeopardy clause. If neither the legislature nor the courts performed the task, the frequency of repeated criminal suits for the same conduct would be greatly increased.

The historical development of double jeopardy is so complex that its genesis provides no sure indication of its meaning. During one period, the doctrine seems to have been a protection only against repeated private prosecution; at another (especially in Puritan Massachusetts) its protection extended to both civil and criminal suits. The public policy of terminating criminal litigation has been

35

confused with the policy of preventing multiple punishment for the commission of a single criminal act.[148] The failure to make this distinction still continues to hamper the formulation of double jeopardy policy.[149]

In order to ascertain at what point double jeopardy may be said to have had its inception, a problem of definition must be overcome. The answer depends on whether one considers the generalized maxim to be the same as a social policy limiting the power of the state to conduct criminal prosecutions. Under the former definition, double jeopardy may be found in Roman law or in the writings of Bracton.[150] Under the latter meaning, adopted here, the existence of double jeopardy requires a developed substantive criminal law and an advanced stage of criminal procedure. Such a position would identify the beginnings of double jeopardy as occurring about the time of Sir Edward Coke. Because certain archaic features of earlier criminal procedure remained in England later than in the United States, however, the development of double jeopardy was divergent after the American Revolution. Although double jeopardy existed in England, it did not achieve the status of a fundamental protection.[151] The principle of double jeopardy is itself merely a general concept without a definite content until the courts or the legislatures supply definite policies.[152]

[148] This distinction is noted by Judge John O. Bigelow in a leading article on double jeopardy entitled, "Former Conviction and Former Acquittal," 11 *Rutg. L. Rev.* 490 (1957). He states that from the failure of judicial opinions to distinguish between a conviction and an acquittal has grown a law "insufficient in sound policy." Judge Bigelow does not give clear historical evidence, although he suggests it. See 57 *Yale L.J.* 133 (1947), which demonstrates that the confusion of these two policies pervades the history of double jeopardy.

[149] 11 *Stan. L. Rev.* 735 (1959), n.

[150] Bracton, *De legibus et consuetudinibus angliae,* ed. Woodbine (London, 1922), pp. 391, 397.

[151] Radin, *Handbook of Anglo-American Legal History* (St. Paul, Minn., 1936), pp. 226–27.

[152] Of course the delusion persists that the double jeopardy clause has a specific content. See *State v. Jones,* 7 Ga. 422, 424 (1849): *"Nemo debet bis vexari pro una et eadem causa;* which rule, for greater caution and in a

History has given American law a double jeopardy concept as a part of its most fundamental principles. That concept, which is directed towards the protection of the criminal defendant and against the state's power, is the product of innumerable cases and writings. But history alone cannot determine the content of the double jeopardy ideal. The conflicting needs of society and the individual which are inherent in double jeopardy must be resolved by each generation. A reconsideration of the policy may reveal that its basis has disappeared, or the contrary. A continued neglect of the task may cause the concept to become obsolescent.

---

stricter vigilance over the rights of the citizens against the State, has been in substance embodied in the Constitution of the United States, thus: 'nor shall any person be subject, for the same offense, to be twice in jeopardy of life or limb.' "

» 2 «

Federal Double Jeopardy Policy*

Understanding the American view of double jeopardy requires, at first, a fresh examination of the decisions of the national courts. The doctrine is related to the system of federalism, which is itself undergoing change.[1] The scope of the fifth [2] and fourth amendments [3] is also being altered. The basic issue of the extent of the fifth amendment's requirements has been re-examined by state courts on the double jeopardy issue.[4] *Malloy* v. *Hogan* [5] recently applied the self-incrimination clause against the states. So it seems likely that double jeopardy will eventually become incorporated as well.[6] However, although an understanding of the nature of federal double jeopardy policy is useful, the federal cases do not provide great wisdom or insight in this area.

The double jeopardy clause may profitably be viewed as a series of problems in social policy which are usually treated as a single problem. Analyzed in this fashion, double jeopardy law may be resolved into five separate policy situations. The first situation con-

---

* This chapter originally appeared in the *Vanderbilt Law Review*, Vol. 19 (1966), pp. 375–405, and is reprinted with the permission of the Vanderbilt University School of Law.

[1] See *United States* v. *Guest*, 383 U.S. 745 (1966).

[2] *Miranda* v. *Arizona*, 384 U.S. 436 (1966).

[3] *Ker* v. *California*, 374 U.S. 23 (1963).

[4] *People* v. *Laws*, 29 Ill. 2d 221, 193 N.E.2d 806 (1963).

[5] 378 U.S. 1 (1964).

[6] See Louis Henkin, "Selective Incorporations in the Fourteenth Amendment," 73 *Yale L. J.* 74 (1963).

cerns the definition of jeopardy and the question of when jeopardy can be said to attach. The second situation concerns the desirability of a uniform national policy and is to be clearly differentiated from the third, which involves the legal significance to be accorded traditional jurisdictional lines. The fourth situation, the scope of the criminal act, is the thorniest and is most closely related to the substantive criminal law. The final problem is that of the significance to be given the use of the criminal appeal, whether employed by the prosecution or the defendant. These separate problems are usually treated together under the rubric "double jeopardy," tending to confuse an already complicated concept.

Definition of Jeopardy: When Jeopardy Attaches

Once the double jeopardy clause had become an accepted part of American constitutions, the phrase "life or limb" began to receive an interpretation broad enough to apply the protection to any criminal penalty so that the threat of death or mutilation was removed as a necessary element of the doctrine.[7] While this development was fairly obvious, the further implications of double jeopardy have been more complicated. History provided some hints with which to guide the judges, but the creation of double jeopardy policy was largely a novel task.

A recent case enunciates the modern formula of federal double jeopardy policy in broad terms:

Once acquitted or convicted of a crime for his conduct in a particular transaction, a defendant should be able to consider the matter closed and plan his life ahead without the threat of subsequent prosecution and possible imprisonment.[8]

Other objectives of that policy might be the avoidance of unnecessary harrassment, the avoidance of social stigma incident upon repeated criminal trials, economy of time and money, and psychologi-

[7] *Ex parte Lange,* 85 U.S. (18 Wall.) 163 (1873). Based upon common law precedents, the case held that both former acquittal and former conviction were comprised in the protection to the accused.

[8] *United States* v. *Candalaria,* 131 F. Supp. 797 (S.D. Cal. 1955).

39

cal security.[9] These meanings of double jeopardy are not derived from its history.

The increasing tendency of modern penal legislation to create more detailed and more numerous criminal offenses has further complicated the problem of setting double jeopardy policy because it has increased the number of offense categories which proscribe a single criminal act.[10] Now one transaction may afford the prosecution a choice of two counts or separate indictments where only one existed previously. This would not be inherently detrimental if the decision to create more overlapping offenses were the fruit of a conscious legislative policy. However, it has been left to the courts to determine legislative intent and, by implication, to repeal or add to the criminal statutes. The decision ultimately determines the powers of the prosecutor's office.

Constitutionally, there is nothing to prevent the legislature from repeatedly incriminating similar acts, but there is a limitation on the judiciary forbidding it from ordering multiple punishment when it appears that the legislature did not so intend.[11] The use of the judge's sentencing power or of the executive's pardoning power may be said to mitigate legislative duplication,[12] but these remedies occur at too late a point in time, that is, after a defendant has been harassed by the state and the damage has been done.

Several distinguishable factual situations account for the overwhelming number of double jeopardy cases and have created disparate policy requirements. These situations may be suggested:

1. The trial of a case is stopped at some point short of its final termination.

2. The trial concludes with an acquittal, and the prosecution begins another trial upon another indictment.

[9] See comment, 65 *Yale L. J.* 339 (1956).

[10] See *Bozza* v. *United States,* 330 U.S. 160 (1947); *Fleischer* v. *United States,* 91 F.2d 404 (6th Cir. 1939).

[11] See *People* v. *Moore,* 143 Cal. App. 2d 333, 299 P.2d 691 (1956).

[12] But see *Samsone* v. *Zerbst,* 73 F.2d 670 (10th Cir. 1934), a case which, in typical fashion, avoids judicial responsibility for separation of offenses by relying without question upon legislative determination of multiple sentencing and multiple punishment for the same act.

3. The trial ends with a conviction, and the defendant appeals and is either later convicted of a greater offense than he was originally indicated for or is convicted of the same offense as well as on other counts not contained in the original indictment.

4. The trial ends with a conviction, and the defendant is later tried for offenses "arising out of the same transaction," but which are technically different from the original charges, in an entirely new proceeding.

5. Overlapping jurisdictional boundaries may result in repeated punishments for the same act. Thus, civil-criminal distinctions or federal-state, civilian-military, or foreign-domestic jurisdictional lines may cause the same action to be tried again as an offense of a different kind or against a different sovereign.

6. One act may constitute conduct directed at several persons or objects. The question arises whether each person or object injured represents a criminally punishable act.

It is very common for judges to confuse these separate situations. Double jeopardy law has become so tangled that in some respects the outcome of a plea is in great doubt. Rarely will a court face the critical policy issues which lie deep beneath the surface. This recent policy statement is an exception:

[The provision of the Fifth Amendment against double jeopardy is] designed to protect an individual from being subjected to the hazards of trial and possible conviction more than once for an alleged offense. . . . [The] underlying idea . . . is that the State with all its resources and power should not be allowed to make repeated attempts to convict an individual for an alleged offense, thereby subjecting him to embarrassment, expense and ordeal, and compelling him to live in a continuing state of anxiety and insecurity, as well as enhancing the possibility that even though innocent he may be found guilty.[13]

Approached chronologically, the first question which can arise in double jeopardy law is whether a prior uncompleted trial had reached such a degree of maturation as to amount to a "jeopardy." While some early cases held to the contrary, the contention that

[13] *Green* v. *United States,* 355 U.S. 184, 187 (1957).

"jeopardy" referred only to a prior conviction or acquittal was rejected in the federal courts because "there is a wide difference between a verdict given and the jeopardy of a verdict," since "hazard, peril, danger, jeopardy of a verdict cannot mean a verdict given." [14] But this rule remained unsettled as late as 1833, when it was held that in order to bar prosecution a former conviction must be pleaded.[15] A judgment of acquittal based on the operation of a statute of limitations as a bar to a prior case is definitely a former jeopardy.[16]

Once it is agreed that jeopardy does not require a final judgment, a host of new issues arises. The most important issue is whether there had been a sufficient amount of risk on the previous trial to amount to a putting in jeopardy. The problem is usually referred to as the "attachment of jeopardy" situation. If there has been no attachment of jeopardy, the prior trial is treated as though it never existed and it is blotted out of legal memory.

Some mystifying results are produced by this theory. For example, in a recent case, the discharge of a jury because of misconduct of a defense counsel was held to bar a retrial.[17] The trial court on its own motion, even over defendant's objection, ordered a mistrial. Subsequently, the defendant moved to dismiss the indictment on the theory that he had been placed in jeopardy. The decision was based on the ground that "dismissing the jury in a criminal action without defendant's consent precludes another trial except where dismissal arises out of circumstances of necessity." As a practical matter, defendant was acquitted virtually because the trial judge had acted hastily in ordering a mistrial.

Despite the complications which are evident, the rule for the attachment of jeopardy has been stated briefly, as follows:

[14] This Pennsylvania decision, *Commonwealth* v. *Cook,* 6 S. & R. 577, 596 (1822), became the federal rationale. But in 1823, *United States* v. *Haskell,* 26 F. Cas. 207 (No. 15,321) (C.C.E.D. Pa. 1823), the federal court still adhered to the English rule requiring final judgment.

[15] *United States* v. *Wilson,* 32 U.S. (7 Pet.) 150, 160 (1833).

[16] *United States* v. *Oppenheimer,* 242 U.S. 85 (1916).

[17] *United States* v. *Whitlow,* 110 F. Supp. 871 (D.C. Cir. 1953).

[A] person has been in jeopardy when he is regularly charged with a crime before a tribunal properly organized and competent to try him. . . . Undoubtedly in those jurisdictions where a trial of one accused of a crime can only be to a jury, and a verdict of acquittal or conviction must be by a jury, no legal jeopardy can attach until a jury has been called and charged with the deliverance of the accused.[18]

After the impaneling of the jury, jeopardy can be said to attach when any evidence is heard, or testimony received, but before the prosecution presents its opening argument to the jury.[19] However, preliminary examination by a magistrate is not a trial,[20] and arraignment and pleadings are not trials.[21] Interestingly, Congress has provided a double jeopardy protection for military personnel tried under the Uniform Code of Military Justice, but it has stipulated that only final judgments would have the effect of prior jeopardy.[22]

In cases of "manifest necessity," exceptions to the attachment rule permit the trial judge to order a new trial without confronting a double jeopardy plea. If the jury cannot agree, or if it is illegally constituted, there is no trial and no former jeopardy.[23] A leading case confused the doctrines of "attachment" and "waiver" by holding that where a conviction was set aside on appeal there had been no jeopardy.[24]

Other instances of "manifest necessity" are a juror's acquaintance

---

[18] *Kepner* v. *United States*, 195 U.S. 100, 128 (1904). This case is better known for Holmes's dissent, in which he proposes the concept of "continuing jeopardy" for appeals by the federal government to be upheld.

[19] *Clawens* v. *Rives*, 104 F.2d 240 (D.C. Cir. 1939).

[20] *Collins* v. *Loisel*, 262 U.S. 426 (1922).

[21] *Bassing* v. *Cady*, 208 U.S. 386 (1907).

[22] Art. 44, 70A Stat. 52, 10 U.S.C. Sec. 844 (1964); S. Rep. No. 486, 81st Cong., 1st Sess. 19 (1949); H.R. Rep. No. 491, 81st Cong., 1st Sess. 23 (1949). This rule was upheld as not violative of the fifth amendment when applied by a military tribunal (*United States* v. *Zimmerman*, 2 C.M.R. 66 [1952]).

[23] *United States* v. *Perez*, 22 U.S. (9 Wheat.) 579 (1824).

[24] *Trono* v. *United States*, 199 U.S. 521 (1905); Corwin, *The Constitution and What It Means Today* (Princeton, N.J., 1958), p. 213, makes the same error, which confuses separate problems.

with the accused,[25] irregularity in the indictment,[26] absence of witnesses for tactical military reasons,[27] illness of a juror,[28] termination of a court term, and other emergencies or unusual circumstances.[29] A double jeopardy plea was not permitted when the previous trial resulted in a mistrial because the state's witnesses pleaded self-incrimination.[30] However, no "manifest necessity" was discerned sufficient to meet a claim of jeopardy having attached when, on the original action, the prosecution had been unable to secure the presence of needed witnesses.[31]

Generally stated, necessity intervening after attachment mitigates against the operation of double jeopardy.[32] The exceptions are legion. The tendency of the appellate courts to leave the discretion of the trial judge undisturbed has been marked. If the judge at the first trial senses the necessity of premature termination, perhaps it is not desirable to permit a defendant to utilize his double jeopardy plea. The dimensions of the "manifest necessity" exception are definitely, if not logically, indicated by the cases.

Several recent decisions have sought to clarify and simplify the rules concerning attachment. In the most important decision, *Downum* v. *United States*,[33] it was held that a second trial was barred where, because of the prosecutor's failure to find a principal witness, the original trial judge dismissed the jury before any evidence had been introduced. In *Gori* v. *United States*,[34] the trial

---

[25] *Simmons* v. *United States*, 142 U.S. 148 (1891).

[26] *Lovato* v. *New Mexico*, 242 U.S. 199 (1916).

[27] *Wade* v. *Hunter*, 336 U.S. 684 (1949).

[28] *United States* v. *Potash*, 118 F.2d 54 (2d Cir. 1941).

[29] *Thompson* v. *United States*, 155 U.S. 271 (1894).

[30] *Brock* v. *North Carolina*, 344 U.S. 424 (1953).

[31] *Correro* v. *United States*, 48 F.2d 69 (9th Cir. 1931). *Contra United States* v. *Coolidge*, 25 F. Cas. 622 (No. 14,858) (C.C.D. Mass. 1815).

[32] *Himmelfarb* v. *United States*, 175 F.2d 924 (9th Cir. 1949).

[33] 372 U.S. 734 (1963).

[34] 367 U.S. 364 (1961). In *Fong Foo* v. *United States*, 369 U.S. 141 (1961), *reversing sub. nom., In re United States*, 286 F.2d 556 (1st Cir. 1961), the trial judge, having discovered that, during the recess of a long and complicated trial the prosecution had refreshed the memory of a witness, called upon the jury to render an acquittal of the defendant. The judge thus

judge had declared a mistrial in order to protect the defendant from irrelevant and prejudical testimony. On retrial a conviction was obtained and was not considered double jeopardy since the judge was acting in the defendant's interest even though over his objection. Although the facts of the cases are irreconcilable, the decisions can be reconciled on the ground that the trial judge's determination regarding the impact of questioning and testimony upon a jury is less reviewable than his decision regarding the prosecutor's failure to proceed with trial. Where the trial judge forces a plea of guilty upon a defendant, however, a new trial is not barred by double jeopardy.[35] It seems, then, that judicial animosity towards the defendant is to be treated differently from a prosecutor's animosity towards the defendant because of the supposed neutral role of the judge.

Despite these cases, the doctrine of "manifest necessity" remains confused.[36] The states differ considerably in their views concerning the attachment of jeopardy. The Supreme Court has held as a matter of due process that a state need not abandon jurisdiction for reasons of double jeopardy because mob violence has rendered a trial abortive.[37] The Court will defer to state law when it permits a new trial in cases where the federal law as to attachment of jeopardy would produce a different result.[38] The case of *Palko* v. *Connecticut* has been relied upon as a source for this permissive attitude, as long as the criminal defendant is not subjected to "unendurable hardship" or a violation of some "fundamental principle of liberty and justice."[39]

A closely related problem, although rarely treated as such, is that

---

aborted the case and caused jeopardy to attach, barring a retrial. The Supreme Court insisted on a distinction between the effects of a mistrial (not effecting jeopardy) and an acquittal (which does).

[35] *United States* v. *Tateo,* 377 U.S. 463 (1964).

[36] See H. Kaminsky, "Double Jeopardy and the Doctrine of Manifest Necessity," 20 *Intra. L. Rev.* 189, 200 (1965).

[37] *Frank* v. *Magnum,* 237 U.S. 309 (1915).

[38] *Brock* v. *North Carolina,* 344 U.S. 424 (1953).

[39] 302 U.S. 319 (1937).

of postconviction sentencing. In such cases it is usually held that jeopardy has not yet attached, because the sentencing process is a part of the original trial. It has been held that a second sentence entered after the reversal of a previous sentence, but without a second trial, is no violation of due process, nor does it place a defendant in double jeopardy.[40] Here, correction of a mandatory legal penalty is not double jeopardy and should not give a defendant his release.[41] The accumulation of sentences does not amount to a putting in double jeopardy, "and a single sentence for several offenses, in excess of that prescribed for one offense, may be authorized by statute." [42]

It is possible to dissect the attachment cases and discover certain policy features which usually escape the eye. The following competing social interests are at stake:

1. The interest in permitting the prosecution to have full and complete opportunity to present all the evidence that the state has available and in preventing an accused from going free solely by virtue of the operation of the double jeopardy clause, regardless of the merits of the case.

2. The interest in preventing the prosecution from harassing a defendant with repeated trials, any of which may be terminated at the whim of the prosecution. Two considerations are: (a) the moral impropriety of permitting the state a second chance to prosecute an accused, and (b) the practical effect of forcing the prosecution to prepare its best case before beginning suit.

3. The interest in preventing an extraneous event, not connected with the merits of a case, from interfering with the prosecuting of a criminal matter (the justification for the exceptions to attachment of jeopardy).

A more realistic and workable distinction in this area would be between extrinsic and intrinsic factors in the presentation of a case which prevent the case from being carried to its normal conclusion.

40 *Murphy* v. *Massachusetts*, 177 U.S. 155 (1900).
41 *Bozza* v. *United States*, 330 U.S. 160 (1947).
42 *Carter* v. *McClaughry*, 183 U.S. 365, 394 (1902).

Using this formula, when a case is halted by an event not caused by the defense or the prosecution, it should be retried. In those cases where the intervening event is caused by the prosecution, and policy requires the single presentation of the prosecution's case, it can be determined as a factual matter whether the prosecution had a reasonable opportunity to present the state's best case. If the intervening factor is caused by the defendant, he should not be heard to object. This suggestion could help eliminate the arbitrary character of this branch of law.

Desirability of a Uniform National Policy

Another aspect of federal double jeopardy law which deserves discussion is the social desirability of a nationally uniform or a federally disparate system of double jeopardy. This involves some of the most sensitive recent developments in the double jeopardy area. When the need for a uniform national policy is perceived to be the underlying problem, however, much of the controversy which has raged over these cases dwindles into insignificance. One of the fundamental questions raised is whether federal double jeopardy principles bind the states through the due process clause of the fifth amendment.

Barron v. Baltimore [43] first indicated that the fifth amendment was largely a federal concern and not a limitation upon state criminal proceedings. When the fourteenth amendment's due process clause was later substituted for this purpose, it became apparent that the fifth amendment still did not apply to the states.[44] Some earlier cases had indicated the contrary,[45] but in 1847 it was held specifically that the double jeopardy provision did not act as a limitation upon the use of state power.[46] That is still the present rule although considerable criticism has recently developed.[47]

[43] 32 U.S. (7 Pet.) 242 (1833).

[44] Hurtado v. California, 110 U.S. 516 (1884).

[45] See State v. Moor, 1 Miss. 134 (1823); accord Phillips v. McCauley, 92 F.2d 790 (1937).

[46] Fox v. Ohio, 46 U.S. (5 How.) 410 (1847).

[47] Justices Black and Douglas hold that the federal double jeopardy clause sets the standard for state criminal proceedings, either directly through the

Until 1900, the door was still open to the possibility of imposing some standards for double jeopardy on the states as an aspect of due process. In that year the Supreme Court hinted that states might have varying standards, but until 1937 the Court always avoided the question whether double jeopardy was protected by the fourteenth amendment.[48] In 1902 the Court refused to pass on the issue when it was squarely presented.[49] By 1915 it seemed clear that "the state [might] conduct successive criminal trials for the same offense" if there is no showing "that the accused [had] been subjected to unendurable hardships, or violations of fundamental principles of liberty and justice." [50] But the basis of this case was narrow, for the Court held that to rule otherwise would "impair the power of the states to repress and punish crime" in a situation in which mob violence had erupted at the first trial. Before the First World War the Supreme Court was willing to review state criminal trials only to the extent necessary to find that the state court had properly exercised its jurisdiction.[51]

States were allowed to weaken the protection against self-incrimination [52] and to alter the common law trial by jury,[53] even

---

fifth amendment or indirectly through the fourteenth. Black dissented with Douglas in *Ciucci* v. *Illinois* 356 U.S. 571 (1958); Douglas dissented with Black in *Hoag* v. *New Jersey*, 356 U.S. 464 (1958); and Black dissented in *Brock* v. *North Carolina*, 344 U.S. 424 (1953). Black's dissent in *Abbate* v. *United States*, 359 U.S. 187 (1959), shows his reliance on the negative historical inference from Partridge's proposed amendment to the original double jeopardy clause, mentioned above.

[48] *Graham* v. *West Virginia*, 224 U.S. 616 (1912); *Brantley* v. *Georgia*, 217 U.S. 284 (1910); *Keerl* v. *Montana*, 213 U.S. 135 (1909); *Shoerer* v. *Pennsylvania*, 207 U.S. 188 (1907); *McDonald* v. *Massachusetts*, 180 U.S. 311 (1901); *Murphy* v. *Massachusetts*, 177 U.S. 155 (1900); *Hawker* v. *New York*, 170 U.S. 189 (1898); *Moore* v. *Missouri*, 159 U.S. 673 (1895).

[49] *Dreyer* v. *Illinois*, 187 U.S. 71 (1902), refused to pass upon the effect of the fourteenth amendment upon double jeopardy, "upon which question we need not now express an opinion."

[50] *Frank* v. *Magnum*, 237 U.S. 309 (1915).

[51] Mason and Beaney, *American Constitutional Law* (2d ed.; Englewood Cliffs, N.J., 1959).

[52] *Twining* v. *New Jersey*, 211 U.S. 78 (1908).

[53] *Maxwell* v. *Dow*, 176 U.S. 581 (1900).

though the Court had long since agreed that the fourteenth amendment included certain of the first amendment freedoms. In 1937 the Supreme Court, through Justice Cardozo, reaffirmed its previous assertions that the entire Bill of Rights was not incorporated into the fourteenth amendment. The decision in *Palko* v. *Connecticut* [54] attempted to justify a selective incorporation and had special reference to double jeopardy.

In *Palko* a Connecticut statute had permitted the prosecution to appeal from the adverse rulings of the state's criminal courts, a practice not permitted in the federal system. Palko, after having been convicted of murder in the second degree and given a life sentence, was retried after a successful state appeal. He was convicted of first degree murder in the second trial and sentenced to death. Palko appealed, claiming that he had been placed twice in jeopardy.

The United States Supreme Court held that the kind of jeopardy to which Connecticut had subjected the defendant "would have to create a hardship so acute and shocking as to be unendurable, and as to violate those fundamental principles of ordered liberty which lie at the base of all our civil and political institutions." [55] In reaching this result the Court placed double jeopardy, as well as most other protections accorded criminal defendants, on a different constitutional plane from certain more fundamental freedoms taken over from the earlier articles of the Bill of Rights. In effect, each federal court must measure each claim of double jeopardy arising out of state courts to see whether it violates fundamental principles of liberty and justice. The answer in the *Palko* case was "no" because the state was not attempting to wear down the defendant by a multitude of cases, but asking only "that the case against him shall go on until there shall be a trial free from substantial legal error." [56]

In no case has the Supreme Court found a due process defect in successive state criminal prosecutions for a single offense. One may ask whether the Court has not ignored a good many other aspects of

[54] 302 U.S. 319 (1937).   [55] *Ibid.*, p. 328.
[56] *Sapir* v. *United States*, 348 U.S. 373 (1955) (by implication).

49

double jeopardy policy by employing a low standard. Justice Black has said that he fears "to see the consequences of the Court's practice of substituting its own concepts of decency and fundamental justice for the language of the Bill of Rights." [57] So far as double jeopardy is concerned, Black's fears are groundless. The Court has imposed such a high degree of self-restraint that many state variations in double jeopardy policy are permitted.

The *Palko* ruling has meant a multiplicity of solutions to the problems of double jeopardy and, by later interpretations, prevented the setting of national minimum standards of double jeopardy. Uniformity of American double jeopardy law was made impossible. By withdrawing federal power in the double jeopardy area, the *Palko* decision runs counter to a general trend toward greater Supreme Court concern with defendant's rights, for "the enhancement of the relative importance of the federal government in many aspects of criminal law administration is one of the most significant developments in the recent history of criminal justice in America." [58]

The *Palko* decision still represents the basic dividing line between the states and the federal government in the double jeopardy area, and there are prospects of its being overruled. The decision was employed as authority in a case in which the defendant claimed that the prosecution had sought a new trial after a mistrial had been obtained, even though the prosecution had supposedly known that the grounds for the mistrial had been present.[59] The *Palko* case was relied upon because of a supposed factual similarity, so it is not entirely clear that dissimilar factual situations will be treated in the same fashion. However, Mr. Justice Frankfurter, concurring in the majority decision, observed:

[A] state falls short of its obligation when it callously subjects an individual to successive retrials on a charge on which he has been acquitted or prevents a trial from proceeding to a termination in favor of the accused

[57] *Adamson* v. *California*, 332 U.S. 46 (1947) (dissenting opinion).

[58] Allen, "The Supreme Court, Federalism, and State Systems of Criminal Justice," 8 *DePaul L. Rev.* 213 (1958).

[59] *Brock* v. *North Carolina*, 344 U.S. 424 (1953).

merely in order to allow a prosecutor who has been incompetent or casual or ineffective to see if he cannot do better a second time.[60]

As it is, a sufficiently flagrant example of harassment might result in application of the fourteenth amendment.

What are the states permitted to do under the *Palko* rule? If a statute permits, the state may appeal in case of error, since "this merely places the state in a positon of equality with the defendant." [61] The rule exists even though the common law did not permit appeals by the state,[62] and even though the federal government may not have this privilege.[63] But a state may not appeal from an acquittal and obtain a new trial in the absence of a statute, even though a defendant may be retried after obtaining a reversal of a conviction following his own appeal.[64] It is settled law that there is no denial of due process when a defendant has a conviction set aside and is later retried for the same offense.[65]

One case involved the failure of an execution pursuant to a death penalty. The subsequent issuance of a new death warrant was held by the Supreme Court to be no infringement of double jeopardy: "We see no difference from a constitutional point of view between a new trial for error of law at the instance of the state that results in a death sentence instead of imprisonment for life and an execution that follows a failure of equipment." [66] The reference to the *Palko* fact situation is really quite strained, unless the holding is taken to mean that only the most heinous transgression by a state prosecutor will be questioned in federal court.

Another case of this type held that a reversal by the Supreme Court of a criminal conviction should be treated in the same way as a reversal of a state court on appeal, and should not serve as a bar to

---

[60] *Ibid.*, 499.   [61] *Palko* v. *Connecticut*, 302 U.S. 319 (1937).

[62] *United States* v. *Rosenwasser*, 145 F.2d 1015 (9th Cir. 1944).

[63] *Kepner* v. *United States*, 195 U.S. 100 (1904), *overruling in part United States* v. *Sanges*, 144 U.S. 310 (1892). See *United States* v. *Janitz*, 161 F.2d 19 (3d Cir. 1947), which seems to prefer the *Sanges* dicta.

[64] *United States* v. *Ball*, 163 U.S. 662 (1896).

[65] *Murphy* v. *Massachusetts*, 177 U.S. 155 (1900).

[66] *Lousiana* ex rel. *Francis* v. *Resweber*, 329 U.S. 459, 463 (1947).

a new trial by the state.[67] Similarly, the discharge of a jury after a failure to agree upon a verdict does not bar the state from beginning a new trial, even in the light of due process requirements.[68]

The Supreme Court has rarely felt hard-pressed to approve a state's version of double jeopardy. Some recent cases have involved such striking state double jeopardy policies that some members of the Court have paused for careful reflection. At times, there are signs that a broader reconsideration may be possible.

In the *Hoag* case, the State of New Jersey indulged in the use of multiple prosecutions with only slight variations in the offense formulas for the purpose of obtaining multiple convictions. The Supreme Court, in rendering a decision favorable to the state, apparently felt that the desirability of leaving the states free to administer their own criminal policies was not outweighed by the unusual severity of the state's policy of double jeopardy. Specifically, the Court held that the fourteenth amendment does not forbid a state from prosecuting separate criminal offenses at separate trials, even though the offenses may arise out of the "same criminal transaction," but the determination of deprivation of due process must be "picked out in the facts and circumstances of each case." [69] The fourteenth amendment does not necessarily prevent a state from allowing different offenses which are phases of the same act or transgression to be prosecuted in separate actions.

Another question considered in *Hoag* was whether the doctrine of "collateral estoppel" applied to these multiple trials. The doctrine, which normally is restricted to civil trials, requires that the determination of a question of fact essential to the judgment of a previous trial should be conclusive in a subsequent trial involving the same parties and the same facts. The Court indicated that the rule might be applicable, but expressed grave doubts as to whether it is a constitutional requirement.[70] The broader civil doctrine of res judi-

[67] *Hill v. Texas,* 316 U.S. 400 (1942).

[68] *Keerl v. Montana,* 213 U.S. 135 (1909).

[69] *Hoag v. New Jersey,* 356 U.S. 464, 466–67 (1958).

[70] *Ibid.,* p. 471. The Court said that "despite its wide employment we entertain grave doubts whether collateral estoppel can be regarded as a

cata has not yet been tested by the Court for its constitutional nature, nor has its application to criminal actions been required as a matter of fundamental fairness.[71] If the Court were to overturn the state's decision in the *Hoag* case, it would have to supply an alternative rule, but since no clear federal rule has emerged to solve questions of overlapping offense categories, no alternative is available. Neither res judicata nor collateral estoppel, being civil doctrines, can serve as adequate replacements of double jeopardy.[72]

In *Ciucci* v. *Illinois*,[73] a companion case to *Hoag*, the Court held that multiple state prosecutions for four murders occurring simultaneously (identical offenses which had been charged in four separate indictments) did not violate the requirements of due process. At each trial the prosecution had introduced evidence of all four deaths. After obtaining two convictions and two jail sentences, the

---

constitutional requirement [because] certainly this Court has never so held." Justice Warren said that the civil concept ought to apply: "The first jury's verdict of acquittal is merely an illusion of justice if its legal significance is not a determination that there was at least a reasonable doubt whether petitioner was present at the scene of the robbery," which was the only important contested issue (*ibid.*, p. 476 [dissenting opinion]). In a case decided in 1959, Justice Brennan in a separate opinion indicated that collateral estoppel should not apply to criminal cases: "The doctrine of collateral estoppel may not provide adequate protection" in practice, and "furthermore, the protection of an essentially procedural concept such as collateral estoppel . . . is less substantial than the constitutional protection of the Double Jeopardy Clause" (*Abbate* v. *United States*, 359 U.S. 187, 200 [1959]).

[71] Justice Holmes concluded that, even if double jeopardy were absent, res judicata was applicable in criminal as well as in civil cases (*United States* v. *Oppenheimer*, 242 U.S. 85, 87 [1916]). The existence of the double jeopardy provision of the fifth amendment does not exclude the use of res judicata. See *Fall* v. *United States*, 49 F.2d 506, 511 (D.C. Cir. 1931), *cert. denied*, 283 U.S. 867 (1931). This does not mean, however, that res judicata will be required of the states as part of the due process clause. See *Mutual Benefit Life Ins. Co.* v. *Tisdale*, 91 U.S. 238 (1876), which seems to indicate that it could be a due process requirement.

[72] The difference in the requisite burden of proof in criminal and civil cases would seem to make the civil doctrines unusable. There is no "reasonable doubt" doctrine in civil law. See *Murray & Sorenson, Inc.* v. *United States*, 207 F.2d 119 (1st Cir. 1953).

[73] 356 U.S. 571 (1958).

prosecution succeeded in obtaining a death sentence. This manuever was sustained by the Court in a per curiam opinion which relied upon the logic of the *Hoag* case, declaring that the state is entitled constitutionally to prosecute individual offenses at separate trials, and to utilize all relevant evidence even if employed at a previous trial. If there were no showing of "fundamental unfairness" in the state's procedure, due process would not be deemed violated.

Justice Douglas, one of four justices dissenting, stated that the prosecution had assured a death sentence by using multiple trials, resulting in an oppressive policy of criminal prosecution. Once again, the Court was faced with a case in which no federal standard was available to replace that of the state. Once again, the Supreme Court deferred to state double jeopardy policy.

Some have explained the *Hoag* result as an attempt by the Supreme Court to create a lenient rule for state prosecutions to counterbalance the state's inability to appeal criminal cases.[74] But more fundamental policies are at stake. The important difference between *Hoag* and *Palko*, which is ignored by the Supreme Court, is that the former involves the prosecutor's discretion solely, while the latter involves the deliberate choice of a state legislature to permit criminal appeals. In both cases the Supreme Court failed to impose federal double jeopardy through the due process clause. The fears of Justice Black have not been realized, for the Court has not substituted its version of concepts of decency and fundamental fairness for the language of the Bill of Rights. Instead, the court has failed to act in the double jeopardy area, failed to impose its standards, because it has not yet decided what those standards should be.

The selective incorporation approach of the *Palko* case has the merit of permitting a pragmatic case-by-case testing of each claim of federal double jeopardy raised in a state court. As a practical matter, though, it has led to a deference to the judgments of state courts and to the actions of state prosecutors as well as to the policies of state legislatures. Once the federal double jeopardy law is itself clarified,

[74] Mayers and Yarbrough, "*Bis Vexari:* New Trials and Successive Prosecutions," 74 *Harv. L. Rev.* 1, 37 (1960).

there may be a reconsideration of the requirements which federal double jeopardy imposes upon the states.

Conflict between Jurisdictional Lines

The next problem area to be considered is that of the conflict of jurisdictional lines. On one level, this issue concerns the delicate interrelationship between the jurisdictions of state and federal governments. On another level, the lines drawn between the civil and military areas and the civil and criminal areas deserve attention. These problems can be treated in the same way because the courts have tended to evolve similar legal rules with respect to them. The policy issue involved is the significance to be accorded traditional jurisdictional distinctions for the purposes of double jeopardy. The cases which fall into this category pose the question: "Is the line drawn between this and that zone so significant that it should permit a man to be incriminated more than once for the commission of a single reprehensible act?"

The problem has been a recurrent one. In one early case a dispute arose concerning jurisdiction over an American who had shot another American in Canada, with death occurring in the United States. The double jeopardy question was never litigated as such because the Canadian officials dropped their demands for extradition once the Michigan courts had agreed to hear the case.[75]

The problem of double jeopardy in international law is often avoided by the use of treaties waiving American claims of jurisdiction.[76] The Supreme Court held, as early as 1820, that a criminal prosecution in the courts of another nation would bar prosecution in the United States federal courts.[77] Since at least the year 1662,

[75] *Tyler* v. *People*, 8 Mich. 320 (1860).

[76] See Harvard Research in International Law, "Jurisdiction with Respect to Crime," 29 *Am. J. Int'l. L.* 435 (Supp. 1935). Article 13 provides: "In exercising jurisdiction under this Convention, no State shall prosecute or punish an alien after it is proved that the alien has been prosecuted in another State for a crime requiring proof of substantially the same acts or omissions." But see *Rocha* v. *United States*, 288 F.2d 245 (9th Cir. 1961).

[77] *United States* v. *Furlong*, 18 U.S. (5 Wheat.) 184 (1820).

England has followed the same rule.[78] The jurisdictional boundaries between nation-states have not been given legal significance sufficient to permit double prosecution. It does not matter that several nations have the ability to try a particular defendant. American courts will not try him if he has been tried by courts of another nation. One may ask: "If American courts can trust foreign courts, is it too much to expect them to trust each other?"[79]

Similar situations frequently arise in conflicts between the states of the federal union. In discussing the effect of the concurrent jurisdiction of Washington and Oregon over the Columbia River, the Supreme Court said that "the one first acquiring jurisdiction of the person may prosecute the offense, and its judgment is a finality in both states, so that one convicted or acquitted in the courts of one state cannot be prosecuted for the same offense in the courts of the other."[80] Thus, as a matter of federal policy, duplicating prosecutions are eliminated and the criminal defendant protected.

In like fashion, the question of federal jurisdiction over crimes committed on the Great Lakes raises double jeopardy problems of a jurisdictional nature. In one case, the court indicated that federal jurisdiction had been extended over the Great Lakes regardless of state jurisdiction and exists even if a state has already prosecuted the offender. But when a crime is committed on a tributary of the Great Lakes, the federal court will have jurisdiction only when a state court does not claim it. Federal criminal jurisdiction seems to depend on the statutes and location of the vessel. Federal admirality law would be applied to vessels plying the Great Lakes, as on the "high seas."[81]

The most famous and most important jurisdictional line is that drawn between state and federal criminal law by the case of *United*

[78] *R.* v. *Thomas,* 1 Sid. 179, 1 Lev. 118 (1662).

[79] Franck, "An International Lawyer Looks at the Bartkus Rule," 34 *N.Y.U.L. Rev.* 1096, 1103 (1959).

[80] *Nielsen* v. *Oregon,* 212 U.S. 315, 320 (1909).

[81] *Hoopengarner* v. *United States,* 270 F.2d 465 (6th Cir. 1959). This was based on *United States* v. *Rodgers,* 150 U.S. 259 (1893), except that in *Rodgers* the offense occurred on the Canadian side of the Detroit River.

States v. *Lanza*.[82] This case held that persons illegally transporting liquor in violation of a state and federal prohibition law may be prosecuted separately by each authority for violating the law of each. The case treated the question of the constitutionality of a federal prosecution following a completed state prosecution, but on grounds so broad as to include the reverse situation. It was ruled that two separate sovereignties which derive their power from separate sources each have the power to punish the same criminal activity. Each could deal with the same subject matter without interference from the other because each should determine what conduct offends its own peace and dignity.

The double jeopardy clause was held inapplicable since it only restricted federal prosecutions. There had been only one prosecution for the violation of the laws incident to its sovereignty. Similarly, the state double jeopardy provision referred only to the state prosecution. The decision had the effect of placing the significance of the federal-state relationship on a higher plane than the interest against double prosecutions.

Dean Roscoe Pound has criticized the *Lanza* rule as "an easy way for prosecutors to make a record for convictions with a minimum of effort." [83] Professor J. A. C. Grant has led the scholarly attack on the decision. Professor Grant maintains that the *Lanza* case is clearly incorrect on historical grounds, wrong in its interpretation of the English and American case law, wrong because of its inherent contradictions, and wrong on policy grounds.[84] Grant points out that

[82] 260 U.S. 377 (1922).

[83] Pound, "Cooperation in Enforcement of Law," 17 *A.B.A.J.* 9, 14 (1931).

[84] Grant, "The Lanza Rule of Successive Prosecutions," 32 *Colum. L. Rev.* 1309, 1317 (1932). As Grant points out, the Supreme Court had declared, at first, that passage of a national criminal act would necessarily render the state law unenforceable. See *Houston* v. *Moore*, 18 U.S. (5 Wheat.) 1 (1820). It would have been in accord with international law and the logic of previous decisions to have applied the double jeopardy principle in the Court's first case of successive state and federal prosecutions. But instead the Court created, in *United States* v. *Lanza*, the "novel doctrine that dual offenses arise merely from the existence of duplicate laws" (Grant, "Successive Prosecutions by State and Nation: Common Law and British Empire Comparisons," 4

extension of the rule has led to the possibility of triple trials for the same conduct—by the federal government, by the state, and by the municipality.[85]

The *Lanza* rule has been consistently followed in the few cases in which it has been tested.[86] Recently, the federal pre-emption doctrine of the *Nelson* case [87] cast slight doubt upon its viability. The Court in the *Nelson* case took pains to distinguish *Lanza* in its holding that the Smith Act superseded the enforceability of a state act proscribing conduct aiding the forcible overthrow of the government. This area of criminal conduct was reserved to the control of the federal government as an area of national concern, the federal government having pre-empted the field by the enactment of the Smith Act. The *Nelson* case was intended to be exceptional, as subsequent decisions have emphasized. Generally, federal and state criminal powers are considered as co-equal.

If there was any doubt created in the *Nelson* ruling, it was dispelled by the *Bartkus* case, which concerned a situation factually the reverse of the *Lanza* case. In this decision the defendant was convicted in a state prosecution which followed a prior federal acquittal, based on substantially the same offense and the same evidence. The Court held, by a five to four vote, that there was no double jeopardy bar to such a threat of double punishment. The decision was justified "in the name of federalism," asserting that it would be in derogation of the federal system to permit the reserved power of the states to be displaced by federal prosecution of minor federal offenses. The majority displayed its motives, stating: "Some recent

---

U.C.L.A.L. Rev. 1, 4 [1956]). Grant goes on to demonstrate that the inconsistency of this rule is based upon an incorrect and unjustifiable interpretation of the common law and of the relevant cases in the United States. He points out, very skillfully, that *Fox* v. *Ohio,* 46 U.S. (5 How.) 410 (1847), upon which *Lanza* claims to be based, is completely misconstrued by the *Lanza* Court. Grant accuses the solicitor general and the defense counsel of not having studied the history of the problem.

[85] Grant, "Penal Ordinances and the Guarantee against Double Jeopardy," 25 *Geo. L.J.* 294 (1937).

[86] *Albrecht* v. *United States,* 273 U.S. 1 (1927).

[87] *Pennsylvania* v. *Nelson,* 350 U.S. 497 (1956).

suggestions that the Constitution was in reality a deft device for establishing a centralized government are . . . without factual justification," [88] hinting that the Nelson rule would not be extended.

Criticism of this decision was outspoken. A leading English journal criticized the view of federalism espoused by the case on the ground that "Justice Frankfurter's opinion . . . seemed sometimes to view federalism as an end in itself, not as a means to a better life for individuals." [89] In its practical impact, the decision opened the door to increased cooperation between federal and state prosecutors to the detriment of defendants. Some procedural devices have been suggested to avoid the possible harsh results. [90]

It seems evident that the majority in *Bartkus* did not have to decide as a matter of federalism that state and federal prosecutions for the same offense do not offend double jeopardy. The reserved powers of the state to determine its criminal laws are not threatened by the application of double jeopardy. The effective use of a double jeopardy plea would not nullify any state laws.

On the other hand, federal-state relations have been on a particularly difficult footing since the *Nelson* decision. The feelings of state courts are as important as the reality of the situation. In such a circumstance it is not surprising that concern with federalism would prevail over the right to plead double jeopardy. Justice Frankfurter was faced with a conflict between the fifth and tenth amendments and sensitively preferred the latter, an act of judicial statesmanship. Justice Brennan, writing in *Abbate* v. *United States*, a companion case to *Bartkus*, discerned the policy issues at stake. He thought that the danger of multiple prosecution was outweighed by the necessities of the federal system, which would otherwise permit a defen-

---

[88] *Bartkus* v. *Illinois,* 359 U.S. 121, 137 (1959).

[89] "Conflicts in Court," 191 *Economist* 233 (1959). The article stresses the division between Frankfurter and Black, the former guided by respect for the political branches of government, the latter by individual rights.

[90] 45 *Corn. L.Q.* 574, 579 (1960), n., proposes negotiation between sovereignties, pre-emptive exclusion, calculation of primary interests, and direct legislative action. None of these seems likely to take place in the foreseeable future.

dant to get off lightly if the state or federal penalty were minor.[91] Whatever the merits of these arguments, it seems undesirable to reverse in the criminal area the achievements of *Erie R.R.* v. *Tompkins* [92] in the civil area. There is no federal common law for civil cases; neither should there be a pre-eminent federal criminal law. Double jeopardy must give way.

The line between civil and criminal law is an important one in double jeopardy law. The federal cases are in conflict on the abstract question of whether a defendant's former acquittal or conviction of a criminal charge bars a civil action against him to recover a statutory penalty for the same course of conduct. The modern federal view is probably that a former acquittal or conviction will not bar a subsequent civil suit.[93] The attempt to reconcile differing case results has been made in terms of a distinction based upon the nature of the penalty. The distinction rests on whether the penalty was intended to be criminal in nature.[94]

Under some circumstances, a civil action to recover taxes may amount to a criminal action because of the nature of the punishment.[95] The distinction can be made on the basis of the statutory exaction between the compensatory or punitive nature of the statute. In some cases neither the defense of double jeopardy nor the defense of res judicata will avail a defendant. This is true under the Federal False Claims Acts.[96]

---

[91] 359 U.S. 187, 195 (1959).   [92] 304 U.S. 64 (1938).

[93] *Rex Trailer Co.* v. *United States,* 350 U.S. 148 (1956); *United States ex rel. Marcus* v. *Hess,* 317 U.S. 537 (1943); *Helvering* v. *Mitchell,* 303 U.S. 391 (1937). *Contra, United States* v. *Ulrici,* 102 U.S. 612 (1881); *United States* v. *Gates,* 25 F. Cas. 1263 (No. 15,191) (S.D.N.Y. 1845). This seems a tenuous distinction at best, since it would imply that any money damages not related to actual damages caused are punitive; hence the proceeding is criminal.

[94] *Helvering* v. *Mitchell,* 303 U.S. 391 (1937). *United States* v. *Ben Grunstein & Sons,* 127 F. Supp. 907 (D.N.J. 1955).

[95] *United States* v. *LaFranca,* 282 U.S. 568 (1931).

[96] *United States ex rel. Ostrager* v. *New Orleans Chapter, Associated Gen. Contractors, Inc.,* 317 U.S. 562 (1943).

A suit on behalf of the United States to recover treble damages under the Emergency Price Control Act of 1942 [97] was considered to be a civil action involving no double jeopardy.[98] Acquittal on a criminal charge is not a bar to a civil action by the government which is remedial in nature, arising out of the same facts on which the criminal proceedings were based.[99] Double jeopardy does not apply to drug misbranding proceedings.[100] A contumacious witness may be punished for contempt of the United States Senate for a refusal to testify after being subpoenaed and separately indicted for a misdemeanor for each refusal.[101] Imposition of the civil sentence for the refusal is no barrier to criminal punishment, because "the civil and criminal sentences served distinct purposes, the one coercive, the other punitive and deterrent; that the same act may give rise to these distinct sanctions presents no double jeopardy problem." [102] Obviously, an *in rem* proceeding is not a criminal action and will not be accorded double jeopardy protection.[103]

The federal courts have made conscious policy judgments in this area of drawing the line between the civil and criminal areas. The difficulty arises with the use of indefinite terms in order to determine whether a statute is "coercive," "deterrent," "remedial," "compensatory," or whatever phrase the court may employ as an aid in delimiting the civil from the criminal. An element of artificiality surrounds

[97] Emergency Price Control Act, 56 Stat. 33 (1942), as amended, 58 Stat. 640 (1944), as amended, 60 Stat. 676 (1946), as amended, 61 Stat. 619 (1947).

[98] *United States* ex rel. *Marcus* v. *Hess,* 317 U.S. 537 (1943).

[99] *Stone* v. *United States,* 167 U.S. 178 (1897).

[100] *United States* v. *42 Jars . . . Bee Royale Capsules,* 160 F. Supp. 818 (D.N.J. 1958).

[101] *In re Chapman,* 166 U.S. 661 (1897). Doubt was cast upon the availability of a double jeopardy defense, on the peculiar ground that a prosecution through Congress' own process was not the same as statutory prosecution, since each is committed "against different jurisdictions."

[102] *Yates* v. *United States,* 355 U.S. 66 (1957).

[103] *Various Items of Personal Property* v. *United States,* 282 U.S. 577 (1931).

the use of these concepts, but they are not entirely lacking in meaningful content.[104]

There is considerable doubt whether the fifth amendment double jeopardy provision is a requirement in military courts-martial. It is clear that a soldier committing a crime in a jurisdiction governed by federal law cannot be tried by a federal court if he has been previously exonerated at a court-martial.[105] It is very uncertain just how far this principle can be extended.[106] Thus, double jeopardy protection is not accorded with any certainty in cases overlapping the military-civil jurisdictional lines. The federal courts seem to have developed no sure policy, nor even a consistent attitude, toward the problems inherent in the conflicts of courts-martial with criminal law.[107]

If the diverse double jeopardy situations are meaningfully grouped together as problems of policy line-drawing in matters of

[104] An example of decisive policy-making in double jeopardy is to be found in *United States* v. *Williams,* 341 U.S. 58 (1951), in which a defendant's acquittal in a criminal prosecution was held not to bar a subsequent prosecution for perjury committed at his former trial on the ground that to decide otherwise would permit a defendant testifying on his own behalf to swear to anything he pleased.

[105] *Grafton* v. *United States,* 206 U.S. 333 (1907); *United States* v. *Block* 262 F. 205 (7th Cir., 1920).

[106] The question of whether the fifth amendment may be invoked in cases arising in the military was unanswered in earlier decisions. See *Carter* v. *McClaughry,* 183 U.S. 365 (1902); *Wrublewski* v. *McInerney,* 166 F.2d 243 (9th Cir. 1948). It does not now seem to be a requirement in courts-martial (*Wade* v. *Hunter,* 336 U.S. 684 [1949]). The Supreme Court has never squarely decided the question of whether the sentence of a court-martial is void and subject to habeas corpus attack merely because the accused was twice placed in jeopardy. It has been assumed that the former conviction or acquittal was in a federal court, since both courts are courts of the same sovereign, but this is only a surmise. See *United States* ex rel. *Pasella* v. *Fenno,* 76 F. Supp. 203 (D. Conn. 1947), *aff'd.,* 167 F.2d 435 (5th Cir. 1940), with *Ex parte Henkes,* 267 F. 276 (D. Kan. 1919).

[107] *Trop* v. *Dulles,* 356 U.S. 86 (1958); *Reid* v. *Covert,* 354 U.S. 1 (1957); Schubert sees a fundamental constitutional trend toward the use of judicial review in this general area, notably in *United States* ex rel. *Toth* v. *Quarles,* 350 U.S. 11 (1955). This may be seen in "scalograms" in Schubert, *Constitutional Politics* (New York, 1960), pp. 204–5.

overlapping jurisdiction, some deficiencies become apparent. Inconsistencies which could be removed from double jeopardy law detract from its significance as a constitutional protection. The federal courts can remedy these defects by a more direct confrontation of the genuine policy issues.

Scope of the Criminal Act

The problem of the multiple consequences of a criminal act and of the multiple prosecutions which might be accorded those single acts is the central problem in the double jeopardy area, and is also the most commonly contested double jeopardy claim. Confusion is rampant in this branch of double jeopardy law. But before the confusion can be dissipated, the separate and distinct nature of the problem must be perceived.

The first strand which must be disentangled from the skein is the problem of the effect of appeal from the judgment of the trial court. That is patently a different question from the scope of the criminal act, the problem now at hand. Yet, the federal courts have tended to treat these problems alike, often using the same language as rationale.

A single criminal act may present the prosecution with opportunities for securing a conviction under several penal statutes which, even though they may overlap and even though they punish conduct of a single sort, provide alternative legal theories on which conviction may be obtained.[108] To complicate the picture further, a single criminal act may injure several persons or things, multiplying the possibilities of conviction. Beyond this, the prosecution has the option of joining the violations as counts in a single indictment before a single jury, or of splitting the violations into separate indictments before several juries.[109]

[108] See Horack, "The Multiple Consequences of a Single Criminal Act," 21 *Minn. L. Rev.* 805 (1937).

[109] This is explored in interesting fashion by Kirchenheimer, "The Act, the Offense, and Double Jeopardy," 58 *Yale L.J.* 513 (1949). Kirchenheimer considers the state and federal law together. Indeed, the problems are the same,

Obviously, double jeopardy objections are sure to arise, but how are the courts to resolve them? For the federal system, the Supreme Court and circuit courts have evolved a completely fictitious series of tests: the "same offense," "same evidence," "same transaction," and the "same act" tests. The result of the use of these convenient fictions has been to add contradictory and unpredictable elements to double jeopardy law.

The great range of choices presented the prosecution is due to the multiplication of legislatively created criminal categories. Every new criminal statute further extends the alternatives available to the prosecution while increasing the number of possible convictions and sentences which a defendant may suffer. A deed which might have violated one criminal proscription in 1800 may violate five today. Thus, the problem is partly one of legislative interpretation. It must be determined whether the legislature "intended" to increase the penalty for a single criminal deed, merely to provide another alternative remedy, or to make actions criminal which were previously legal.

Traditionally, the courts have had the task of determining legislative intent. All too often courts must assume that a conscious policy exists where there is none. They must read criminal statutes to discover whether they are "intended" to repeal by implication or to add to the criminal punishment meted out to a particular activity. This is no easy task. One judge astutely complained:

The areas in which the legislator has attempted to carve out several offenses from one transaction by varying the legal description so as to embrace all varieties and stages of performance, have created in those areas, a host of semi-independent, yet generally identical offenses.[110]

Another court concludes:

The confusion in the decisions is intelligible only as an expression of conflicting views on the desirability of leaving an absolute discretion with the

---

although a bit different in the significance accorded to double jeopardy itself. Still, the same formulas are employed.

[110] *District of Columbia* v. *Buckley,* 128 F.2d 17 (D.C. Cir. 1942).

trial court. It is not difficult to understand the considerations which have led many courts to inspect the record carefully and to restrict the use of consecutive sentences.[111]

Normally, the courts will not examine probable legislative intent in situations where new crimes and subdivided old crimes accumulate and apply to the same facts.[112] In the absence of repeal, legislative intent appears to make all such provisions cumulatively applicable.[113] Congress may separate a conspiracy to commit a substantive offense from the commission of the offense and affix to each a different penalty.[114] Only if the substantive offense and the conspiracy "are identical" does a conviction for both constitute double jeopardy.[115] In actuality, the courts cannot merely defer to legislative judgment. The task of interpretation cannot be evaded.

The dilemma is best revealed by the example of a recent case, *Gore* v. *United States,* where the defendant, by one criminal act, violated at least three statutes: selling narcotics without a written order; selling in a container other than the original stamped package; and facilitating the concealment and sale of narcotics. By a five to four decision, the majority accepted these similar offense cate-

[111] 45 *Harv. L. Rev.* 533, 540 (1932), n.

[112] *Burton* v. *United States,* 202 U.S. 344 (1906).

[113] *Bozza* v. *United States,* 330 U.S. 160 (1947).

[114] *United States* v. *Bayer,* 331 U.S. 532 (1947); *Pinkerton* v. *United States,* 328 U.S. 640 (1946). In a relatively recent decision, Justice Frankfurter discussed the underlying policy considerations, saying: "We attribute to Congress a tacit purpose—in the absence of any inconsistent expression—to maintain a long-established distinction between offenses essentially different," and "this settled principle derives from the reason of things in dealing with socially reprehensible conduct: collective criminal agreement—partnership in crime—presents a greater potential threat to the public than individual delicts" (*Callanan* v. *United States,* 364 U.S. 587 [1961]). Similarly, separate convictions for a conspiracy to monopolize trade do not amount to double jeopardy, since they are separate statutory offenses, each punishable as separable violations of the Sherman Act (*Am. Tobacco Co.* v. *United States,* 328 U.S. 781 [1946]). The courts may uphold attempts to punish as two conspiracies, under separate counts in a single indictment, that which amounts to one conspiracy to remove liquor from a bonded warehouse. See *Murphy* v. *United States,* 285 F. 801 (7th Cir. 1923).

[115] *Ladner* v. *United States,* 358 U.S. 169 (1958).

gories as separate offenses. Justice Douglas entered a vigorous dissent, saying, "I think it is time that the Double Jeopardy Clause was liberally construed in light of its great historic purpose to protect the citizen from more than one trial for the same act." [116]

The federal courts have developed interpretive aids to solve presumed legislative intent. Actually, these tests take the place of conscious policy and provide an arbitrary device to solve the dilemma of overlapping offenses. Even those jurists who prefer not to be legal activists must assert the court's role of interpretation and creation of law.

One test which is employed is the "same evidence" test. Where the act constitutes a violation of two distinct statutory provisions, the test to determine whether there are two offenses or one is whether either statute requires proof of facts which the other does not.[117] In cases involving two violations of congressional enactments, the test would be whether the two offenses are distinguishable by requiring somewhat different evidence in proving each.[118]

An extension of the same evidence rule provides that a person may not be tried for first degree murder and, after acquittal, be tried for manslaughter.[119] But the "same evidence" test, in requiring that the second accusation utilize substantially the same evidence in order for the defendant to have the benefit of double jeopardy protection, is a very narrow view of double jeopardy. The rule amounts to a broad grant of discretion to the prosecutor. Accordingly, the test has often been qualified by the use of res judicata and the "lesser included offense" doctrine.[120]

Another frequently employed but narrower test is the "same offense" test, which requires a plea of double jeopardy to be based upon a prosecution for the same offense.[121] The test of identity of offenses is whether there is a separate definition in the statutes. One court added to the confusion by ruling that the test of the identity of

[116] 357 U.S. 386, 396 (1958).
[117] *Blockenburger* v. *United States*, 284 U.S. 299 (1932).
[118] *Gavieres* v. *United States*, 220 U.S. 338 (1911).
[119] *Helvering* v. *Mitchell*, 303 U.S. 391 (1937).
[120] See Kirchenheimer, *op. cit.*, pp. 527–530.
[121] *Burton* v. *United States*, 202 U.S. 344 (1906).

66

the offenses is whether the same evidence is required to sustain both charges,[122] a common error.[123]

Until quite recently, the "same offense" dogma was a very popular one.[124] In its best phraseology, the Supreme Court has declared: "A single act may be an offense against two statutes, and if each statute requires proof of an additional fact which the other does not, an acquittal or conviction under either statute does not exempt the defendant from prosecution and punishment under the other." [125] In a 1955 case, however, the Court decided that so far as the Mann Act was concerned, the single offense doctrine did not apply.[126] This case may indicate the Supreme Court's distaste for the "same offense" rule.

The "same transaction" test seems to have been applied in an 1897 case which has never been overruled.[127] This generous test would forbid a new trial based on any occurrence which may be said to arise out of the same criminal transaction. Some of the circuit courts seem to have adopted this rule as their guide in the double jeopardy area.[128] In so doing, they have relied upon dicta appearing in the case of *Holiday* v. *Johnson*.[129] The "same transaction" test is favorable to the defendant, since it permits a second prosecution only in cases in which the proof does not show that the second case concerns the same criminal transaction as the first.

The "same act" test is not easy to isolate as a separate criterion and is usually posed as a rationale with other tests. No significant Supreme Court case may be found dealing with this point. A similar but vaguer test has been developed by lower courts under the hazy guise of a "common essential element" test.[130]

[122] *Morgan* v. *Devine*, 237 U.S. 632 (1915).
[123] See *Albrecht* v. *United States*, 273 U.S. 1 (1927).
[124] *Ex parte Lange*, 85 U.S. (18 Wall.) 163 (1873).
[125] *Carter* v. *McClaughry*, 183 U.S. 365, 395 (1901).
[126] *Bell* v. *United States*, 349 U.S. 81 (1955).
[127] *United States* v. *Ball*, 163 U.S. 662 (1896).
[128] *Goetz* v. *United States*, 39 F.2d 902 (5th Cir. 1930); *Tritico* v. *United States*, 4 F.2d 664 (5th Cir. 125).
[129] 313 U.S. 342 (1940).
[130] *Copperthwaite* v. *United States*, 37 F.2d 846 (6th Cir. 1930); *Lewis* v. *United States*, 4 F.2d 520 (5th Cir. 1925).

Lower federal courts have been given no guide by the Supreme Court to resolve this problem in double jeopardy. In this bewildering situation, some circuit courts, as indicated above, have adopted the "same transaction" test. Others employ the "same offense" test or some intermediate variation. A few courts have discovered an almost unique formula: "A plea of double jeopardy is unavailing unless the offense to which it is interposed is precisely the same in law and in fact as a former one relied upon under the plea." [131] This test is almost formless and consequently of little value.

This important area of double jeopardy law seems to be largely in the hands of the trial judge. He is left relatively free to employ the test of his choice, and his decision is usually affirmed. The intangible nature of the tests and the flexibility of their applications give the trial judge unusual discretionary powers.[132] The Supreme Court has failed to set a guiding policy. In cases in which a single physical movement has produced several statutory violations, the "single act," "single transaction," "same offense," and "same evidence" rules have been used more as a justification and rationalization of desired results than as an analytical tool.

The same tests appear again in cases in which a single physical movement has produced several consequences.[133] In this area one event injures more than one person or object, and the question arises as to the number of theories which are to be made available to the prosecution. In one decision in which the defendant was charged with violating the Mann Act by transporting two different women across state lines for immoral purposes, it was held that only one offense had been committed which could not be subjected to cumulative punishment under two separate counts.[134]

[131] *Bartlett* v. *United States,* 166 F.2d 928, 931 (10th Cir. 1948).

[132] Jones, "What Constitutes Double Jeopardy?" 38 *J. Crim. L.C. P.S.* 383, 385 (1947). This article gives a good brief summary of traditional double jeopardy approaches, but is not analytical.

[133] Of course, the problem is really more fundamental, requiring formal restriction on the prosecution as a matter of policy. Now the courts each set the policy for themselves. The language of the tests is similar, but the policy decision is really quite different in this subarea.

[134] *Bell* v. *United States,* 349 U.S. 81 (1955).

In *Ladner* v. *United States,* the defendant wounded two federal revenue agents with what was alleged to have been a single shotgun blast. The Court held that there was no constitutional issue presented. The question for decision was the construction of a section of the criminal code, which section was interpreted by the court "to mean that the single discharge of the shotgun would constitute an 'assault' without regard to the number of federal officers." [135] The Court avoided the double jeopardy issue by adopting a policy of deference in interpreting the statute, asserting that when choice is to be made between two readings of what conduct Congress has made a crime, it is appropriate that Congress should have spoken in language that is clear and definite.

The approach of direct statutory interpretation is more forthright than the use of the double jeopardy tests. Since most of the problems have been created by multiplicity of criminal legislation, this approach discerns the policy issue. However, it does not necessarily solve the problems better than fictional tests.

Use of the Criminal Appeal

The final aspect of double jeopardy law to be treated is the effect of an appeal by the defendant or the state upon the issues to be litigated at the new trial. The situation is to be sharply distinguished from that in the preceding section, which was concerned with an entirely different criminal suit, connected with the first only by virtue of the similarity of facts. The problem of appeal is less delicate, since it may be said that the voluntary appeal of the defendant has provided the prosecution with a "second crack" at a conviction.

Appeals by the federal government are extremely unusual and are looked upon with disfavor by the Supreme Court.[136] Congress has enacted laws granting the prosecution a right of appeal in criminal cases, and such legislation is not directly violative of any constitu-

[135] 358 U.S. 169 (1958).
[136] *Carroll* v. *United States,* 354 U.S. 394 (1957); *Peters* v. *Hobby,* 349 U.S. 331, 344–45 (1955) (appears even stronger).

tional prohibition.[137] A provision of the Criminal Appeals Act of 1907 states that if a demurrer or a motion to quash an indictment is sustained when a federal statute is construed or its validity is denied, the government may then bring the matter of its construction and validity directly to the Supreme Court.[138]

One early case held that the prohibition against double jeopardy applies equally whether the defendant has been acquitted or convicted. No exception to the applicability of the double jeopardy clause would be made merely because the new trial had been sought by the defendant for his own benefit.[139] The problem is narrowed to the question of the limitation upon the second indictment.[140]

One of the first formulas to be developed was the "lesser included offense" doctrine. The doctrine states that acquittal or conviction of a greater offense is not a bar to subsequent conviction of a minor offense included within the former whenever, under the indictment for the greater offense, the defendant could have been convicted of the lesser. But if the lesser offense is tried first, this will be a bar to the greater charge on the new trial. Although one-half the states have accepted this defendant-oriented doctrine, or some portion of it, many others have not.[141] The Supreme Court has not expressed its attitude on the matter but lower federal courts apply the doctrine on occasion. In *Goodall* v. *United States*,[142] an appellate court held

[137] *United States* v. *Heinze*, 218 U.S. 532 (1910); *United States* v. *Bitty*, 208 U.S. 393 (1907); *United States* v. *Sanges*, 144 U.S. 310 (1892); *United States* v. *Janitz*, 161 F.2d 19 (Cir. 1947).

[138] Act of March 2, 1907, ch. 2564, Sec. 587, 34 Stat. 1246. Upheld in *United States* v. *Curtiss-Wright Export Corp.*, 299 U.S. 304 (1936).

[139] *United States* v. *Gilbert*, 25 F. Cas. 1287 (No. 15,204) (C.C.D. Mass. 1834).

[140] Other limitations upon appeal have been set by Congress which condition the double jeopardy situation. So far as the Supreme Court itself is concerned, only limited criminal appeals by the government are permitted under the Criminal Appeals Act of 1948, 62 Stat. 844, as amended, 28 U.S.C. Sec. 3731 (1949). This statute permits direct appeal by the government from decisions or judgments setting aside an indictment where the decision is based upon the invalidity of a statute.

[141] See compilation by Frankfurter, J., in *Green* v. *United States*, 355 U.S. 184, 211 (1957).

[142] 180 F.2d 397 (D.C. Cir. 1950).

that second-degree murder is a lesser offense which can be proven under a charge of felony-murder.

A more troublesome, and more frequently used, test is the "waiver" rule. The doctrine rests upon the theory that when a new trial is granted, the defendant is in the same position as if there had been no trial and thus cannot plead his prior conviction as double jeopardy. He is, in effect, held to have waived the plea of former jeopardy by his appeal.

The Supreme Court ruled in 1905, in passing upon a case arising under a Philippine statute prohibiting the infliction of double jeopardy, that by appealing a conviction for assault the defendants have waived the right to plead double jeopardy in a new trial for the charge of murder. In this famous case, *Trono v. United States*,[143] it was not made clear whether the waiver doctrine was accepted as a part of constitutional law or was merely a matter of statutory interpretation.

Five years later the Court considered the question again. In *Brantley v. Georgia*[144] it was held that the Supreme Court of Georgia could permit a new trial for murder after an appeal conviction of manslaughter had been reversed without violating the fifth amendment double jeopardy provision. More recently, in *Hill v. Texas*,[145] the Supreme Court commented that a prisoner whose conviction in a state court is reversed by the state supreme court need not go free, for a state may indict and try him again. Thus, the states are granted broad discretion in this area.

The *Trono* case remained the federal law for some time. In 1919 the United States Supreme Court, relying expressly upon *Trono*, upheld the imposition of the death penalty in a new trial following the successful appeal of the first trial in which the jury had not recommended capital punishment.[146]

---

[143] 199 U.S. 521 (1905).   [144] 217 U.S. 284 (1910).
[145] 316 U.S. 400 (1942).
[146] *Stroud v. United States*, 251 U.S. 15 (1919). Frankfurther's dissent in *Green* v. *United States*, 355 U.S. 184, 211 (1957), rested in part on this case. The Justice could find no distinction between allowing a man to be retried at the risk of a greater punishment and being retried at the risk of a

Waiver of a plea of double jeopardy, however, must be a voluntary and knowing relinquishment of rights.[147] In its normal meaning, the Court has held that the word "waiver" indicates a conscious gamble; thus it forces the defendant to choose to accept a lesser penalty or to enter an appeal and take the risk that the second charge might be much more serious.

In 1957 much of the doctrine was discarded in the important case of *Green* v. *United States*.[148] Green had been found guilty of the commission of arson and second-degree murder in his first trial. The jury had made no finding as to first-degree murder. The court of appeals reversed and remanded the case for a new trial.[149] On remand Green was tried again, but this time for first-degree murder, when the Court overruled his plea of former jeopardy. The new jury found him guilty of first-degree murder, and he was given the mandatory death penalty. A divided court of appeals rejected the defense of double jeopardy and affirmed the decision.[150]

The Supreme Court reversed the decision, stating that the conviction of a lesser offense is a bar to any further prosecution for the greater offense on retrial after the appeal by the accused and reversal of the conviction. The Government had contended that the accused had "waived" his constitutional defense by obtaining a successful appeal of his improper conviction. To condition an appeal of one offense on a coerced surrender of a valid plea of former jeopardy on another, however, conflicts with the constitutional bar against double jeopardy.[151] Justice Black, for the majority, distinguished the *Trono* case on the ground that the defendant could not have intentionally consented to be tried for more than was contained in the first prosecution.[152] Justice Frankfurter insisted that

---

greater punishment for a higher crime. *Stroud* v. *United States* was not overruled.

[147] *Johnson* v. *Zerbst*, 304 U.S. 458 (1938).

[148] 355 U.S. 184, 211 (1957).

[149] *Green* v. *United States*, 218 F.2d 856 (D.C. Cir. 1955).

[150] *Green* v. *United States*, 236 F.2d 708 (D.C. Cir. 1956).

[151] *Green* v. *United States*, 355 U.S. 184, 191, 193.

[152] As a matter of fact, the defendant did know the possible consequences of his appeal, but he said that he preferred death to spending the rest of his life in prison.

by distinguishing *Trono* the majority was really overruling it indirectly.[153]

In *Forman* v. *United States*,[154] a 1960 case, the Supreme Court demonstrated that the "waiver" doctrine of the *Trono* case still applied to cases in which the new trial after defendant's appeal was for the same offense. Although the decision rested on other grounds, there is good reason for assuming that if the "waiver" doctrine is still viable, it cannot be used to bar a plea of double jeopardy when the defendant is being retried for an offense greater than that contained in the original indictment. The result suggests that the *Green* case is the most significant precedent in this area. The policy question seems to be in the process of being resolved so as to permit appeal free from coercive risk.

Judicial Behavior in Double Jeopardy Cases

It would be incomplete to leave the case study of federal double jeopardy law without considering the judicial behavior aspects. In this regard, the work of Glendon Schubert has great utility. He creates a "scalogram" of the seven double jeopardy decisions of the Warren court from *Green* v. *United States* in 1957 through *Williams* v. *Oklahoma* [155] in 1959. From this he concludes: "During this brief but relatively homogenous period, the attitudes of the justices toward the equity of double jeopardy practices seemed to have a much more important bearing upon their decision-making than did the constitutional theories and concepts with which the opinions of the justices are concerned." [156]

Unfortunately, the evidence provided by the cases does not seem to support Schubert's conclusions. The Court has rather consistently

---

[153] *Green* v. *United States,* 355 U.S. 184, 213, 214.

[154] 361 U.S. 416 (1960).

[155] *Williams* v. *Oklahoma,* 358 U.S. 576 (1959), is a case concerning the due process meaning of double jeopardy as a restriction on the states. Like every other such case, the fourteenth amendment was no limitation upon the state's interpretation of the double jeopardy protection. The defendant, after having been convicted of murder and sentenced to life, pleaded guilty to a kidnapping charge and was sentenced to death.

[156] Schubert, *op. cit.,* pp. 608–9.

applied first one, then another series of constitutional tests. If anything, the fault has been that insufficient consideration has been given to the "equity of double jeopardy," the policy levels which lie beneath the legal rules.

Schubert's analysis is more useful in locating the "swing man" on the Court in double jeopardy questions:

The separation of the justices into two groups is rather sharply and consistently defined . . . the disposition of the cases is in perfect accord with the voting of only one justice, Whittaker; and in a majority of four of the seven cases, Whittaker's vote was determinative, which made him the equipoise of the Court on this issue. Thus the freshman justice of the 1956 Term became, in the decision of this set of cases, the most powerful justice on the Court.[157]

This is interesting information, even if one need not have constructed a scalogram to discover it. The more important issue of the personal philosophies of the judges tends to be overlooked, however.

Conclusion

Several inconsistencies in federal double jeopardy law appear as a result of this examination. First, the internal inconsistencies inherent in the doctrine of attachment are so great that they immediately give rise to qualifications and exceptions. The intrinsic-extrinsic formula suggested above seems much closer to the real policy considerations in this area. Its adoption would have solved the *Gori* case and similar problems.

Second, the inconsistencies flowing from the effect of the *Palko* case and subsequent failures to define due process limitations upon state double jeopardy has increased the tendency to proliferate double jeopardy rules. Uniformity itself may not be possible, especially in the absence of uniform state procedures, but some standards could be federally established to prevent extreme abuses, as in the *Hoag* situation.

[157] *Ibid.*, pp. 607, 669.

74

Third, the problem of conflicting jurisdictional zones, as it has been denoted here, must be seen as separate from other double jeopardy problems. The delineation between zones should be made after conscious deliberation and not by means of unconscious traditional distinctions. Better drafting of statutes to indicate their civil or criminal nature would help relieve the courts of the task of guessing at legislative intent.

Fourth, the central confusion surrounding the problem of the scope of the criminal act is so serious that it requires a more exhaustive treatment. Here, too, presumptions of legislative intent have been utilized by the courts, except that the resort to test of jeopardy has introduced even greater artificiality. Many of these problems would be removed by better legislative drafting, but what is primarily needed is a more complete consideration of the social policies which underlie double jeopardy. In the absence of a broad legislative reconsideration, a single standard should be applied by courts. This would help remove some of the uncertainties in this problem area.

Fifth, the question of the impact of the defendant's appeal should be resolved in such a way that the defendant would not be forced to gamble with his future. Although the *Green* case is a long step in this direction, conflicting precedents still exist which retain some force. The resolution cannot be accomplished by the courts alone.

But the dominant policy issue in double jeopardy is that of the extent of the defendant's protection against state prosecution, represented by the power of the state prosecutor. How many times should the prosecution be permitted a chance to proceed against a criminal defendant? The answer is not simple, especially since the prosecution's advantages are offset somewhat by the burden of overturning the presumption of the defendant's innocence. The language of the double jeopardy clause is definite, if not clear. Ultimately, courts and legislatures must decide if this doctrine is absolute or conditional.

As it is now, the outcome of a double jeopardy plea in the federal courts is not always predictable. Even where it is relatively certain, the legal rule seems often unrelated to any conscious social goal.[158] History will not cure the deficiencies of law. The social policy of double jeopardy requires a more conscious consideration by Congress and the federal courts.

[158] Unfortunately, denial of certiorari by the Supreme Court has been a deliberate policy in this area according to Hanus, "Denial of Certiorari and Supreme Court Policy-Making," 17 *Amer. U.L. Rev.* 41 (1967).

»3«

State Double Jeopardy
Policy

Although federal double jeopardy policy could have served as a model, the states have each developed their own versions of double jeopardy policy, with variations sharing a common pattern. A remarkable similarity in approach is apparent, despite divergent formulas. Legislative activity in the field of double jeopardy is more noticeable in the states than at the national level, especially in the area of overlapping jurisdictions, to be noted below. Many states have provided a statutory basis for double jeopardy. Nonetheless, state courts have been left without legislative guideposts in most of the areas of double jeopardy. Because of the silence of the legislatures, the courts have been driven to improvisation, resulting in the creation of more complicated "tests" than those employed by federal courts.

The role of the state prosecutor, which is treated in Chapter 5, is of great significance in state double jeopardy policy. The double jeopardy provision is usually the most formidable obstacle to the initiation of repeated criminal suits. For the defendant the issue of double jeopardy, which precedes all matters of substantive criminal law, is especially important because it determines the number of times he may be forced to withstand the risks and rigors of a criminal trial. Since the corpus of state criminal law is much larger than that of federal criminal law, double jeopardy situations are much more frequent in the states. State legislatures continue to create new criminal statutues, usually without any reference to offenses already extant, making state double jeopardy policy more significant each day.

The Constitutional Basis of Double Jeopardy

Once double jeopardy had been incorporated into the Bill of Rights of the federal constitution, the idea of double jeopardy as a fundamental right was accepted by most states. Many states adopted as part of their constitutions declarations of rights which included provisions identical to the federal clause. The first state to do so was Pennsylvania in 1790; [1] Kentucky adopted the clause in 1792,[2] and Delaware followed later in the same year.[3] Rhode Island chose to copy the phraseology of the New Hampshire Bill of Rights, which differed from the federal double jeopardy clause in that it restricted the protection to prior acquittals.[4]

In the New Jersey Constitutional Convention of 1844, the Committee on the Bill of Rights produced a provision similar to that of the fifth amendment: "No person shall be twice put in danger of punishment for the same offense." This wording was bitterly opposed by several delegates, including the Chief Justice of New Jersey, Joseph C. Hornblower, who argued that the language might be held to imply that any situation which occurred after the attachment of jeopardy and prevented the completion of trial would fall under this clause.[5] A motion to substitute the provision which had been adopted by Rhode Island prevailed. The clause became part of paragraph 10 of Article I of the 1844 constitution and was retained in the current constitution.

All but five states now have a constitutional provision against a

[1] Pennsylvania Constitution of 1790, Art. IX, Sec. 10.

[2] Kentucky Constitution of 1792, Art. XII, para. 12.

[3] Delaware Constitution of 1792, Art. I, Sec. 8.

[4] Art. I, Sec. 7, which provides that "no person shall, after acquittal, be tried for the same offense" (1842 Constitution).

[5] New Jersey Constitutional Convention of 1844, *Proceedings,* J. Bebout (ed.) pp. 52, 413 (Trenton, 1942).

second trial for the same offense.[6] The constitutions of thirty-seven states follow the federal formula that no person shall be twice put in "jeopardy," while eight provide that after an acquittal a person shall not be tried again for the same offense (the New Hampshire formula). There is nothing in any constitution, however, to indicate what constitutes "jeopardy" or what is meant by the "same offense." Despite considerable resemblance, state constitutional phraseology does differ significantly in the wording of double jeopardy, so that it must be admitted that although the federal concept has been accepted, it has been constitutionally limited by most of the states.[7] In some cases the state double jeopardy provisions are far more precise than the federal.[8]

Beyond the differences in constitutional provisions, state double

[6] Maryland, Connecticut, Massachusetts, North Carolina, and Vermont. In New Jersey it was held that since the double jeopardy provisions of the state and federal constitutions in regard to double jeopardy are nearly coextensive, United States Supreme Court views would be persuasive though not controlling (*State* v. *Farmer*, 48 N.J. 145, 224 A.2d 481 [1966]). The Pennsylvania Constitution applies double jeopardy only to capital cases (see *Commonwealth* v. *Warfield*, 227 A.2d 177 [Pa., 1967]).

[7] Two states provide: "nor shall any person, after once being acquitted by a jury, be again put in jeopardy of life and liberty" (Missouri, Constitution of 1875, Art. II, Sec. 23, "for the same offense," and Oklahoma, Constitution of 1907, Art. II, Sec. 21 "for that of which he has been acquitted"). One constitution, that of Mississippi, provides explicitly the need for an actual acquittal on the merits to bar another prosecution (Constitution of 1890, Art. II, Sec. 22). Six states provide, with some variations, that "no person after acquittal, be tried for the same offense" (Iowa, Constitution of 1857, Art. I, Sec. 12; Michigan, Constitution of 1908, Art. II, Sec. 14; New Hampshire, Constitution of 1912, Pt. First, Art. 16; New Jersey, Constitution of 1844, Art. I, Sec. 7, and in present constitution; Rhode Island, Constitution of 1842, Art. I, Sec. 7; Texas, Constitution of 1876, Art. I, Sec. 14).

[8] Various express limitations upon the use of double jeopardy in situations of mistrials and discharge of juries are set forth constitutionally (Georgia, Constitution of 1877, Art. I, Sec. 1, para. VIII; Louisiana, Constitution of 1921, Art. I, Sec. 9; and as to hung juries, Arkansas, Constitution of 1874, Art. II, Sec. 8; Colorado, Constitution of 1875, Art. II, Sec. 23; Wyoming, Constitution of 1889, Art. I, Sec. 11.) The most express constitutional provision is that of New Mexico, which prohibits a new trial for a greater offense or degree of an offense when the indictment charges different offenses (Constitution of 1912, Art. II, Sec. 15).

79

jeopardy differs from the federal in the fact that some of it has a statutory base. In those states a defendant may have to look to a statute for his protection. A typical statute provides: "No person can be subjected to a second prosecution for a public offense for which he has once been prosecuted and convicted or acquitted." [9] In states where the constitution is silent on the matter, state statutes may recognize double jeopardy, or the concept may be adopted by state courts from the common law.[10] Mere variation in the wording of double jeopardy itself may have no material effect upon the doctrine, so that a court may hold that "twice in jeopardy" and "twice in jeopardy of punishment" mean the same thing.[11] It should be obvious that placing double jeopardy on a statutory or common law base makes alteration of the doctrine to suit policy needs much easier than where it may be enshrined in a constitutional provision.

Exceptions to the double jeopardy rule are sometimes specifically set forth in the states—some by constitutional declaration, which often specifically shapes the contours of that state's policy,[12] others

[9] California, Penal Code, 1931, Sec. 687, with minor variations in: Idaho, Compiled Statutes, 1919, Sec. 8622; Montana, Revised Codes, 1921, Sec. 11,612; Nevada, Compiled Laws, 1929, Sec. 10,655; New York, Criminal Code, 1930, Criminal Procedure, Sec. 9; Oklahoma, Compiled Statutes, 1921, Sec. 2350; South Dakota, Revised Code, 1919, Sec. 4411. The statutory formula which emulates the federal clause, that "no person can be twice put in jeopardy for the same offense," is found in North Dakota, Compiled Laws, 1913, Sec. 10,394; Georgia, Penal Code, Sec. 11; Louisiana, Code of Criminal Procedure, 1929, Art. 274; Texas, Revised Criminal Statutes, 1925, Art. 8; Utah, Compiled Laws, 1917, Sec. 8555.

[10] See *Holt* v. *State*, 160 Tenn. 366, 367, 24 S.W. 824, 886, 887 (1930), and *State* v. *Benham*, 7 Conn. 414 (1829), applying the doctrine although Connecticut has no constitutional provision.

[11] In *State* v. *Findling*, 123 Minn. 413, 416, 144 N.W. 142, 145 (1913), the court rejects the contention that the provision in the Minnesota constitution differs materially from those of many other states. Of course, wide differences in double jeopardy language will not be treated in this fashion.

[12] Colorado, Constitution of 1876, Art. I, Sec. 18: "If the jury disagree, or if the judgment be arrested after verdict, or if the judgment be reversed for error in law, the accused shall not be deemed to have been in jeopardy"; Georgia, Constitution of 1877, Art. I, Sec. 1, para. VIII: "No person shall be put in jeopardy of life, or liberty, more than once for the same offense, save on his or her own motion for a new trial after conviction, or in the case of

by statutory prescription.[13] On the other hand, the use of legislation to prevent the undue comulation of sentences has been rare. Some statutes provide that a conviction or acquittal of an act charged as an offense under any statute bars any further prosecution for the same act.[14]

Generally, the words of the clause of the fifth amendment which restricts double jeopardy to dangers to "life and limb" have been ignored, and a majority of states have not adopted the original federal rule which restricts double jeopardy to felonies.[15] Instead, most states have extended the doctrine to cover all classes of criminal and indictable offenses, including misdemeanors.[16] The contrary rule, narrowing the scope of double jeopardy, rests upon a literal and historical meaning of the phrase.[17] On the frontier, judges were

---

mistrial"; Louisiana, Constitution of 1921, Art. I, Sec. 9: "Nor shall any person be twice put in jeopardy of life or liberty for the same offense, except on his own application for a new trial, or where there is a mistrial, or a motion in arrest of judgment is sustained"; Wyoming, Constitution of 1889, Art. I, Sec. 11: "If the jury disagree, or if the judgment be reversed for error in law, the accused shall not be deemed to have been in jeopardy."

[13] The section of the California Penal Code, for example, which provides for a separate trial of the issue upon a defendant's plea of insanity (California Penal Code of 1927, Sec. 1026), was upheld as constitutional, not violative of the state's double jeopardy clause, in *People* v. *Hickman,* 204 Cal. 470, 268 P. 909 (1928). Some statutes specifically declare a prior conviction a double jeopardy bar to subsequent prosecution; Arkansas Statutes Annotated, Sec. 43-1224, of 1947 and Wisconsin Statutes, Sec. 939.71, of 1955 are examples of statutes which both declare and limit the scope of double jeopardy.

[14] New York, Penal Code of 1919, Sec. 1938, and Idaho, Compiled Statutes of 1919, Sec. 8602, are typical of a growing tendency.

[15] *Ex parte Lange,* 85 U.S. (18 Wall.) 163 (1873).

[16] *Scalf* v. *Commonwealth,* 95 Ky. 830, 243 S.W. 1034 (1922); *Commonwealth* v. *Perrow,* 124 Va. 806, 97 S.E. 280 (1919); *Dragan* v. *State,* 243 Ala. 102, 8 So. 2d 596 (1941). Separate investigations by the State Commission for Human Rights and the Department of State do not involve double jeopardy since both proceedings are civil actions involving remedial administrative proceedings (*Neidlich* v. *State Comm. for Human Rights,* 280 N.Y.S.2d 463 [Sup. Ct. 1967]).

[17] The most notable exponent of this rule is Pennsylvania (see *Commonwealth* v. *Simpson,* 310 Pa. 580, 165 A. 498 [1932]). It has been said that the Pennsylvania double jeopardy clause, though identical to the federal clause in its wording, applies only to cases of capital felonies (*Commonwealth*

applying precedents derived from the more restrictive English law, even though earlier democratic Anglophobia had, in part, been directed against the common law.[18] The divergence between more restrictive and more generous double jeopardy may be due to the diverse sources of double jeopardy as much as to different policy evaluations.

At times, double jeopardy has been assumed to exist even in the absence of any specific statute or case:

> If this Court has not said in so many words that this principle was embodied in our [Vermont] Constitution, it is because it has never been questioned before. Whenever the plea has been made, and the court has found, that a person had been either acquitted or convicted of the same offense, it has enforced the principle and discharged the respondent.[19]

In Louisiana, the common law is resorted to in order to ascertain the true meaning of the provision of the Louisiana Constitution setting forth the double jeopardy clause.[20]

The terms "Jeopardy of life and liberty for the same offense,"

---

ex. rel. *Backus* v. *Cavell*, 186 Pa. Super. 48, 410 A. 355 [1958]). Maryland, Arkansas, and Missouri also have double jeopardy rules which limit the scope of the protection.

[18] See *Territory* v. *Darling Bradly*, Adams County Circuit Court, Miss. Terr. (1807), in which the defendant pleaded a former acquittal and demurred, arguing that he had been acquitted for assault and battery and could not be tried for another assult and battery arising out of the same transaction. The court cited Hawkins, *A Treatise of the Pleas of the Crown* (London, 1716), an eighteenth-century English law treatise and collection, in deciding to adopt a restrictive rule and overrule the plea of former acquittal. The case may be read in William Baskerville Hamilton's *Anglo-American Law on the Frontier: Thomas Rodney and His Territorial Cases* [Durham, N.C., 1953], p. 271.) There is considerable disagreement as to the manner of the reception of English law into the American colonies, but by the eighteenth century the common law was definitely reasserting itself despite its English sources (*ibid.*, p. 117). Double jeopardy may not have been effected by Anglophobia.

[19] *State* v. *Felch*, 92 Vt. 477, 105 A. 23, 26 (1918). Of necessity, this attitude must oversimplify the double jeopardy problem, since it implies that double jeopardy has been the same throughout the ages.

[20] *State* v. *Duvall*, 135 La. 710, 165 So. 904 (1914).

"jeopardy of life and limb," "jeopardy for the same offense," "twice in jeopardy of punishment," and other similar provisions employed in the various constitutions may mean substantially the same thing,[21] but the states do not agree, either as a matter of constitutional provisions or of statute, upon the scope of the double jeopardy protection itself. Of course, in those states which have constitutional double jeopardy, the legislature may not deprive citizens of the constitutional right by statutory enactment.[22]

Attachment of Jeopardy

Attachment of jeopardy, considered from the federal viewpoint as the first problem in the preceding chapter, presents a confused pattern when projected from the point of view of state double jeopardy law. Several states have constitutional provisions embodying the English rule requiring a final judgment of acquittal or conviction. New Jersey's constitution of 1844, which limited double jeopardy to situations of prior acquittal, was held to imply that only a final and complete acquittal could cause jeopardy to attach.[23] Mississippi's constitution of 1890 has been similarly interpreted.[24] The adoption of the English rule has been cogently justified:

In the decisions of the English courts antecedent to the Constitution [twice in jeopardy] had been construed as equivalent to 'autrefois acquit' or 'autrefois convict'. Contemporaneous construction is the true interpreter of language. Being transformed from a legal maxim to a constitutional clause, does not, it is apprehended, change the meaning of words, although it makes the right they guaranty, more solemn and sacred.[25]

It has been held that a discharge of a jury at any time before a final verdict is rendered cannot be pleaded as a former judgment,

[21] Strout v. State, 36 Okla. 744, 130 P. 553 (1913).

[22] United States v. Aurandt, 15 N.M. 292, 107 P. 1064 (1909).

[23] Smith v. State, 41 N.J.L. 598 (1879).

[24] Lovern v. State, 140 Miss. 635, 105 So. 769 (1925); Smith v. State, 158 Miss. 355, 128 So. 891 (1930).

[25] Hoffman v. State, 20 Md. 425, 533 (1863).

jeopardy not having attached.[26] But in Iowa, even though the constitutional double jeopardy clause is virtually identical, it was held that jeopardy attaches when a jury is sworn in a trial before a court of competent jurisdiction, and if a jury is thereafter improperly discharged the situation constitutes an "acquittal" sufficient to bar a second prosecution.[27] The same interpretation prevails in Michigan, Missouri, and Rhode Island despite similar constitutional clauses.[28] South Carolina only gives double jeopardy effect to an acquittal, strictly interpreting the state constitution. It was held that a defendant could be put on trial a second time for the same offense, following a conviction, because the constitutional prohibition was only against a second trial after an acquittal.[29] The case was decided under the Constitution of 1868. But under the previous constitution, a contrary result was obtained by applying the common law maxim.[30]

As a general rule, jeopardy attaches when a person has been placed on trial on a valid indictment or information before a court of competent jurisdiction. After arraignment [31] and after a jury has

[26] See *Anderson* v. *State*, 86 Md. 479, 38 A. 937 (1897). But in the celebrated case of *Martinis* v. *Supreme Court*, 15 N.Y.2d 246, 206 N.E.2d 165, 258 N.Y.S.2d 65 (1965), an acquittal for a reckless driving charge in a local city court was held not to bar a subsequent prosecution and conviction of the more serious offense of vehicular homicide. The judges may have been motivated by fear that the defendant would escape with little or no punishment because he had rapidly rushed into a local court to obtain a prompt result which would place him in jeopardy on a minor charge. Clearly, this is a procedural matter in which the local judge or the police could notify the prosecutor of the possible major violations and suspend trial on the minor charges until a later date.

[27] *State* v. *Dickson*, 200 Iowa 17, 202 N.W. 225 (1925).

[28] *People* v. *Taylor*, 117 Mich. 583, 176 N.W. 158 (1898); *State* v. *Linton*, 283 Mo. 1, 222 S.W. 847 (1920); *State* v. *Nelson*, 19 R.I. 467, 34 A. 990 (1896).

[29] *State* v. *Wyse*, 33 S.C. 582, 10 S.E. 827 (1890).

[30] *State* v. *M'Kee*, 17 S.C.L. 651, 655 (1830).

[31] This technicality acts as a further protection to the accused and is ignored federally because of the simpler Federal Rules of Criminal Procedure (see *Clawans* v. *Rives*, 104 F.2d 240 [D.C. Cir. 1939]).

been impaneled and sworn, jeopardy can be said to attach at some point.[32] The proceedings before a grand jury do not amount to jeopardy.[33] Neither could the mere pendency of an indictment.[34] A few states have adopted the English requirement of a final judgment, either with respect to acquittal or conviction, or both.[35] The latter rule, although having the benefit of consistency with the historical tradition of double jeopardy in England, although logically better founded, clearly favors the prosecution over the accused, since it prevents late dismissal or discharge obtained by the prosecution from barring a subsequent prosecution. There may be more justification for this in England, where the scheme of prosecution is

[32] Almost every state accepts this minimum concept.

[33] *State* v. *Lewis*, 226 N.C. 249, 37 S.E. 691 (1946); *State* v. *Swain*, 147 Ore. 207, 36 P.2d 211 (1934).

[34] *People* v. *Head*, 103 Cal. App. 465, 234 P.2d 103 (1951); *State* v. *Preto*, 51 N.J. Super. 175, 144 A. 2919 (1958). A presentence investigation required retroactively is not a jeopardy (*State* v. *Morse*, 229 A.2d 232 [Vt. 1967]).

[35] *State* v. *Pace*, 210 Miss. 448, 49 So. 2d 710 (1950); *Anderson* v. *State*, 86 Md. 479, 38 A. 937 (1897); *State* v. *Whipple*, 57 Vt. 637 (1884); *State* v. *Deso*, 110 Vt. 1, 1 A.2d 710 (1938); *Commonwealth* v. *Rogers*, 58 Lack. Jur. 217 (Pa. 1820). Those states in which a verdict of acquittal or conviction is required for attachment usually hold, further, that if a conviction has been reversed by an appellate court because of an error in law, the defendant will not have been in jeopardy and may be tried again (*State* v. *Kennedy*, 96 Miss. 624, 50 So. 978 [1910], based upon the language of the Mississippi Constitution: *Smith and Bennett* v. *State*, 41 N.J.L. 598 [1879]; *Perkins* v. *State*, 65 Tex. Crim. 311, 144 S.W. 241 [1912]). One jurisdiction, Kentucky, having constitutional language similar to the great majority of American jurisdictions, yet holds that jeopardy does not attach until a verdict has been rendered (*Hobbs* v. *Commonwealth*, 156 Ky. 847, 162 S.W. 104 [1914]). Of those five states whose constitutions contain no provisions against double jeopardy, but which have adopted the doctrine as a part of the common law, there are two which follow the minority rule that jeopardy does not attach until a verdict of acquittal or conviction has been given (*Anderson* v. *State*, 86 Md. 479, 38 A. 937 [1897]; *State* v. *Deso*, 110 Vt. 1, 1 A.2d 710 [1938]). The diversity of common law sources, English and American, makes the finding of precedent for the minority position rather difficult. It should be remembered, however, that the majority rule is almost unique to the American version of double jeopardy.

distinctly different, as will be noted later. But in most states, the quashing or dismissing of an indictment or sustaining a demurrer does not amount to jeopardy.[36]

Usually, the mere fact that witnesses have been examined or that other steps preliminary to trial have been taken will not amount to jeopardy until the stage when "the issue is joined," which requires an arraignment and plea of the accused.[37] In still other jurisdictions, the additional element that evidence must have been offered against the accused has become the determining factor.[38] The Iowa view places the defendant in jeopardy once a demurrer to an indictment has been sustained, perhaps even before the impaneling of a jury.[39] Others find that jeopardy sets in with the charging of the jury,[40] with commencement of trial,[41] and, of course, with the impaneling of the jury.[42]

Perhaps the most unusual attachment decision was reached in *Commonwealth* v. *Simpson*,[43] a Pennsylvania case. There, after jeopardy had attached on a prosecution for a capital offense, a discharge of the jury without absolute necessity and without the defendant's consent was held to prevent a second prosecution for murder, but it did not prevent a second prosecution for a lesser offense

[36] *State* v. *Reinhard*, 202 Iowa 168, 209 N.W. 419 (1926). Most states agree, except when statutes provide differently as they do in the Iowa case cited here. Virginia seems to be the only nonstatutory exception to the rule (*Adkins* v. *Commonwealth*, 175 Va. 590, 9 S.E.2d 349 [1940]). Dismissal of a speeding charge for lack of prosecution was held to bar a subsequent trial for the same offense in *Flahaven* v. *Allen*, 5 Misc. 2d 1063, 274 N.Y.S.2d 703 (Sup. Ct. 1966).

[37] *Steen* v. *State*, 92 Tex. Crim. 99, 242 S.W. 1047 (1922); *McLeod* v. *State*, 128 Fla. 35, 174 So. 66 (1937); *Peavey* v. *State*, 153 Ga. 119, 111 S.E. 420 (1922).

[38] This is the New York rule, *People* v. *Zendano*, 136 N.Y.S.2d 106 (1954); *People* ex. rel. *Meyer* v. *Warden of Nassau County Jail*, 269 N.Y. 426 (1935).

[39] See Love and Thistle, "Double Jeopardy and the Necessity Rule," 14 *U. Pitt. L. Rev.* 588 (1953).

[40] *State* v. *Crook*, 16 Utah 212, 51 P. 1091 (1898); *contra*, *Commonwealth* v. *Bressant*, 126 Mass. 246 (1879).

[41] *Gillespie* v. *State*, 168 Ind. 298, 180 N.E. 829 (1907).

[42] *State* v. *Lee*, 65 Conn. 265, 30 A. 1110 (1894).

[43] 310 Pa. 580, 165 A. 498 (1933).

included in the first indictment. Pennsylvania reached this result because of its highly restrictive view of the double jeopardy protection.

The usual American position as to double jeopardy stresses the event of impaneling the jury for the moment when jeopardy can be said to attach. Some writers suggest that the only basis for holding that jeopardy attaches at the time when the jury is sworn is the English rule of practice which compelled a jury, once sworn, to be kept together until it rendered a verdict; "however, a further consideration may have been the possibility, recognized by some courts, not only of a second trial after a verdict has once been rendered, but also of the prosecution commencing and discontinuing as many proceedings as may be necessary to get evidence sufficient and a jury favorable for conviction." [44] If the difference between English and American double jeopardy law is to be understood, then the legal context of the entire situation must be envisaged. The state of double jeopardy law is conditioned by the state of criminal procedure and particularly by the functioning of the prosecutor.

To remedy the social disadvantages created by the strict application of the attachment rules, the states have developed numerous exceptions, similar to those of the federal courts. But a second trial will not be permitted the prosecution for failure of evidence except only in the most extreme circumstances, as for example, where it was the defendant's fault that the crucial testimony was not available at the first trial. As Justice Douglas notes: "This is in accordance with the British rule, finally adopted in 1746, after the contrary practice had been abusively employed during the reign of the Stuarts." [45]

It would be impossible to set forth a list of the reasons which would justify a discharge of a jury as an exception to the attachment of double jeopardy.[46] Usually, the cases indicate, the appellate

[44] 24 *Minn. L. Rev.* 525 (1940), n.; see also *State* v. *Calendine,* 8 Iowa 288, 292 (1859).

[45] Douglas, *An Almanac of Liberty* (Garden City, N.Y., 1954), p. 143.

[46] *Commonwealth* v. *Purchase,* 2 Pick. 521, 524 (Mass. 1824). See also, *United States* v. *Perez,* 22 U.S. (9 Wheat.) 379 (1824).

court will assert that the power of jury discharge and its exercise is a matter for the discretion of the trial judge.[47] There has been some tendency, however, to delineate the exercise of this discretion through the passage of statutes permitting discharge in special situations.[48] The rule of "manifest necessity" is an exception to the attachment of jeopardy, but it is for the courts to determine whether such a necessity exists. Whether the discharge resulted from some mere whim of the judge or jury or some other accident is immaterial, states one court, with very weak policy justification.[49] Probably the manifest necessity exception touches upon a sensitive judicial nerve, the matter of the discretion of the trial court judge in discharging a case. The policy question is whether such dismissal should be given double jeopardy significance.

The circumstances must be "forceful" to justify the exception, and must be in the nature of an uncontrollable emergency.[50] In some jurisdictions the reasons for which the court granted a jury discharge must be on record to permit a plea of double jeopardy to be entered.[51] The same exceptions familiar in federal cases are made in the state cases: illness of a juror, illness of the accused or of the judge, misconduct of a juror or court officer. An interesting situation arises when the accused is absent and the jury discharged in his absence. This acts as an acquittal[52] unless the accused has run away.[53] It has been held that the absence of the accused was "a

[47] *State* v. *Van Ness*, 82 N.J.L. 181, 182, 83 A. 195, 196 (1912). But if the jury were discharged without indicating that agreement was impossible and in spite of the wishes of the prosecutor and defense, a jeopardy would result (*Adamo* v. *Several Justices of Supreme Court*, 280 N.Y.S.2d 749 [A.D. 1967]).

[48] There is an extensive number of such statutes. A typical example permits discharge when on the trial of an offense there is a variance between the evidence and the charge (South Carolina, Code of Laws, 1922, Cr. Pr., Sec. 91; also, Mississippi, Code, 1930, Sec. 1289).

[49] *State* ex. rel. *Dato* v. *Himes*, 134 Fla. 675, 184 So. 244 (1938).

[50] *State* v. *Phillips*, 27 Ariz. 349, 223 P. 568 (1925).

[51] *Garrison* v. *State*, 9 Ohio 77 (1839); *contra*, *Hurdock* v. *State*, 165 Tex. Crim. 359, 235 S.W.2d 163 (1950).

[52] *Stough* v. *State*, 75 Okla. Crim. 62, 128 P.2d 1028 (1943).

[53] *People* v. *Higgins*, 59 Cal. 357 (1881).

waiver of the right to be present,"[54] and that his right to be present may[55] or may not be waived by his counsel.[56] The exception might also be created by statute.[57]

Perhaps the most common discharge situation is that of the hung jury. The situation has been generally held to be no bar against a second trial, but some states have held to the contrary in capital cases.[58] The recent operation of this exception is obvious in the California murder trial of Bernard Finch, which involved two hung juries.

But the courts differ widely as to what constitutes an "untoward accident" or "overwhelming physical or legal necessity" to justify a suspension of the normal rule of double jeopardy.[59] For each exception to the attachment of double jeopardy a specific precedent must be found. The law of manifest necessity as an exception to double jeopardy is a piecemeal creation.

One explanation which has been offered to justify the manifest necessity exception is that in such cases jeopardy did not, in fact really attach, that jeopardy is only apparent, becoming real only if it later appears that a verdict could never have been rendered.[60] Or it is argued that jeopardy depends upon a presumption of a regular and complete proceeding.[61] There appear to be a number of inconsistencies in operation. These exceptions, made in the name of "manifest necessity" are not real exceptions but the admission of other considerations to bar the operation of double jeopardy, for reasons that are only dimly conceived.[62] As demonstrated earlier,

[54] *State* v. *McCrary*, 365 Mo. 799, 287 S.W.2d 785 (1956).

[55] *People* v. *Smalling*, 94 Cal. 119, 29 F. 421 (1892).

[56] *Cook* v. *State*, 60 Ala. 39 (1877).

[57] California, Penal Code, Sec. 1387, declares dismissal of a misdemeanor complaint a bar to further prosecution unless an order is explicitly made for the purpose of amending a pleading.

[58] *Commonwealth* v. *Fitzpatrick*, 121 Pa. 109, 165 A. 498 (1888).

[59] See 14 *U. Pitt. L. Rev.* 587 (1953), n.

[60] *People* v. *Hunckeler*, 48 Cal. 331, 334 (1874).

[61] *State* v. *Emery*, 59 Vt. 84, 88, 7 A. 129, 133 (1886).

[62] *Commonwealth* v. *Purchase*, 2 Pick. 521, 526 (Mass. 1824), is an example.

the attachment doctrine necessarily leads to exceptions, and it would be preferable to substitute a clear-cut standard by which exceptions might be made, such as the extrinsic-intrinsic test proposed in the previous chapter, than to continue the present lack of clear policy guides.[63]

Several jurisdictions, in an attempt to reform the double jeopardy doctrine, have applied res judicata in criminal prosecutions.[64] Res judicata is the legal concept that all factual matters necessarily resolved by a prior suit between two parties are binding upon the parties in all future suits between them. Although resting upon some dubious reasoning from an analogy with the civil law, some state courts have been quick to declare that if an issue was actually and fully litigated on the former trial, the judgment should be conclusive as to that time, even in a criminal case.[65] Yet, "res judicata does

[63] In certain areas statutes have carved out exceptions to double jeopardy. A Kentucky statute authorized a second trial after a dismissal. This statute was declared by the Kentucky courts to be unconstitutional in *Williams* v. *Commonwealth*, 78 Ky. 93 (1879). This may hold true even in a state where acquittal is necessary to constitute a bar to a second prosecution, on the ground that a new trial might present the possibility of oppression of persons charged with crime (*People* v. *Barrett*, 2 Cai. R. 304 [N.Y. 1805]). Certain areas have been excluded from double jeopardy by the courts for policy reasons. One of these is that of the sanity hearing preceding the judgment of guilt or innocence. So, an inquiry which was made into the sanity of the accused at the time his case was first called for trial resulted in committal to a hospital for the insane and was not a jeopardy barring his subsequent trial for the crime after regaining his sanity (*McNaren* v. *State*, 20 Ala. App. 529, 104 So. 339 [1939]). A verdict of insanity at the time of the commission of the crime does not operate as an acquittal (*People* v. *Perry*, 99 Cal. App. 90, 221 P.2d 120 [1950]).

[64] *Jay* v. *State*, 15 Ala. App. 255, 73 So. 137 (1916); *Harris* v. *State*, 193 Ga. 109, 17 S.E.2d 573 (1941); *People* v. *Grzesezak*, 77 Misc. 202, 137 N.Y.S. 538 (Nassau County Ct. 1912). See McLaren, "The Doctrine of Res Judicata as Applied to the Trial of Criminal Cases," 10 *Wash. L. Rev.* 198 (1935), which calls for the use of res judicata where double jeopardy fails, as statutory penalties continue to multiply. Collateral estoppel was applied in New Jersey in 1966 in *State* v. *Corimer*, 46 N.J. 494, 218 A.2d 138.

[65] *People* v. *Albers*, 137 Mich. 678, 100 N.W. 903 (1914); see also *In re Cottesfeld*, 245 Pa. 314, 291 A. 494, 497 (1914); *State* v. *Coblentz*, 169 Md. 159, 180 A. 266 (1935); *Mitchell* v. *State*, 140 Ala. 118, 37 S. 76 (1904);

rest not upon any constitutional provision," but "is a rule of evidence." [66] Res judicata may, unlike double jeopardy, be used by the prosecution against the defendant. Justice Holmes argued eloquently, if not logically, that the defendant in a criminal case ought to have the same protection on this score as a civil litigant, for "the safeguards of the person, so often and so rightly mentioned with solemn reverence, are less than those that protect from liability for debt." [67]

Considerable overlap exists between the doctrines of former jeopardy and res judicata, cases in which either might be pleaded. And "because of this overlap, there is some danger that the applicability of the plea of double jeopardy may be disregarded in favor of the plea of res judicata in cases where both seem applicable," says one journal.[68] This danger seems unimportant when compared with the more serious effect of watering down the protection available to the defendant through the drawing of an analogy from the civil law which implies that, somehow, civil protections contained in evidence law are on a par with constitutional protections. An example of the possible bad effects of such reasoning is the case of *People* v. *Majado*,[69] where res judicata was used in its civil law role. In this case, a prior conviction for nonsupport of an illegitimate child was

---

Commonwealth v. *Ellis*, 160 Mass. 165, 135 N.E. 455 (1893); *Altenburg* v. *Commonwealth*, 126 Pa. 602, 117 A. 799 (1889). *State* v. *Coblentz* holds it effective only where a plea of double jeopardy would be effective, as does *State* v. *Vandemark*, 77 Conn. 201, 58 A. 715 (1904).

[66] *N.Y.L.J.*, Dec. 18, 19, and 20, 1939, quoted in *United States* v. *Carlisi*, 32 F. Supp. 479, 482 (E.D.N.Y. 1940). "Former jeopardy is to be distinguished from *res judicata*" (*State* v. *Witte*, 243 Wis. 243, 10 N.W.2d 117 (1943).

[67] In *United States* v. *Oppenheimer*, 242 U.S. 85, 87 (1916).

[68] "Res Judicata as a Plea in Bar in Criminal Prosecutions," 26 *Va. L. Rev.* 841 (1939), n.

[69] 22 Cal. App. 2d 323, 70 P.2d 1015 (1937); see also *State* v. *Seingood*, 80 Vt. 412, 68 A. 51 (1907); *Commonwealth* v. *Ellis*, 160 Mass. 165, 35 N.E. 455 (1893). In *Ex parte Dusenberg* v. *Rudolph*, 325 Mo. 881, 30 S.W.2d 94 (1930), the conviction of robbery in a prior prosecution was held to establish res judicata as to the place where the robbery was committed (really collateral estoppel).

held to have conclusively established the defendant's parentage for the purposes of a second prosecution.

Overlapping Jurisdictional Boundaries

Just as the federal government has problems drawing lines indicating the significance which traditional legal boundaries are to have for double jeopardy, the states, through their courts and legislatures, must resolve this question with respect to their subordinate units, the municipalities. As we shall see, the resolution of the problem has not been any more satisfactory, as conscious policy, than the parallel federal solution. This aspect of double jeopardy presents the potentiality not only of double prosecutions by city and state, but, by virtue of the *Lanza* and *Bartkus* cases, of triple prosecutions as well.

It is well-settled that, in the absence of state constitutional limitations upon the actions of state legislatures, municipalities are wholly controlled by the state legislature.[70] The power of the legislature over the municipalities is not limited by any provisions of the federal constitution. A municipal corporation has "no privileges or immunities under the federal constitution which it may invoke in opposition to the will of its creator." [71] The well-known doctrine of Judge Cooley, asserting an inherent right of municipalities to self-government, has never been accepted.[72]

Many states have provided for municipal home rule which would permit the cities more sovereignty over their own affairs.[73] Whether the motive was a desire to free the municipalities from the absolute will of legislatures or to rid the legislatures of the task of prescribing

[70] *City of Trenton* v. *New Jersey*, 262 U.S. 182 (1923).

[71] *Williams* v. *Mayor and City Council of Baltimore*, 289 U.S. 36 (1928).

[72] In *People* ex. rel. *LeRoy* v. *Hurlbut*, 24 Mich. 44, 95–100 (1871), rejected in *City of Trenton* v. *New Jersey*, cited above, the Court declaring that "municipalities have no inherent right of self-government which is beyond the legislative control of the state. . . . [The] state may withhold, grant or withdraw powers and priviliges as it sees fit" (p. 187).

[73] Twenty-four states have some constitutional variant; many have legislative home rule.

for petty matters, some states have extended considerable powers to their municipalities. Although the scope of municipal powers under home rule is far from clear [74] as a legal matter, the states have permitted some municipal criminal powers. The double jeopardy problem arises from the conflict of state criminal statutes with municipal ordinances.

At the turn of the century it seemed certain that the same act might constitute an offense against both the state and a municipality. An accused might be punished by either or both.[75] Basing its reasoning upon the logic of a dictum in the federal case of *Fox* v. *Ohio*,[76] a leading state case held:

The offenses against the corporation and the state . . . are distinguishable, and wholly disconnected, and the prosecution at the suit of each proceeds upon a different hypothesis—the one contemplates the observance of the peace and good order of the city—the other has a more enlarged object in view, the maintenance of the peace and dignity of the state.[77]

The case was decided before the home rule movement gained impetus, so that the notion of separate sovereignties is hard to justify. Such cases have led one commentator to observe that "to this extent, at least, our vaunted constitutional guarantees against a second prosecution for the same offense have dropped out of our living constitutions and have been relegated to the realm of constitutional mythology." [78]

The weight of authority is to the effect that prosecution by both the state and the municipality does not constitute double jeopardy.[79] Some courts have held that the violation of a municipal

---

[74] See Baker, *Urban Government* (Princeton, 1957), p. 321–25.

[75] 92 Am. St. R. 89, 100 (1902), n., has a collection of cases.

[76] 46 U.S. (5 How.) 410, 434, 439 (1847).

[77] *Mayor of Mobile* v. *Allaire*, 14 Ala. 400, 403 (1848).

[78] Grant, "Penal Ordinances and the Guarantee against Double Jeopardy," 25 *Geo. L. J.*, 294 (1937).

[79] See *McCarn* v. *State*, 82 Okla. Crim. 374, 170 P.2d 526 (1949); cf. *Ancrim* v. *Camden Water, Light and Ice Co.*, 82 S.C. 284, 64 S.E. 151 (1909).

ordinance is not really a crime at all, but, instead, that punishment by way of fine for the violation of a municipal ordinance "implies a mere forfeiture or penalty collectible by civil action in the name of the city." [80] It is clear that a new evaluation of this rule is needed, especially in view of the changing nature of city life and the growing seriousness of urban crime. Legal policy must eventually conform to social reality. The fact is that the greater number of serious crimes take place within cities, and that fact should not be the basis of the evasion of double jeopardy.[81]

Certain states, have, by statute, restricted the possibility of multiple punishment by forbidding cities to make acts punishable by ordinance which are already made public offenses punishable by the state.[82] Kentucky makes conviction or acquittal under either a statute or a municipal ordinance a bar to another prosecution for the same offense, as a matter of constitutional right.[83] Even though some states have tried to prevent multiple prosecutions, most have not. One way to avoid the problem might be to allow the ordinance and the statute to coexist but to permit the state to intervene, if it chose, or else be foreclosed from further prosecution.

The conflict between city and state in the criminal law area is not really inevitable,[84] but "from the point of view of policy it seems to

[80] *City of Milwaukee* v. *Johnson*, 192 Wis. 585, 213 N.E. 335 (1927).

[81] See Gross, "Successive Prosecution by City and State," 43 *Ore. L. Rev.* 281 (1964). Only the New Jersey courts have refuted the majority rule in this century by reversing the earlier, commonly held rule (*State* v. *Labato*, 7 N.J. 137, 80 A.2d 617 [1951], and *State* v. *Mark*, 23 N.J. 162, 128 A.2d 487 [1957]).

[82] Indiana, as in *City of Frankfort* v. *Aughie*, 114 Ind. 77, 15 N.E. 902 (1888); Arkansas, as in *Richardson* v. *State*, 56 Ark. 367, 19 S.W. 1052 (1892); and Texas, as in *Davis* v. *State*, 37 Tex. Crim. 359, 38 S.W. 616 (1897).

[83] Constitution, Sec. 168.

[84] The similarity with the problem of federalism is striking in home rule states: "It is difficult to draw a distinction between the situation in home rule jurisdictions and that existing in the federal state context, in which the double jeopardy defense has been held unavailable. In both situations, one of two prosecuting bodies is a government of delegated powers, initially created by a state (or states), and in both cases these powers derive from a constitution

be doubtful justice to provide for prosecution by both state and municipality for the same act." [85] This possibility of double or even of triple prosecutions is heightened by the constant extension of municipal jurisdiction. A system of municipal corporations with some power to impose severe criminal penalties can be integrated into a state's legal system without sacrificing the concept of double jeopardy.[86]

Conviction of a crime in one county is a bar to prosecution in the other.[87] In this situation, of course, the county, not being a criminal-law-creating authority, is important only for jurisdictional considerations. But a prosecution for operating a lottery in one county has been held no bar to subsequent prosecution in another county.[88] It could be argued that the legal position of the municipality is not so different from that of the county for purposes of double jeopardy, but no such holding exists.

There is no double jeopardy when a person is tried by both a state court and a court-martial, it has been declared,[89] although a recent case seems to hold to the contrary.[90] The policy problem in this situation seems clearly distinguishable from the preceding. The sources and purposes of the Uniform Code of Military Justice are quite different from those of state and local law.

Perhaps the least satisfactory aspect of jurisdictional line-drawing in state double jeopardy law is that concerning offenses against two or more states. Generally, where an act violates the laws of two

---

not subject to legislative modification" ("Conflicts between State Statutes and Municipal Ordinances," 72 *Harv. L. Rev.* 747 [1958]. n. 70).

[85] Kneier, "Prosecution under State Law and Municipal Ordinance as Double Jeopardy," 16 *Corn. L.Q.* 208, 209 (1931).

[86] Grant, "Penal Ordinances and the Guarantee against Double Jeopardy," p. 312.

[87] *State* v. *Roberts,* 152 La. 283, 93 So. 95 (1922).

[88] *Lunsford* v. *State,* 18 Ga. 162, 199 S.E. 808 (1939); similarly in a case involving a rape, *Hall* v. *State,* 41 Ga. App. 455, 150 S.E. 465 (1936).

[89] Crowe, "Double Jeopardy and Courts-Martial," 3 *Minn. L. Rev.* 181, 187 (1919) summarizes much of the law.

[90] *Perry* v. *Harper,* 180 Okla. 211, 307 P.2d 168 (1957); noted in 11 *Okla. L. Rev.* 212 (1958).

states, the offender may be subjected to multiple prosecution in the absence of a statute or an interstate compact.[91] This rule has been criticized as contrary to the common law of England.[92] In order to offset the harshness of the rule, courts will indirectly recognize the fact of the former prosecution in another jurisdiction by use of the sentencing power in the imposition of punishment.[93]

The undesirability of the encouragement of multiple prosecutions because of jurisdictional lines has been so obvious to many state legislatures and drafters of constitutions that they have taken direct action to set state policy to protect the defendant. Many state statutes provide that a prosecution in a foreign country should be a bar to subsequent state proceedings. These statutes may also bar the duplication of prosecutions when these have already been completed in other states or by other governments.[94]

The Virginia Code has the effect of reversing the federal Supreme Court, since it makes federal prosecution for an act a bar to state prosecution for the same act.[95] Illinois, in 1959, became the eighteenth state to bar state prosecution if there has been a prior federal prosecution for the same crime. This statute was in direct reaction to the *Bartkus* case.[96] But even though the legislature may seek to

[91] *Strobhan* v. *State,* 55 Fla. 167, 47 So. 4 (1908); *Marshall* v. *State,* 6 Neb. 120 (1877); *State* v. *Johnson,* 212 N.C. 566, 194 S.E. 319 (1937).

[92] Grant, "The Lanza Rule of Successive Prosecutions," 32 *Colum. L. Rev.* 1309 (1932).

[93] *McInerney* v. *City of Denver,* 17 Colo. 302, 77 P. 862 (1892); *Marshall* v. *State,* 6 Neb. 120 (1877).

[94] See Arizona Code, 1939, Sec. 43-6102 (the United States or another state or country); Indiana, Statutes Annotated, Burns, 1933, Sec. 9-215 (another state, territory or country); North Dakota, Revised Code, 1943, Sec. 12-0505 (another state, government, or country); see also, Texas, Code of Criminal Procedure, Vernon, 1954, Art. 208 (under the laws of the place where the offense was committed).

[95] Virginia, Code of 1950, Sec. 19-232. See Chapter 2 above for the federal rule, especially *Bartkus* v. *United States,* 359 U.S. 121 (1959).

[96] The statute reads: "Whenever on the trial of an accused person for the violation of any criminal law of this state it is shown that he has previously been tried and convicted or acquitted under the laws of the Federal government, which former trial was based on the act or omission for which he is being tried in this state, it is a sufficient defense" (Illinois, Revised Statutes,

assert such a purpose, the courts still must finally interpret the meaning of the policy declaration. The language of the statutes usually requires a final verdict of acquittal or conviction.[97] The meaning of the phrase requiring a "same act," "same charge," or "same omission" presents such great interpretative difficulties that a court-made test may be applied.[98] Small differences in the wording of criminal statutes may prevent a plea of double jeopardy.[99] The court may find that an "identical fact" accusation will be required of the accused wishing to avail himself of the plea.[100] The result is that the attempts of the state legislatures to set double jeopardy policy have not been entirely successful, usually because the terms of the legislation have not been sufficiently specific.[101]

Multiple Punishment and New Trials

State courts sometimes have difficulty discerning the policy needs which double jeopardy seems best fitted to serve. In the two largest jurisdictions mere multiple punishment has been treated as double jeopardy in situations where most states would have found separate criminal offenses.[102] The error is part of a larger failure to distinguish between the question of multiplicity of trials and multiplicity

---

Ch. 38, Sec. 601.1 [1959]). Of course, there is nothing to prevent a trial in a state court from being followed by a federal prosecution, the *Lanza* case decision.

[97] See Sears, "The Illinois Double Jeopardy Act: An Empty Gesture," 51 *J. Crim. L.C. & P.S.* 236 (1960).

[98] *State* v. *Thompson,* 62 N.W.2d 512 (Minn. 1954), and *Perry* v. *Harper,* 180 Okla. 211, 307 P.2d 168 (1957), are illustrations of this kind of difficulty. The Oklahoma statute has been narrowly interpreted. The fact that indictments were differently worded and differently proved was enough to avoid the supposed operation of the statute.

[99] See especially *United States* v. *Candalaria,* 139 Cal. App. 2d 432, 294 P.2d 120 (1956); *People* v. *Arenstein,* 128 Misc. 176, 218 N.Y.S. 633 (Ct. Gen. Sess. 1926).

[100] *People* v. *Eklof,* 179 Misc. 536, 41 N.Y.S.2d 557 (1942).

[101] A statutory defense of double jeopardy has been held not to be the same as "double jeopardy," but to be equivalent to it (*Sigmon* v. *Commonwealth,* 200 Va. 258, 105 S.E.2d 171 [1958]).

[102] *People* v. *Knowles,* 35 Cal. 2d 175, 217 P.2d 11 (1950).

of punishments.[103] Such a confusion runs counter to the root meaning of double jeopardy, either as a historical matter or as a problem of setting public policy.

The significance to be accorded the defendant's own motion for a new trial is a problem more obviously relevant for double jeopardy. The policy struggle which was described in the federal *Trono* and *Green* decisions is mirrored in the state courts. This situation involves a second opportunity to prosecute which may have been provided by the defendant himself. The question remains whether the defendant should be forced to some sort of election, a gamble on a possible favorable future verdict, or to take the risk of taking the judgment he has.

In the state courts, where the defendant moves for a new trial, it is usually held that the motion is no bar to a second prosecution.[104] Most of the states adopt some sort of "waiver" theory, declaring either that the defendant had "waived" his double jeopardy protection [105] or that he had "annulled" the first trial on his own motion [106] or that the first trial had become "nonexistent." [107] The majority rule also finds no double jeopardy where the defendant succeeds in his motion in arrest of judgment or to set aside the judgment.[108]

---

[103] *State* v. *Roberts*, 170 La. 727, 129 So. 144 (1930), should be compared with *Spannell* v. *State*, 83 Tex. Crim. 418, 203 S.E. 357 (1918).

[104] *Jeffries* v. *State*, 40 Ala. 381 (1867), is an example. A federal grant of habeas corpus has the same effect (*Kessinger* v. *State*, 423 P.2d 888 [Okla. 1967]).

[105] This is the theory of the federal *Trono* case and is subject to the objections made in the previous chapter.

[106] *State* v. *McGarrity*, 140 La. 436, 73 So. 259 (1916). A plea of guilty may have this effect (*State* v. *Ward*, 422 P.2d 961 [Kan. 1967]).

[107] *People* v. *Rulloff*, 5 Park. Crim. 77, 83 (N.Y. 1860).

[108] *Joy* v. *State*, 14 Ind. 139, 147 (1860); *Jones* v. *Commonwealth*, 124 Ky. 26, 30, 197 S.W. 1118, 1122 (1906). Two states hold the contrary view, which extends double jeopardy protection to the defendant even though he caused the event (*State* v. *Norvell*, 2 Yerg. 24 [Tenn. 1820]; *State* v. *Parish*, 43 Wis. 395 [1877]). The minority position would seem more correct and more consistent with recent federal developments, which reject a gambling

The real question in this area is whether, upon a new trial procured on the defendant's own motion, the defendant may be convicted of a higher degree of the offense than the degree of which he was convicted on the first trial. The federal rule has changed, but the states are quite divided on the issue. Nineteen states permit the second trial to charge crimes of a higher degree.[109] Five directly prohibit the conviction of a higher degree of crime on the second trial than in the first.[110] Five hold that the defendant may not be charged on the second trial with a higher degree of the *same offense* for which he had been previously convicted.[111] The remaining states do not seem to have a clear rule on the matter.

---

theory of justice. However, there is no state equivalent of the federal case of *Green* v. *United States,* 355 U.S. 184 (1957). The defendant may not be forced to waive his double jeopardy plea by manipulation of the sentencing power (*Whaley* v. *North Carolina,* 379 F.2d 22 [Ct. App. 1967]).

[109] *People* v. *Keeper,* 65 Cal. 232 (1884); *Young* v. *People,* 54 Colo. 293, 299, 130 P. 1011 (1913); *Perdue* v. *State,* 134 Ga. 300, 67 S.E. 810 (1910); *State* v. *McCord,* 8 Kan. 232 (1871); *Commonwealth* v. *Arnold,* 83 Ky. 1 (1884); *Jones* v. *State,* 144 Miss. 52, 109 So. 265 (1926); *State* v. *Simms,* 71 Mo. 538 (1880); *Bohanan* v. *State,* 18 Neb. 57, 61, 73 (1885); *In the matter of Somers,* 31 Nev. 531, 103 P. 1073 (1909); *People* v. *Dowling,* 84 N.Y. 478 (1881); *State* v. *Matthews,* 142 N.C. 621, 55 S.E. 342 (1906); *State* v. *Beheimer,* 20 Ohio St. 572 (1870); *Turner* v. *Territory,* 16 Okla. 357, 82 P. 650 (1905); *State* v. *Kessler,* 15 Utah 142, 49 P. 293 (1897); *State* v. *Gillis,* 73 S.C. 318, 323, 53 S.E. 487, 491 (1905); *State* v. *Bradley,* 67 Vt. 465, 32 A. 238 (1894); *State* v. *Ash,* 68 Wash. 194, 122 P. 995 (1912). There is considerable similarity between this and the lesser-included offense area. The latter is discussed, for logical coherence, after the consideration of the scope of the criminal act. The same rationale would seem to apply, in that the second trial, although instituted by the prosecution, still raises the question of the breadth of the first judgment.

[110] *People* v. *McFarlane,* 138 Cal. 481, 71 P. 568 (1903); *State* v. *Naylor,* 28 Del. 99, 115, 90 A. 880, 895 (1914); *State* v. *Walker,* 133 Iowa 489, 110 N.W. (1907); *State* v. *Steeves,* 29 Ore. 85, 43 P. 947 (1896); *Slaughter* v. *State,* 6 Humph. 410 (Tenn. 1846).

[111] *Johnson* v. *State,* 29 Ark. 31, 44 (1874); *West* v. *State,* 55 Fla. 20, 46 S. 93 (1908); *Barnett* v. *People,* 54 Ill. 325, 331 (1870); *People* v. *Farrell,* 146 Mich. 264, 109 N.W. 440 (1906); *State* v. *Cross,* 44 W. Va. 315, 29 S.E. 527 (1897).

Scope of the Criminal Act

The greatest puzzle in state double jeopardy law involves the dilemma which also seems to bedevil the federal courts—the policy question of the scope of the criminal act. This concerns the meaning of the concept "same offense," which is contained in most state constitutions. One writer observes that "although courts and writers unanimously agree that to try a culprit twice for the same offense would be deplorable action, great diversity of opinion exists as to the meaning of the phrase 'same offense.'" [112] If anything, this is a supreme understatement, for the careful reader would almost have to conclude that there is virtually no predictability of judicial decision-making in this area, that many of the decisions seem to dwell in some mathematical limbo removed from the real social needs, from the balancing of policies which a resolution of the problem would require. In the previous chapter this matter was discussed from the point of view of statutory interpretation by the judiciary. Because of the greater diversity of case material presented in state reports, it will be simpler to dissect carefully only a sample of the various so-called "tests" which have evolved to aid the courts in their interpretations. The policy issue remains: the legal significance to be accorded to statutory multiplication of incriminated actions.

The most commonly accepted rule is that laid down by Justice Buller in the old English case of *Rex* v. *Vandercomb and Abbott,* decided in 1796: "Unless the first indictment were such as the prisoner might have been convicted by proof of the facts contained in the second indictment, an acquittal on the first indictment can be no bar to the second." [113] Under this rationale, it was held that an acquittal of breaking and entering a dwelling and stealing property therein was no bar to a subsequent prosecution for breaking and entering the same dwelling, at the same time, with intent to steal.

[112] "Double Jeopardy and the Concept of Identity of Offenses," 7 *Brook. L. Rev.* 80 (1937), n.
[113] 2 Leach. C.C. 708, 720 (1796).

The logical structure of the analysis is undermined by a confusion of the term "indictment" (a legal list of charges) with the phrase "proof of facts" (a strictly evidentiary matter for jury determination). From the outset, the solution to the problem of the scope of double jeopardy became beclouded by a logical paradox. The common law predilection for pat legal formulas has led to an impasse in double jeopardy law.

But perhaps the courts deserve sympathy more than censure. The problem has been created for them by the lack of legislative circumspection. As a result, "no phase of the double jeopardy field has proved to be more troublesome than the question whether in a given case the offenses charged are sufficiently similar to be within the prohibition or sufficiently distinct to be prosecuted separately." [114] The American Law Institute recognized the quandary of the courts in its 1935 study of the administration of criminal law. The study observes that when "fair play and public policy seem to demand that a court forbid multiple prosecution, the only rule to which it can turn is that which states that no person shall be prosecuted twice for the 'same offense.'" [115] The development of stopgap "tests" to determine the meaning of "same offense" is obviously an expedient, pending the necessary recodification and integration of criminal law sanctions such as will be proposed in succeeding chapters. Until then, the problem is virtually insoluble.[116]

[114] 24 *Minn. L. Rev.* 516 (1940), n.

[115] American Law Institute, *Administration of the Criminal Law, Draft No. 1* (Chicago, 1935), p. 10. The multiplicity of criminal statutes has created important problems as a recent commentator observed: "[A] factor prompting concern for these statutory developments is that the administration of penal law poses major difficulties, as in the great degree of choice possessed by prosecutors concerning enforcement of the criminal law" (Fox, "Statutory Criminal Law," 52 *J. Crim. L.C. & P.S.* 392, 395 [1961]).

[116] See Mueller, *Annual Survey of American Law—1958* (New York, 1959) p. 122, where the author concludes that: "Courts encounter difficulties whenever one offense is not totally included in another, but factually there is little, if any chance that one can ever be committed without the other. To subject a defendant to multiple punishments for such legislative constructs is legalism carried to an extreme and subverts the legality and double jeopardy principles in spirit."

Buller's rule has been applied by many state courts. Its effect, rigidly applied, is to arm the state with great powers. In sex crimes it has been held that on the basis of a single act of illicit intercourse a defendant could be convicted of both rape and seduction,[117] or rape and incest,[118] or adultery and seduction,[119] and some indictments combining counts of lewd and lascivious conduct with adultery have been upheld.[120] If carried to its logical limits, a defendant could be convicted on a single count of seduction, adultery, and incest.[121] Some people may be upset by this apparent multiplicity of prosecutions, but one court rejected questions of fair play, concluding:

The question of the justice of punishing the offender for two distinct offenses growing out of the same act was a matter for the consideration of the grand jury and the attorney for the Commonwealth in the presentment and prosecution, of the court below in imposing sentence, or of the executive of the pardoning power. It is not within the jurisdiction of this court as a court of error.[122]

Saying this, the court simply washed its hands of the matter by applying a strict rule of interpretation of legislative intent.

But Buller's rule has been applied in reverse as well as in a forward direction, so that a former trial will not be a bar to a subsequent prosecution unless the defendant could have been convicted of the offense charged in the subsequent trial by employing evidence which had been offered in the former.[123] This procedure will be discussed later as an American doctrine, the so-called "same evidence" rule.

[117] *Hall* v. *State,* 134 Ala. 90, 32 S. 750 (1902).
[118] *State* v. *Learned,* 73 Kan. 328, 85 P. 293 (1906) and *Burdue* v. *Commonwealth,* 144 Ky. 428, 138 S.W. 296 (1911); but *contra, State* v. *Price,* 127 Iowa 301, 103 N.W. 195 (1905).
[119] *Smith* v. *Commonwealth,* 17 Ky. L. Rep. 541, 32 S.W. 137 (1895).
[120] *State* v. *Brooks,* 107 Wash. 264, 254 N.W. 374 (1934).
[121] *Commonwealth* v. *Burk,* 2 Pa. County Ct. 12 (1885).
[122] *Morey* v. *Commonwealth,* 108 Mass. 433, 436 (1871).
[123] *State* v. *Brownrigg,* 87 Me. 500, 33 A. 11 (1895); *Ex parte Gano,* 90 Kan. 134, 132 P. 999 (1913).

Buller's rule backward can be combined with Buller's rule forward. The result would be a ruling to the effect that jeopardy upon one indictment is no bar to jeopardy upon a subsequent indictment unless the evidence which is required to support a conviction upon either of them would have been sufficient to warrant a conviction upon the subsequent prosecution.[124] In another twist, it has been said that "the best test of the identity of the offense is the admissibility of the same evidence in both trials." [125] and the possibility of a conviction being obtained thereon at either trial. Some states profess to follow the rule laid down by Blackstone in which he says "that the pleas of auterfoits acquit and auterfoits convict, or a former acquittal and a former conviction, must be upon a prosecution for the same identical act and crime." [126] This rule is virtually identical with the original Buller's rule.[127] In 1907 one law writer suggested a simple solution to all this, remarking that "it is clear that the state has been injured but once; and where there is only one transaction and one injury to the state, the offenses are identical within the meaning of the double jeopardy guarantee." [128] But, unfortunately, it is not clear at all.

The search for viable tests for the identity of offenses seems to be a favorite pastime of some law note writers. Perhaps the best of a poor lot is the following:

Two offenses are identical so as to render a second prosecution double jeopardy, if:

[124] *State* v. *Waterman,* 87 Iowa 255, 54 N.W. 359 (1893); *Morey* v. *Commonwealth,* 108 Mass. 433 (1871); see also 12 *Corn. L.Q.* 212 (1927), n. 12.
[125] See Dangel, "Double Jeopardy in Massachusetts," 16 *B.U.L. Rev.* 380, 401 (1936).
[126] Blackstone, *Commentaries on the Laws of England* (Worcester, Mass., 1790), Vol. IV, Sec. 336. It is supposedly followed in *State* v. *Elder,* 41 Me. 165 (1865); *Commonwealth* v. *Roby,* 14 Pick. 496 (Mass. 1832); *State* v. *Empey,* 65 Utah 609, 239 P. 25 (1925).
[127] This is apparent in the following cases, which apply the two rules interchangeably: *McCrosky* v. *State,* 17 Ala. App. 523, 87 So. 219 (1920); *Foran* v. *State,* 195 Ind. 55, 144 N.E. 529 (1924); *Winn* v. *State,* 82 Wis. 571, 52 N.W. 775 (1892).
[128] 20 *Harv. L. Rev.* 643 (1907), n.

(1) The essential facts alleged in the second indictment were admissible under the first indictment, and, if proved, would of necessity, have convicted of the offense charged in the first indictment, or

(2) The offense charged in the second indictment as included in its entirety in the greater offense charged in the first indictment and there was a conviction of the greater offense under the indictment charging the greater offense.[129]

Such a rule has the merit of combining the lesser-included offense doctrine (mentioned below) with a variant of Buller's rule which is now known as the "same fact" or "same evidentiary fact" rule. Although logically consistent, the test simply does not delve deeply into underlying policy considerations, but replaces the profusion of extant tests with one simple test (simple in wording). The generally accepted rule of identity of offenses "has proved to be inadequate to explain the decisions involving certain combinations of offenses or to offer a guide to the decisions to the future"; [130] yet this proposed test is based upon the same inadequate foundation.

The use and abuse of Bullers' rule can be studied with more accuracy by employing the names for these tests which are utilized in the preceding chapters: the "same act," the "same transaction," the "same evidence," and their variants. Firstly, a distinction should be made between the "same act" and the "same transaction" tests. The former is the more generous to the defendant, since an acquittal of the murder of one person would be an acquittal as to the murder of other persons.[131] The same transaction test is supposed to be a reaction to the harsh results obtained under the Buller rule. It has been declared that the Buller rule should not be applied to lump together distinct offenses, whose only similarity is that they

---

[129] 40 *Yale L.J.* 469 (1931), n.

[130] *Ibid.*, p. 470. The identity rule, which concerns the question of the meaning of the phrase "same offense," or the policy question of the scope of the criminal act, must fail, since it is an attempt to balance a constitutional right against the exigencies of statutory interpretation, usually in the absence of a clearly expressed legislative intent.

[131] *Gunter* v. *State,* 111 Ala. 23, 20 So. 632 (1896); *Clem* v. *State,* 42 Ind. 420 (1873). But *contra: People* v. *Majors,* 65 Cal. 138, 3 P. 597 (1884); *State* v. *Nash,* 86 N.C. 650 (1882).

grew out of the same criminal enterprise.[132] But some states which normally employ Buller's rule, will, on occasion, use the same transaction test.[133] On the other hand, some states which normally use the same transaction test sometimes find the Buller rule more to their liking. Of course, there is no explicit meaning of the term "same transaction." [134] Legal scholars are of little aid, some having approved the "same transaction" test heartily,[135] others have strongly disapproved it.[136] The policy behind the test is supposed to be that "when a man has done a criminal thing, the commonwealth may not carve from it a number of offenses for which it will convict him," for "it may cut but once." [137]

The "same evidence" rule is closest to the original Buller rule. This rule has been best expressed in a Massachusetts case:

A conviction or an acquittal upon one indictment is no bar to a subsequent conviction and sentence upon another, unless the evidence re-

[132] *Alarion* v. *State,* 92 Tex. Crim. 288, 242 S.W. 1056 (1922).

[133] *People* v. *Stephens,* 79 Cal. 428, 21 P. 856 (1889); *State* v. *Colgate,* 31 Kan. 511, 3 P. 346 (1884); *Mullins* v. *Commonwealth,* 216 Ky. 182, 286 S.W. 1072 (1926). New Jersey has been much more consistent in its use of the "same transaction" tests, although the *Hoag* case indicates a new departure: *State* v. *Cooper,* 13 N.J.L. 361 (1883); *State* v. *Rose,* 72 N.J.L. 462, 62 A. 695 (1905); *State* v. *Mowser,* 92 N.J.L. 474, 106 A. 416 (1919); *State* v. *Cosgrove,* 103 N.J.L. 412, 131 A. 402 (1927). This test is also applied in *Roberts* v. *State,* 14 Ga. 8 (1853), and *State* v. *Shedrick,* 69 Vt. 429, 38 A. 75 (1897).

[134] The trouble has been that there is a need for a test to determine what the same transaction test means. One case suggests that "the rule does not extend to unrelated substantive offenses arising out of the same transaction" (*Dandy* v. *State,* 138 Tenn. 364, 367, 13 S.W.2d 794, 797 [1929]).

[135] 33 *Harv. L. Rev.* 10 (1920).

[136] It has been criticized upon the ground that it would have the effect of preventing more than one prosecution in *any* case where the defendant is charged with multiple offenses arising out of the same transaction. This would seriously hamper the state (32 *Mich. L. Rev.* 512, 515 [1934]). It is a defendant's rule which is inappropriate as a criterion for determining multiple punishment (57 *Yale L.J.* 132, 137 [1947]).

[137] *Mullins* v. *Commonwealth,* 216 Ky. 182, 286 S.W. 1042 (1926); see also, *State* v. *Elder,* 65 Ind. 282 (1879). But *contra: Foran* v. *State,* 195 Ind. 55, 144 N.E. 429 (1924); *People* v. *Johnson,* 81 Mich. 573, 45 N.W. 1119 (1890); *Estep* v. *State,* 11 Okla. Crim. 103, 143 P. 64 (1914).

quired to support a conviction upon one of them would have been sufficient to warrant a conviction upon the other. The test is not whether the
defendant has already been tried for the same act, but whether he has
been put in jeopardy for the same offense. A single act may be an offense
against two statutes; and if each statute require proof of an additional
fact which the other does not, an acquittal or conviction under either
statute does not exempt from prosecution and punishment under the
other.[138]

The rule when strictly applied means that the two crimes "must of
necessity constitute separate offenses in view of the fact that the
grand jury and the district attorney chose to make them separate." [139] Applied in this way, the same evidence rule would dis-
allow the defense of double jeopardy, as in *State* v. *Pianfetti*,[140]
where the defendant was convicted of successive, continuous acts of
selling liquor. It has also been liberally applied, as in *People* v.
Dugas,[141] where the defendant was acquitted of murder and the
test barred a subsequent prosecution of assault with intent to
murder.

The same evidence rule has been criticized upon the ground that
it may cause the issue of double jeopardy to turn upon the presence
or absence of superfluous allegations in an indictment.[142] It has
long been settled that the double jeopardy plea rests upon the facts
alleged rather than those proved in the evidence at the second trial,
or as put in *State* v. *Nash:* "The true test is . . . could the defendant have been convicted upon proof of the facts, not as brought
forward in evidence, but as alleged in the record of the second." [143]
Under such a test, the criticism would seem to be well taken. But
the same evidence test also has the fault of being easily confused
with other tests.[144]

[138] *Morey* v. *Commonwealth,* 108 Mass. 433 (1871).
[139] *Piquett* v. *United States,* 81 F.2d 75, 80 (7th Cir., 1936).
[140] 79 Vt. 236, 65 A. 84 (1906).   [141] 310 Ill. 291, 141 N.E. 769 (1923).
[142] 40 *Yale L.J.* 462 (1931), n.   [143] 86 N.C. 650, 651 (1882).
[144] Thus, one Texas case held that an acquittal is a bar to a subsequent
prosecution in situations where the transaction is the same and the several
indictments could be sustained by the same proof (*Irvin* v. *State,* 7 Tex. Ct.
App. 78 [1879]). This is a confusion of "same evidence" and "same transaction" tests.

A rather rare test stresses the common mental element in the dual prosecutions. Thus if the criminal intent was a material element of the crime, a second prosecution is barred if the criminal intent involved is the same as that which was involved in the prior prosecution.[145] Using such a test, two offenses are to be treated as one, the second being barred for further prosecution if they involve a single act and a single intent.[146] This "single intent test" has the disadvantage of being unavailable in cases of accusations not based upon criminal intent.

A subsidiary problem which has further beclouded the problem of the scope of the criminal act is usually described with the term "the lesser-included offense doctrine." The question of when the doctrine may be applied arises when a trial for a greater offense is later followed by another, and different, prosecution for an offense which is legally a constituent part of the greater offense, or the reverse. The general view is that a lesser offense is necessarily included in a charge of the greater if the proof necessary to establish the greater offense will of necessity establish every element of the lesser offense, without regard to the nature of the offenses.[147]

But the various jurisdictions have arrived at different solutions to the problem of what constitutes a "necessarily included offense." It is difficult to know just what position has been adopted by most courts, or indeed if there is a majority and minority view on the matter. California has recently stated one of the few intelligible tests, based upon its view of public policy needs. The appellate court in *People* v. *Marshall* [148] chose as the ultimate yardstick for

[145] *State* v. *DeGraffenreid,* 9 Baxt. 287 (Tenn. 1878).

[146] *Cook* v. *State,* 43 Tex. Crim. 182, 63 S.W. 872 (1901).

[147] This is codified by Louisiana, Revised Statutes, 15:406 (1950): "When the crime charged includes another of lesser grade, a verdict of guilty of the lesser crime is responsive to the indictment, and it is of no moment that the greater offense is a felony and the lesser a misdemeanor." See 65 *Yale L.J.* 339–68 (1956), n.

[148] 48 A.C. 392, 309 P.2d 456 (1957). This is in accord with *People* v. *Miller,* 143 App. Div. 251, 128 N.Y.S. 549 (1911); *Ex parte McLeod,* 23 Idaho 257, 128 P. 1106 (1913); *Barton* v. *State,* 58 Ga. App. 354, 199 S.E. 357 (1938); *State* v. *Way,* 76 Kan. 928, 93 P. 159 (1907). This is hardly a rule which penetrates deeply into policy questions, but it is at least a rule

determining the inclusion of lesser-included offenses the allegations of the accusatory pleading, rather than other tests which may have been more favorable to the defendant.

On specific matters, confusion is still the rule. Thus, although the federal courts have held that the possession of liquors or of a still are essential ingredients of the greater offense of manufacture or sale and wholly included therein,[149] the states have split upon this question quite irreconcilably.[150] Often the problem is seen as one solely of degrees of offenses. Using this sort of approach, some courts have ruled that a prosecution for the higher degree of an offense would bar a prosecution for a lower.[151] Others, going further, have held that a conviction of a greater crime bars a prosecution for a lesser crime necessarily included with the greater.[152] These considerations have nothing to do with Buller's rule and are probably inconsistent with the results which would be obtained under it.[153]

---

which has some predictability. Like previously discussed rules, it is an attempt at statutory interpretation in the absence of declared intent.

[149] *Gray* v. *State*, 14 F.2d 366 (8th Cir. 1926); *Goetz* v. *United States*, 39 F.2d 903 (5th Cir. 1930).

[150] *Burton* v. *State*, 26 Okla. Crim. 150, 222 P. 1019 (1924); but *contra: Morgan* v. *State*, 28 Ga. App. 358, 111 S.E. 72 (1922), and *French* v. *State*, 139 Tenn. 451, 288 S.W. 601 (1929).

[151] *Fox* v. *State*, 50 Ark. 528, 8 S.W. 836 (1888); *People* ex. rel. *Thornewall* v. *Heacox*, 231 App. Div. 617 (N.Y. 1931).

[152] This may be true even though the defendant could not have been convicted of the lesser crime in the trial for the greater crime (*Commonwealth* v. *Ladusaw*, 226 Ky. 386, 10 S.W.2d 1089 [1928]; *Guenther* v. *People*, 24 N.Y. 100 [1861]).

[153] Bishop says that there is "some apparent authority, therefore, English and American, that a jeopardy for the less is no bar to an indictment for the greater" (Sec. 1057, Bishop, *Commentaries on the Criminal Law* [6th ed.; Boston, 1923]). Some courts have gone beyond this, have gone to the extreme of saying that a prosecution for a smaller crime will bar a prosecution for a greater committed at the same time, even if there could not have been a conviction of the lesser on the trial for the greater (*Territory* v. *Silva*, 27 Haw. 270 [1923]; *State* v. *Clemmons*, 207 N.C. 276, 176 S.E. 760 [1934]). A Texas case says "that there can be no repugnance between the constituent elements of the lesser offense and those of the offense charged" (*Tomlin* v. *State*, 155 Tex. Crim. 207, 220, 233 S.W.2d 333, 336 [1950]); see also *Wright* v. *State*, 7 Tex. Crim. 152 (1884); *Winn* v. *State*, 82 Wis. 571, 52 N.W. 775 (1892);

Many state statutes clearly permit conviction for an offense not specifically charged in the pleadings when that offense is an included offense.[154] Louisiana has adopted the position that the statutory definitions of the two offenses provide the sole test of inclusion.[155] But it must be kept in mind that many states have statutory provisions touching in one way or another upon the problem of lesser-included offenses, even if it is not directly set forth. These statutes have the effect of conditioning the constitutional right of double jeopardy. Many decisions of state courts seem to show a tendency toward protecting the constitutional rights of the accused.[156]

Multiple Injury and Conspiracy

Two significant problems which are a part of the policy question of the scope of the criminal offense remain to be treated: multiple injury flowing from a single act, and the relation of criminal conspiracy charges to other substantive offenses. These two have been singled out because they are the most difficult and most litigated subareas of double jeopardy. They present problems in logic as well as in legal policy.

As a logical matter, two offenses or more cannot be made out of a single act, although if that act injures more than one person logic and law may meet to find as many offenses as there are people injured. In one case the defendant fired four shots at an intended victim. One killed the victim, another killed a bystander acciden-

---

McCrosky v. *State*, 17 Ala. App. 523, 87 So. 219 (1920). In fact, Buller's rule usually could be used in the same cases in which the lesser offense test is utilized.

[154] Alabama, Code, Title 15, Sec. 323 (1940); Arizona, Code Annotated, Sec. 44-1943 (1939); and eleven others. A typical California provision specifically bars a second prosecution after a conviction, acquittal, or putting in jeopardy and bars retrial of prior offenses "or for an offense necessarily included therein" (California, Penal Code, Sec. 1023).

[155] *State* v. *Poe*, 214 La. 606, 38 So. 2d 359 (1948); see also *State* v. *Soloman*, 93 Utah 70, 71 P.2d 104 (1937).

[156] *People* v. *Webb*, 211 Cal. 143, 323 P.2d 141 (1958); *People* v. *McDaniel*, 154 Cal. App. 2d 475, 316 P.2d 660 (1957).

tally. It was held that an acquittal of the murder of the intended victim was a bar to a prosecution for the murder of the bystander.[157] Although this is probably the English rule,[158] many courts have held that separate prosecution could be had because the violations were not the "same offense." Employing this rationale, the acquittal of the murder of X may not have the effect of barring prosecution for the murder of Y, who was killed by two bullets fired from the weapon of the defendant in the same action.[159]

There is a hopeless split of state authority on the question. Some states, probably the majority, have discerned as many separate and distinct acts as there are persons who are injured by the act.[160] Others view this logical problem in completely opposite fashion.[161] A Louisiana statute attempts to solve the problem by providing that in such cases there may be but one indictment, which must contain all the crimes for which the state desires to prosecute, if directed against different persons or property.[162] Of course, if a defendant assaults or kills two or more persons with several separate strokes, there is little problem finding several criminal acts, although some states have held to the contrary when the intent was to injure one person only.[163]

The most striking example of the situation of multiple injury is still the *Hoag* case. In *State* v. *Hoag* the defendant was indicted for the robbery of A, B, and C. The three indictments were consolidated

[157] *Moss* v. *State*, 16 Ala. App. 34, 75 So. 179 (1917); see also *Ellis* v. *State*, 105 Ala. 72, 17 So. 179 (1894); *People* v. *Stephens*, 79 Cal. 428, 21 P. 856 (1889); *Ruffin* v. *State*, 29 Ga. App. 214, 114 S.E. 581 (1922).

[158] *Rex* v. *Birdseye*, 4 Ct. P. 386, 172 Eng. Rep. 751 (Gt. Brit. 1830).

[159] *State* v. *Billette*, 104 Ohio St. 13, 135 N.E. 285 (1922); *State* v. *Vines*, 34 La. App. 1079 (1882); *State* v. *Corbett*, 117 S.C. 356, 109 S.E. 133 (1921).

[160] See *People* v. *Kelly*, 168 C.A.2d 387, 335 P.2d 955 (1959); Illinois, Kansas, Kentucky, Minnesota, Mississippi, Ohio, Oklahoma, Virginia, and Washington seem to agree.

[161] *Hurst* v. *State*, 24 Ala. App. 47, 129 So. 714 (1930); *State* v. *Wheelock*, 216 Iowa 1428, 250 N.W. 617 (1933).

[162] See *State* v. *Roberts*, 170 La. 727, 129 So. 144 (1930).

[163] *Dykes* v. *State*, 232 Miss. 379, 299 So. 2d 602 (1957); *State* v. *Houchins*, 102 W. Va. 169, 134 S.E. 790 (1926).

into one, but the defendant was acquitted on May 27, 1952. The county grand jury was not satisfied with the verdict, and the defendant was later indicted again for the robbery of E, who had been a prosecution witness in the first trial. E had been a victim of Hoag's original deed and was one of twelve persons who were robbed at the same time and place. On October 18, 1954, forty-nine months after the crime, Hoag was again tried, but this time he was convicted.[164] In order to reach this result the court had to reverse or ignore most of the earlier New Jersey precedents.[165]

The sole remaining problem concerning the scope of the criminal act is that of separate charges of conspiracy. It is apparent that the law of conspiracy covers much the same area as that of the substantive offenses, presenting many double jeopardy situations. At early common law, if a felony was committed in furtherance of a conspiracy, the conspiracy (which was a misdemeanor) was treated as merging with the felony itself. Thus there could be no separate and subsequent punishment for the conspiracy and the completed offense, nor if the felony was proven could there be a conviction for conspiracy.[166] There was no merger, however, if the completed offense was a misdemeanor, for reasons of procedure.[167] There was no merger if the conspiracy was a statutory offense, specifically enacted.[168] With the decline of common law crimes, the common law justification for the rule has disappeared, and the rule has been virtually abandoned in both this country and in England.[169]

---

[164] 21 N.J. 496, 122 A.2d 628 (1955).

[165] See the cases listed above in footnote 133. This change was forseeable from the decision in *State* v. *Pa. R.R.*, 9 N.J. 194, 87 A.2d 709 (1952), in which eighty-four victims died as a result of defendant's criminal neglect, which was held by the court to constitute eighty-four separate acts, although joined in one proceeding.

[166] *Commonwealth* v. *Kingsbury*, 5 Mass. 106 (1809).

[167] *People* v. *Tavormina*, 257 N.Y. 84, 90, 177 N.E. 317, 323, dictum (1931), and *Graff* v. *People*, 208 Ill. 321, 70 N.E. 299, 317, dictum (1904).

[168] *State* v. *Mayberry*, 48 Me. 218 (1839); *Davis* v. *People*, 22 Colo. 1, 125 P. 855 (1895).

[169] *Graff* v. *People*, 209 Ill. 321, 70 N.E. 299 (1848); *Queen* v. *Button*, 11 Q.B. 929 (1848).

Some writers have maintained that merger is an effective means of avoiding punishment for both conspiracy and the substantive offense.[170] But, should a conspiracy prosecution be more appropriate, the prosecutor would be forced, under the merger rule, to prosecute for substantive offense, if he prosecuted at all.[171] Several policy questions are posed here: Will the additional punishment for conspiracy operate as a deterrent against wrongful conduct? Will an increase in the severity of punishment for an offense act as a substantial deterrent to both substantive crimes and conspiracies? Should the question of severity of punishment be left to the judge as part of his sentencing power or be determined by the prosecutor who frames the indictment? Yet these questions are rarely weighed by the courts.

As a general rule, where there are successive prosecutions, or a prosecution on separate counts in the same indictment for a conspiracy to commit a substantive offense and for the commission of the offense itself, the plea of double jeopardy will not be successful.[172] A statute may change this situation by declaring an offense and a conspiracy to commit that offense degrees of each other, permitting conviction for either offense under an indictment charging the other.[173] But with rare exceptions the conviction of both conspiracy and the substantive offense is allowed under present law in the states.[174] By way of example, if there are successive prosecutions for murder occurring during the commission of a felony and for the

[170] See 31 *Colum. L. Rev.* 708 (1931).

[171] See *People* v. *Tavormina,* 257 N.Y. 84, 93, 177 N.E. 317, 321 (1931), in which merger resulted in the escape of the defendant from prosecution although he was guilty of the conspiracy.

[172] *People* v. *Clensey,* 97 Cal. App. 71, 274 P. 1018 (1929); *Gilpin* v. *State,* 142 Md. 464, 121 A. 354 (1923); *State* v. *Nolon,* 129 Wash. 284, 224 P. 932 (1924).

[173] *Ex parte Resler,* 115 Neb. 335, 212 N.W. 765 (1927); *Ex parte Berman,* 201 Cal. 17, 286 P. 1043 (1930).

[174] *State* v. *Blackledge,* 216 Iowa 199, 243 N.W. 534 (1932); see *Preeman* v. *United States,* 244 F. 1 (2d Cir. 1917), for an expression of the opposite point of view.

felony itself, the prosecution for burglary or robbery following a prosecution for murder does not constitute double jeopardy.[175]

Now that the major problems in state double jeopardy law have been examined, the condition of uncertainty in which that law is lodged should be obvious. As in federal double jeopardy law, the test which is applied is really a matter of statutory interpretation, except that a trial judge at the state court level must try to follow the tests which have been approved by the higher state courts. The analytical uselessness of these tests has been demonstrated again. In the absence of legislative leadership to determine the scope of the criminal act, the courts have been forced to improvise policy, but they have frequently failed in that task.

State Appeal

The final area of state double jeopardy law to be scrutinized here will be that of the effect of an appeal by the state upon the plea of double jeopardy. Beyond the effect of the defendant's own appeal, it must now be asked whether the right given to the state prosecutor to appeal from the defendant's acquittal amounts to subjecting him to harassment sufficient to be considered double jeopardy.

In England neither the king nor the accused could take an appeal at the common law, but modern England and modern America have moved away from this procedure, or the lack of it.[176] Today, the state usually has no right to appeal a criminal case.[177] Although a statute granting the state such a right may be upheld on the ground

[175] *People* v. *Andrae*, 305 Ill. 530, 137 N.E. 496 (1922); *Duvall* v. *State*, 111 Ohio St. 657, 146 N.E. 90 (1924); *State* v. *Ragan*, 123 Kan. 399, 256 P. 169 (1927); *Commonwealth* v. *Crecorian*, 264 Mass. 94, 162 A. 7 (1928). Many other examples of consistent holdings could be cited. State courts seem to have formed their policy in this matter with considerably less difficulty than in most other double jeopardy areas, but the choice is not so different from the meaning of the "same offense" phrase.

[176] Miller, "Appeal by the State in Criminal Cases," 36 *Yale L.J.* 493 (1927).

[177] *State* v. *Van Horton*, 26 Iowa 402 (1868), resembles the federal *Kepner* case, noted in Chapter 2.

that it is a mere continuation of the original jeopardy,[178] most courts consider such statutes to be unconstitutional and violative of their respective double jeopardy provisions. It has been held that a statute may permit appeals from acquittals in misdemeanor cases, however, since they do not involve a threat to life or limb (according to most interpretations).[179]

Connecticut, one of the pioneers in state appeals, as the *Palko* case bears witness, requires the prosecution to request the right to appeal at the time of defendant's acquittal or to forego the right.[180] Other safeguards are provided the defendant: "Appeals . . . upon all questions of law . . . may be taken by the state, with permission of the presiding judge . . . in the same manner and to the same effect as if made by the accused." [181] But Connecticut has no double jeopardy provision in its constitution. The state of Wisconsin has established double jeopardy as a constitutional right, but its statute, similar to Connecticut's in wording,[182] was upheld as being consistent with the state's double jeopardy provision.[183] Most state courts deny the state this procedure of appeal. Some go so far as to decline even to consider points raised by the state in the course of the defendant's appeal.[184]

The wisdom of forbidding the state a right which is available to the defendant as a matter of constitutional law seems questionable. After all, if the state legislature decides, as a matter of policy, to permit the prosecution a full chance to have the state's case heard

[178] *State* v. *Lee,* 65 Conn. 265, 30 A. 1110 (1894); *Palko* v. *Connecticut,* 302 U.S. 319 (1937); *State* v. *Felch,* 92 Vt. 477, 105 A. 23 (1918). The statutes granting the state the right of appeal must be carefully drawn to avoid a constitutional challenge (*Smith* v. *State,* 94 Ark. 368, 128 So. 484 [1910]; *State* v. *Thierfelder,* 114 Mont. 104, 132 P.2d 1035 [1942]; *State* v. *Midgely,* 28 N.J. Super. 491, 101 A.2d 51 [1953]).

[179] *People* v. *Miner,* 144 Ill. 308, 33 N.E. 40 (1893); *Ex parte Bornee,* 76 W. Va. 360, 85 S.E. 529 (1915).

[180] *State* v. *Carabetta,* 106 Conn. 114, 137 A. 394 (1927).

[181] Connecticut, General Statutes Revised, Sec. 54–96 (1958).

[182] Wisconsin, Statutes Annotated, Sec. 958.1(1)(d) (1958).

[183] *State* v. *Witte,* 243 Wis. 423, 210 N.W.2d 117 (1943).

[184] *Prescott* v. *State,* 52 Tex. Crim. 35, 105 S.W. 192 (1907); *Parks* v. *State,* 21 Ga. App. 506, 94 S.E. 581 (1917).

and considered, the courts are replacing that policy judgment with their own when they strike such a statute down. But the courts have not evolved better tests of double jeopardy than have the legislatures; instead they have acted when the legislators have been silent. Besides, there is a social interest in controlling crime which is an object of legitimate legislative concern. For "the use of the jeopardy doctrine to prevent appeal by the state results in an absurdity," and "calling it an application of the rule of former jeopardy is merely hiding behind convenient terminology." [185] There is no sound reason why the jury's verdict should be conclusive when it favors the defendant, but not conclusive when it favors the state.[186]

Summary

The observations made about double jeopardy law in Chapter 2 have been amplified and strengthened by the evidence of the status of the double jeopardy law of the states. The inconsistency between the law of "attachment" and the "waiver" concept, although not stressed in this chapter, remains to weaken the meaning of double jeopardy. The exceptions to the attachment of double jeopardy are legion.

Again, the need for a more meaningful distinction, such as the proposed "extrinsic-intrinsic" test emerges from a study of the cases. The multiple jurisdiction problem, appearing in the federal *Lanza* and *Bartkus* cases, have their counterparts in the states. But the justification for creating the possibility for multiple prosecution because of the existence of municipal corporations seems to be even flimsier, as a matter of policy, than the federal justification of the nature of the federal system itself.

[185] Miller, "Appeal by the State," p. 496. See Justice Holmes's eloquent dissent in *Kepner* v. *United States*, 195 U.S. 100 (1904), for persuasive presentation of the view suggested here. Holmes suggests that jeopardy continues until a case is brought to a full and final resolution, which includes an appeal by the defendant or the state.

[186] But New York state courts still consider any statute which extends the right of appeal to the state from a prior acquittal to be unconstitutional on its face (*Peabody* v. *Kauffman*, 93 App. Div. 401, 61 N.Y.S.2d 313 [1946]). See also, *State* v. *Horville*, 171 La. 258, 130 So. 348 (1930).

The problem of the scope of the criminal act has been, perhaps, the most hopelessly confused area in double jeopardy. As we have noted, it is really a problem in interpretation of legislation created by the absence of the expression of a clear legislative intent to give the prosecutor, or to deny him, new theories of action against the criminal defendant. The problem cannot be solved by makeshift attempts at judicial legislation, but requires a more far-reaching reorientation of double jeopardy policy and a sweeping codification of criminal laws.

The states have played a role as laboratories experimenting with varied solutions to double jeopardy situations. In the legislative arena many states have been extremely active in conscious creation of policy. The states have, to some degree, redefined double jeopardy to restrict the possibility of harsh results (particularly from the operation of common law doctrines of multiple jurisdictions) even to the extent of effectively reversing the impact of the federal *Bartkus* case. It is to be hoped that this kind of experimentation will continue, particularly along lines similar to those advocated here. This development would have two advantages: it might revive the weakened double jeopardy clause, long overburdened with historical contents, and it would replace the uncertain contours of that law with a definite and concrete public policy created by the interaction of those legal bodies properly charged with setting policy.

One area in which states have felt free to experiment has been in the granting to the prosecution of the right of appeal from the defendant's acquittal. Those states which have extended that right to the prosecution seem not to have had any unduly harsh results, nor has much criticism developed. In departing from the common law history, they have not created a new version of the Inquisition. Instead, those states have sought to redress the balance which the double jeopardy law had tipped in favor of the defendant. In doing so they rescued double jeopardy from the effects of undue historicism.

Courts and legislatures have had difficulty in coming to grips with the fundamental intricacies in double jeopardy. The easier path has frequently been the blind acceptance of precedent, a not uncommon temptation of those trained in the common law. The law must frequently balance the advantage of a new theory against the certainty of a long-held rule. In the area of double jeopardy, the ancient rules, as they have developed in the United States, seem to have proven wholly inadequate to the tasks which double jeopardy could perform. The double jeopardy clause has been the source of more confusion than enlightenment. The reason for this is to be found in the history of double jeopardy, in its varied sources, in its uneven development, in its deceptively simple phraseology. It is easier to pay lip service to a principle than to give that principle life and meaning.

It will be necessary to observe double jeopardy, or similar provisions, in operation in other countries. It will be necessary to examine the function of the prosecutor in order to determine the policy needs which underlie the constitutional clause. The legislative aspects of the problem can hardly be ignored, nor should the suggestions for double jeopardy reform go unheeded. Having reviewed the major problems in double jeopardy, the feeling persists that much more needs to be done. The tools of the political scientist include more than a study of cases. The succeeding chapters are an attempt to expand the horizons of double jeopardy.

» 4 «

Double Jeopardy
Abroad

Double jeopardy policy is concerned with problems of a universal nature which are prevalent in all criminal law systems. The codes and statutes of other nations provide a fresh perspective upon the problem of double jeopardy policy. In addition, such a study will shed light upon the allegedly fundamental character of the doctrine.

The quest for double jeopardy abroad may run counter to the nationalistic tendencies of American courts and lawyers who have been steeped in the common law tradition.[1] American jurists are extremely hesitant to permit the use or introduction of foreign law into American courts or lawbooks. Suspicion of foreign legal systems is especially noticeable in the realm of the criminal law. These attitudes make the need for a comparative study of double jeopardy policy all the more pressing, for, as will be demonstrated, the problem has been treated more successfully in some other countries.

Jerome Frank would have regarded comparative jurisprudence as another much-needed antidote to the Langdell-produced "neurotic escapist character" of the case-study method of the contemporary American law school curriculum.[2] Frank seems to have thought that

---

[1] Pound, "A Comparison of Ideals of Law," in Pars. IV, Tome II, *Mémoires de l'Académie Internationale de Droit Comparé*, II, (Paris, 1935), 209.

[2] Frank, "A Plea for Lawyer-Schools," 56 *Yale Law Journal* 1303, 1304 (1947).

the main emphasis in American law should be put on comparative and integrative jurisprudence.[3] But, despite all these exhortations, comparative law remains an area in which "little important work is presently being done in our law schools or elsewhere."[4] What is needed is a conception of law as a decision-making process, "a process in which the decision-makers are influenced by many variables."[5] Law cannot be studied as a mere abstract body of doctrine; those doctrines must be related to social processes.

The advantages for research of comparing legal systems is especially evident in the area of double jeopardy policy. Norms of international law and of municipal legal systems may be contrasted with American standards. The contrast permits an objective evaluation of the concept of double jeopardy and provides a possible source of fresh remedies for the inadequacies of American double jeopardy. The technique seems simple:

Having found out, by comparing, what our rule of law is technically, we can then ascertain whether, with that technical concept, our system achieves results which are equally acceptable, morally, economically, etc., as the results achieved elsewhere with a technically different concept. . . . [One] may, after discussion of the case book opinions in point, direct the discussion to some seemingly hypothetical alternative ways of solving the particular problem, which is usually one with an unsatisfactory solution in our own law. We then consider the advantages and disadvantages of the alternative and . . . come to the conclusion that the alternative is bound to achieve the more acceptable results. Then I will conclude with a reference to the foreign law which has actually adopted the alternative position: "This, gentlemen, is the way the problem has been dealt with under Section 124 of the Swiss Federal Penal Code of 1937."[6]

[3] Frank, "Civil Law Influence in the Common Law—Some Reflections on 'Comparative' and 'Constrative' Law," 104 *U. Pa. L. Rev.* 887 (1956).

[4] McDougal, "The Comparative Study of Law for Policy Purposes: Value Clarification as an Instrument of Democratic World Order," 1 *Am. J. Comp. L.* 24, 29 (1952).

[5] *Ibid.*, p. 28.

[6] Mueller, "Teaching Comparative Law," 49 *J. Comp. L.* 103, 104 (1958).

Yet the problem of comparing unlike systems of law is one of considerable difficulty because even the significance to be ascribed to judicial decisions varies, depending on whether the particular country follows the code system or the common law. It is said that "continental lawyers do not search for a precedent applicable to the particular facts of the dispute with which they are concerned, but consider how far the facts are covered by some general principle or principles." [7] Although there is considerable case law in the code nations, the common law comparative lawyer must resist the temptation to approach the study of legal problems through the cases.[8] Hence, when considering the code nations in this chapter, stress will be placed upon the codes themselves as the best guide to the policies of those nations.

Double Jeopardy and International Law

Some writers have said that the principle that a person should not be punished more than once for the same offense is part of the "universal law of nations." What that phrase means is uncertain, but the maxim *non bis in idem* is an announced aim of many countries. It is, at least, well established in international criminal law.[9] The relevance of international rules of double jeopardy to the internal law of federal systems has been emphasized by the writings of many legal writers, especially Professor J. A. C. Grant. Grant has urged that since most nations agree that a previous judgment in a foreign court prevents a subsequent suit for the same offense in any other country's courts, the American federal system should recognize the same rule.[10] Even beyond this, a brief treatment of international rules of double jeopardy reveals that despite the primitive develop-

[7] Gutteridge, *Comparative Law* (Cambridge, Eng., 1946), p. 89.

[8] *Ibid.*, p. 91.

[9] Elstrodt, *Das Anrechnungs und Erleidigungsprinzip (ne bis in idem) im internationalen Strafrecht der Schweiz* (Zurich, 1932), *passim*, for Switzerland.

[10] Grant, "The Lanza Rule of Successive Prosecutions," 32 *Colum. L. Rev.* 1309, 1317 (1932), assumes that the maxim is firmly opposed to the possibility of multiple prosecutions where two or more sovereigns exist.

ment of international criminal rules, the concept is commonly shared by most nations in their dealings with one another.

English views on international law have been fairly consistent in holding that a judgment of a foreign court should be conclusive of a criminal matter.[11] The American interpretation is not dissimilar. In *United States* v. *Pirates* a plea of *autrefoits acquit* was upheld, "though resting on a prosecution instituted in the courts of any other civilized state."[12] Yet, despite protestations to the contrary,[13] international law does recognize the possibility of the existence of two concurrent sovereigns, one having personal supremacy over the individual, the other over the place where the offense was committed.[14]

Nonetheless, the usual international practice has been to yield and surrender nationals who have returned home after committing a crime abroad by way of extradition, unless some treaty should provide the contrary.[15] It is usually required that the extraditable offense be a crime in the requesting state and the yielding state as well.[16] The effect of this practice is to prevent the possibility of multiple punishment from arising in international law, except in unusual cases. If double jeopardy is a part of international law, it rarely comes into play.

Some treaties have recognized the principle of double jeopardy. An example of this is the NATO Status of Forces Agreement, which maintains American troops (among others) on the soil of the allies in the treaty. The Agreement provides: "Where an accused has been

[11] *R.* v. *Aughet*, 26 Cox Crim. Cas. 232, 238 (1918).

[12] 18 U.S. 184, 197 (1820).

[13] Grant, "Successive Prosecution by State and Nation," 4 *U.C.L.A.L. Rev.* 4 (1956), esp. pp. 6–8.

[14] Oppenheim, *International Law* (7th ed.; London, 1948), Sec. 145.

[15] Corbett, *Law and Society in the Relations of States* (New York, 1951), p. 180.

[16] But this principle was discarded by the American Supreme Court in *Factor* v. *Laubenheimer*, 290 U.S. 276 (1933), which permitted extradition from an American state even though the crime might not have existed in that state. Here, an act criminal in federal law was not criminal in state law, and the treaty prevailed over the lack of state law.

tried in accordance with the provisions of this Article" by one of the contracting parties, "he may not be tried again for the same offense within the same territory by the authorities of another Contracting Party." [17] Under this provision, an American soldier convicted for contempt before a coroner's inquest in Canada was held not to have been in jeopardy, since the federal rule in America treats a criminal contempt as to trial and Canada, being a common law country, was presumed to have the same rule.[18] Probably, the ultimate interpretation of double jeopardy under this treaty still rests in the courts of each nation which is a signatory, each indulging in the convenient fiction that its own notion of double jeopardy is shared by the other nation.

But the concept of double jeopardy is not frequently encountered in international law. For a more instructive study, the municipal law (in the international law sense) must be considered. Historically, the English common law is most important for an understanding of the law of those jurisdictions which have fallen under its influence. Its views, so far as double jeopardy is concerned, have been traced in Chapter 1.

Double Jeopardy as a Civil Law Doctrine

Those nations which employ code law (the civil law systems) are more related to the Roman and the modern French legal systems. The French law is more closely tied to the Roman than is the English. The Roman jurists, the Code of Justinian, and similar sources have provided the matrix in terms of which French law has developed. In France the principle of *non bis in idem* came down through the medieval jurisconsults and was carried into French law in rules applying to both criminal and civil actions as the rules of the *choses jugées*.[19] The Napoleonic Code expressly provided that no person legally acquitted could be held again or reaccused for the same act.[20]

[17] Art. VII, para. 8.
[18] *United States* v. *Sinigar,* 6 U.S.C.M.A. 330, C.M.R. 46 (1955).
[19] Sirey, *Code d'instruction criminelle* (4th ed.; Paris, 1903).
[20] Art. 360, Sirey, *op. cit.* (1808).

The prewar German criminal law applied the unusual principle of the absorption of the penalty, *poena major absorbet minorem,* to several crimes committed by the same person in the course of the same transaction (not to be confused with the American "lesser-included offense" doctrine). An accused might be indicted for and could be convicted of all of them, but his punishment was to be only for that penalty which might be the most severe.[21] This provision, virtually unknown to the common law, is typical of the solutions available to the code jurisdictions.

In Spain the Siete Partidas of 1263 provided for criminal cases that: "If a man has been acquitted by a valid judgment of some offense of which he was accused, no one can afterward charge him with the same offense." [22] The modern Spanish law treats civil and criminal law in similar fashion, considering them both as a matter of *cosa juzgada,* requiring identity of persons and actions.[23] The Latin-American countries, however, omit mention of double jeopardy in the bills of rights in their constitutions, which are otherwise copies of the American constitutional provisions. In this respect, they may be more under the influence of Spanish code law.

The time necessary to treat fully the rise of double jeopardy in the civil law nations need not be spent because the concept arose in such a different context as to be almost altogether another rule than that familiar to those trained in the common law. The concept and its meaning have been conditioned by the historically different modes of criminal procedure:

Since the prosecution and punishment of criminals was taken out of the hands of the church and given over to secular governmental authorities, the civil law countries have never had to seek meticulous excuses and fine-drawn pretences to protect an accused person from the severe harshness of the law, as in the early history of the criminal law in England; and with the judge as trier of fact instead of a jury capable of being unduly

[21] Schwenk, "Criminal Law in Germany," 15 *Tul. L. Rev.* 541, 563 (1941). The 1908 Japanese Penal Code was deliberately modeled after the German (2 *Am. J. Int'l. L.* 845 [1908]).

[22] Partido VII, Titulo I, Ley 12.

[23] J. Pozo, *Leyes y jurisprudencia vigentes* (Madrid, 1890), p. 409.

swayed by sympathy or emotion it has not been necessary for the prosecution to multiply serious charges in order for justice to be done.[24]

It can be said, with some truthfulness, that double jeopardy is a part of most advanced systems of law,[25] but to the statement one must append the cautionary notice that the phrase does bear a different meaning in different places. In both common law and civil law jurisdictions, the rule that a man must not be put in jeopardy twice, *non bis in idem*, was accepted in theory, both systems having borrowed from the canon law to some extent, so that "in England it became a fundamental principle, finally enshrined in constitutional declarations, while on the Continent it was disregarded in the practice of most police investigations, especially where interests of the state were alleged against a defendant, and it is not now an accepted doctrine in Continental systems." [26] Such a disparity in the significance of double jeopardy is actually quite salutary, since it permits a critical analysis of various solutions to the public policy problem.

But the greatest difficulties inherent in a study of comparative law are those of terminology, for "it is obvious that the translation of a legal term from one language to another is still a constant source of error." [27] Equivalents for usual criminal categories, such as burglary or embezzlement, are never precise. A comparative study can be undertaken in the double jeopardy area, although these hazards must be kept in mind. Histories and languages may differ, but the problems of criminal law are the same.

For purposes of understanding the subject it is convenient to treat as members of separate legal categories the common law nations, the civil law nations, and the totalitarian nations. Such a classification of their criminal statutes is consistent with their legal his-

[24] Ireland, "Double Jeopardy and Conspiracy in the Federal Courts," 40 *J. Crim. L.C. & P.S.* 447 (1949).

[25] American Law Institute, "Double Jeopardy," *Administration of the Criminal Law, Draft No. 1* (Chicago, 1935), p. 7.

[26] Radin, *Handbook of Anglo-American Legal History* (St. Paul, Minn., 1936), p. 228.

[27] Ancel, "Observations on the International Comparison of Criminal Statistics," 1 *Int'd. Rev. Crim. Policy* 43 (1952).

tories. In addition, each of the nations within the systems tends to borrow concepts from others within the same legal systems. This scheme of analysis is arbitrary and not completely accurate. Poland and Somaliland provide illustrations of its inadequacies. Nonetheless, the approach does yield more meaningful results than a more random technique.

Double Jeopardy in England

The closest parallel to American double jeopardy law is to be found, of course, in the English law. Once the departure from English law had been taken, double jeopardy in the two largest common law jurisdictions developed separately. Thus, as early as 1744, England had made of double jeopardy a limited statutory plea. The Piracy Act of that year provided that persons tried and acquitted or convicted for piracy, felony and robbery under the Act should not be tried again for "the same fact" as high treason.[28] The Incitement to Mutiny Act of 1797 also contains this provision.[29] The Criminal Procedure Act of 1851 [30] and the Evidence Act [31] of the same year are later statutory descriptions of double jeopardy. But the greater part of English double jeopardy law is to be found in the cases, so that double jeopardy lacks the firm entrenchment provided for by the American bills of rights. In England the plea is considered to be primarily procedural, although still fundamental. To give a brief summary:

In England there is a common law prohibition against a person being twice in peril for the same offense. Statutory provision is made that no offender shall be liable to be punished twice for the same offense, even as to summary proceedings in the magistrate's courts. The Crown has no right of appeal in the case of an acquittal or where the trial court has sustained a demurrer or motion to quash.[32]

---

[28] 18 Geo. II, c. 30 (1744).   [29] 37 Geo. III, c. 70, Sec. 2 (1797).
[30] Sec. 28 contains the clause written at length below.
[31] Tested in *R.* v. *Emden,* 9 East. 437, 103 Eng. Rep. 640 (1808); *R.* v. *King,* 1 Q.B. 214 (1897); *R.* v. *Barron,* 2 K.B. 570 (1914).
[32] From National Association of County and Prosecuting Attorneys, "Report," 50 *J. Crim. L.C. & P.S.* 67 (1959).

The English position on double jeopardy in international law has been consistent, for if a person has been acquitted by a foreign court having competent jurisdiction, he may not be tried for the same offense in an English court.[33] In domestic law the clearest expression of the double jeopardy doctrine is to be found in the 1851 Procedure Act referred to above. It states, in language familiar to American courts:

Where an act or omission constitutes an offense under two or more Acts, or both under an Act and at common law . . . the offender shall, unless the contrary intention appears, be liable to be prosecuted and punished under either or any of those Acts or at common law, but shall not be punished twice for the same offense.[34]

Although this language seems to be clear, a little close reading reveals the same kind of ambiguity which prevails in the American law. The phrase "either or any" encourages the development of confused standards for the meaning of the phrase "same offense" which is a problem in the American policy.

One great difference between English and American double jeopardy is found in the divergent doctrines of attachment of jeopardy. English law does not place the accused in jeopardy until the final judgment after a trial, whether an acquittal or a conviction. In England, "when we talk of a man being twice tried, we mean a trial which proceeds to its legitimate and lawful conclusion by verdict," and "when we speak of a man being twice put in jeopardy by a verdict of a jury," we mean that "he is not tried nor put in jeopardy until the verdict is given." [35]

Following this rule, if the jury is discharged for any cause, the defendant may be tried again because he has not been put in jeop-

---

[33] *Rex* v. *Roche*, 1 Leach C.C. 134 (1775). This case is still considered to represent the best statement of the general rule.

[34] 52 and 53 Vict., c. 63, Sec. 33 (1851).

[35] *Reg.* v. *Charlesworth*, 1 B. and S. 460, 507, 121 Eng. Rep. 786 (1861), misdemeanor.

ardy.[36] The mere fact of the prisoner's illness,[37] or the illness of a juror,[38] or even the intoxication of a juror [39] will not justify a plea of double jeopardy. The decision in the leading case proceeds upon the ground that the defendant may be retried for the same cause but may be given equitable ground for a pardon by the Crown if there should be serious doubt as to the propriety of the discharge by the court on the first trial. To the American view that jeopardy should attach when the jury is sworn, Whightman, J., replies with a question:

If he is placed in jeopardy when the jury is sworn and evidence given, he has been in jeopardy though a juryman may be taken ill, or some unforeseen accident occur, which would be within the ordinary expected cases in which a jury trial may properly be discharged. . . . Has he been more in jeopardy when the jury is wholly discharged, as in the present case? [40]

Such a result would be inconsistent (thus, the need for the American attachment exceptions). It is more logical to employ a broad rule requiring final judgment, since logic itself is a policy consideration. On the other hand, the English rule leaves the protection of the defendant effectively in the hands of the trial judge, because he decides when to discharge the case.

In *Winsor* v. *Queen,* the history of the development of the English rule is traced to the history of English criminal procedure. This quotation provides further proof, if it be needed, that the significance of the double jeopardy plea is dependent upon the state of criminal procedure:

We find from a statement of Lord Hale . . . that the practice universally prevailed in the administration of criminal justice, where proof

[36] In felony cases (*Winsor* v. *Queen,* 1 Q.B. 289, 303, 122 Eng. Rep. 1150 [1866]).

[37] *King* v. *Stevenson,* 2 Leach C.C. 546 (1791).

[38] *King* v. *Edwards,* 4 Taunt. Rep. 309, 128 Eng. Rep. 348 (1812).

[39] *King* v. *Scalbert,* 2 Leach C.C. 706, 707 (1794).

[40] *Reg.* v. *Charlesworth,* 1 B. and S. 459, 512, 121 Eng. Rep. 786 (1861).

turned out upon the trial to be defective, to discharge the jury, in order that the prosecution might come on a future occasion better prepared; and we find that great and eminent lawyer . . . speaking with approbation of that practice, as one essential to prevent frustration of justice in cases where evidence might have been forthcoming but happened to be temporarily absent; and he speaks of that practice having prevailed for many years. Afterwards in consequence of this practice having been abused in political trials, and possibly also in consideration of the great hardship that might be occasioned to an accused person . . . the judges appear to have adopted a different practice.[41]

The judges decided to restrict an abusive practice which they had permitted for many years, thus strengthening the defendant's protections. At any rate, the fact of a jury discharge in a previous trial has been no ground for a double jeopardy plea in England since 1679.[42]

There are other unusual features of the English practice which will be unfamiliar to Americans. In England, if the prosecution replies to a plea of autrefois convict or autrefois acquit (the phrase "double jeopardy" is unknown to the practice), a jury is sworn to try the issue.[43] The question for the jury is whether the defendant has previously been in jeopardy with regard to the charge on which he is arraigned.[44] Thus, many of the vital decisions in double jeopardy law are made by the jury, rather than by the judge.

For the plea to be entered successfully, it is necessary that the defense meet the several tests of identity of offenses. The subsequent indictments must be based upon the same acts or omissions upon which the previous acquittal or conviction was based.[45] But, despite the long history of double jeopardy, the English tests resemble the American in their variety and futility. The standard which is

[41] *Winsor* v. *Queen*, 1 Q.B. 289, 305, 306, 122 Eng. Rep. 1150 (1866).

[42] See *R.* v. *Whitebread*, 7 State Tr. 311 (1679). But it was not until the passage of the Interpretation Act of 1889, Sec. 33, that the rule was extended to statutory offenses.

[43] *R.* v. *Sheen*, 2 C. and P. 634, 172 Eng. Rep. 287 (1827).

[44] *R.* v. *Lester*, 27 Crim. App. 8 (1938).

[45] See Palmer and Palmer, *Wilshere's Criminal Procedure* (London, 1954), p. 68.

usually enunciated is a negative version of the familiar American "same evidence" test: "Unless the first indictment were such as the prisoner might have been convicted upon by proof of the facts contained in the second indictment, an acquittal on the first indictment can be no bar to the second." [46]

Of course, this test has not been followed with consistency. In *R. v. Sheen* it was held that acquittal of the murder of child X was a bar to prosecution for the murder of child Y where the jury found that only one child was killed, although he was known under both names.[47] When the same transaction affected two different persons, however, it constituted two different offenses, as where putting poison in a kettle injured two people.[48] A doctrine of the "continuous offense" seems to have been used in some older cases. A 1777 decision construed the offense of "exercising his ordinary trade upon the Lord's day" as a continuing offense for the duration of the whole day, and not to be split up into four offenses for any one day.[49] In still another well-known case, the theft of two pigs belonging to the same person was tried first for the theft of one. Conviction and punishment for that theft was held no bar to indictment for theft of the second, although it was said that the second prosecution ought not to be proceeded with.[50]

Obviously, the problem of the scope of the criminal act has not been solved in England any more than it has in the United States. The tests are necessary to common law jurisdictions in order to interpret the intention of the legislatures in creating new criminal offenses. Since the English lack the neatness of a code, it is left to the courts to supply an order, which the courts must improvise in the absence of legislative declaration. However, some English statutes, unlike most American statutes, contain specific provisions for situations of overlapping offense categories. The Road Traffic Act of

---

[46] *Vandercomb's Cases,* 2 Leach C.C. 780, 720 (1796).

[47] 2 C. and P. 634 (1827); also *King v. Clark,* 1 B. and B. 473 (1820).

[48] *R. v. Dagnes,* 3 J.P. 293 (1839).

[49] *Crepps* v. *Durden,* Comb. 640 (1777).

[50] *R. v. Brettel,* Car. and M. 609 (1842); this is contrary to another case decided in the same year, *R. v. Pyne,* 6 J.P. 508 (1842).

1930, for example, makes an acquittal on a charge of manslaughter a bar to an indictment on the same facts for the offense of driving to the danger of the public.[51]

The failure to separate res judicata from double jeopardy also adds confusion to English law. In 1684 a conviction by the Privy Council for refusing to take an oath as to harboring rebels could not be pleaded as double jeopardy, but as res judicata, although the plea failed in any event.[52] Res judicata has been used in Scotland in place of autrefois convict and autrefois acquit.[53] This confusion of the civil law doctrine demonstrates a lack of prevision in English double jeopardy formulation which parallels the American.

The English law of appeals extends to the Crown no right of appeal in the case of an acquittal or where the trial court has sustained a demurrer or motion to quash or arrest judgment.[54] Where a conviction has been quashed on appeal, the appellant is in the same position as if he had been acquitted by the jury on the trial level. Thus, when the Crown appealed on a writ of error from an acquittal of a bigamy charge, the only question argued was the validity of the first marriage. But although this was a clear case of Crown appeal, no question was raised of the validity or the right of the Crown in bringing a writ of error.[55] The case illustrates the court's willingness to overlook a double jeopardy doctrine when it suited its purpose. Such a position is similar to that adopted by the American federal courts, although it is denied by most states.

At the present time, the Court of Criminal Appeal has no power to order a new trial of a convicted person who has appealed to the Court. A committee was established in 1952 to consider whether this power should be granted the Court. In its report, issued on April 10, 1954, the committee decided that no such power should be given,

[51] 20 and 21 Geo. V, c. 43, Sec. 11 (1930).

[52] R. v. Baillie, 10 State Tr. 647 (1684).

[53] H.M. Advocate v. Stewart, 5 Irv. 310 (1866); H.M. Advocate v. Cobb, 1 Swin. 354 (1836).

[54] "A Comparative Study of Criminal Law Administration in the United States and Great Britain," 50 J. Crim. L.C. & P.S. 67 (1959), n.

[55] Queen v. Chadwick, 11 Ad. and El. N.S. 205, 115 Eng. Rep. 751 (1847).

largely on the ground that to do otherwise would constitute double jeopardy. The report has been the subject of bitter attack.[56] Thus, the English position is entirely contrary to the American *Trono-Ball-Green* cases, which clearly dismiss the contention of double jeopardy, either on the basis of a waiver doctrine or some similar rule. The American rule also applies in Canada, Australia, New Zealand, and Ceylon.[57]

Drawing from a shared source, the English common law, the American and later English law of double jeopardy have developed in similar fashion, although differing on several fundamentals, particularly on the law of attachment and defendant's appeal. Within this common tradition, little experimentation has been undertaken which might be of substantial aid in solving double jeopardy policy situations. To the student of comparative law, the English double jeopardy law is interesting at least in demonstrating the limitations of the criminal policy of the two greatest common law jurisdictions in the area of double jeopardy.

Double Jeopardy in Other Common Law Jurisdictions

Next to England's, the Canadian law of double jeopardy is the closest to American experience. What makes Canada especially interesting is the existence of a federal system, which, though almost the reverse of the American, still meets the same double jeopardy problem in the same manner as does the United States. In Canada the criminal law for the entire country is made exclusively by the Dominion Parliament at Ottawa. In each province the attorney-general is virtually the commander-in-chief of the entire law enforcement personnel. This fact assures cooperation on the part of every unit of the local enforcement agencies,[58] and "it is the fact of unitary jurisdiction in the Dominion Parliament, coupled with the expression of the law through the medium of a uniform uncompli-

[56] See Goodhart, "Acquitting the Guilty," 70 *L.Q. Rev.* 514 (1954).
[57] See Appendix 5 of the committee report, Cmd. 9150 (1954).
[58] Callison, *Courts of Injustice* (New York, 1956), p. 377.

cated code that largely accounts for the consistency which, by and large, prevails throughout Canada in the field of criminal law and its application." [59]

Despite the unitary criminal system, Canadian courts have not resolved the problems with which American courts have wrestled so vainly, those of overlapping federal and state legal boundaries. Just as the American federal system seems to require multiple incrimination, in the minds of some justices, so some Canadian judges have reached the same result, despite an entirely different state-federal relationship. In a leading case, an acquittal under a Dominion statute was held to be no bar to conviction under a provincial statute, on the ground that the offense under the provincial statute was distinct from, and not in conflict with, the offense created by the Dominion statute.[60] Specifically, the conflict was between the Excise Act of 1934 and the Manitoba Government Liquor Control Act of 1940, which punished the possession of liquor not purchased from the Liquor Commission. The similarity of this decision to the American *Lanza* case is almost startling, even to the violations of laws controlling liquor. It is possible, however, to argue that the offenses are not exactly identical.

The reverse situation, identical to the American *Bartkus* ruling, is the decision in *Buller* v. *Windover*. That case held that a conviction under a provincial statute was no bar to conviction under a federal statute.[61] The case rested somewhat upon an English decision, *The King* v. *Tonks*,[62] which does not seem to be particularly on point. The rationale was set forth by Dennistoun, J.A., in simple terms: "The first involves an offense against the Dominion excise law," but "the second involves an offense against the provincial liquor law,"

---

[59] MacKay, "Criminal Law in Canada," in McWhinney (ed.), *Canadian Jurisprudence* (Toronto, 1958), p. 287. For "the criminal law is the same throughout Canada and if respect is to be maintained for the administration of it the courts of the different provinces should place different interpretations on it but leave it for the Supreme Court of Canada or Parliament to correct any wrong decisions" (*R.* v. *Glenfield*, 1 D.L.R. 37, 39 [1935]).

[60] *R.* v. *Kissick*, 3 D.L.R. 431, 78 Can. Crim. Cas. 34 (1942).

[61] 1 D.L.R. 986 (1931).   [62] 1 K.B. 443 (1916).

and "these offenses are quite different." [63] It can be said that despite the great differences in the federal systems, Canadian judges tend to reach results similar to those obtained by their American counterparts. The same objections which were raised to the American decisions seem valid here.

The sources of Canadian double jeopardy are much the same as the English and American. One justice, after quoting the traditional Latin maxims, concluded that "these maxims state a fundamental rule of our criminal law, which does not permit a person to be put in jeopardy twice for one and the same offense." [64] But the Canadian law follows the English example in requiring a final judgment for the attachment of jeopardy itself.[65] The Canadian law is subject to the same inconsistencies in this regard as the American. It can be generalized that the permission of the court to withdraw a charge is not equivalent to a dismissal which can be pleaded as a bar to subsequent proceedings.[66] A quashed indictment, a mistrial, or a nolle prosequi will not entitle the accused to plead double jeopardy.[67]

As in the other common law countries, the problem of the scope of the criminal deed has given rise to almost unintelligible tests. The general rule still requires the discharge of a prisoner if he can show that he has been autrefois acquit or autrefois convict for what is substantially the same offense.[68] The Canadian Criminal Code of 1955 sets forth one test of identity which, at least, provides a guide for the courts:

[63] *Buller* v. *Windover*, as quoted in *R.* v. *Kissick*, 3 D.L.R. 431, 433, 78 Can. Crim. Cas. 34 (1942).

[64] Haultain, C.J.S., in *R.* v. *Quinn*, 10 Can. Crim. Cas. 412 (1904).

[65] *R.* v. *Carrier*, 104 Can. Crim. Cas. 75 (1951).

[66] See decision of Martin, J.A., in *R.* v. *Tyrone*, 2 Ir. R. 44, 13 Mews 78 (1912); *Re Bond*, 3 D.L.R. 769 (1936); *R.* v. *Chew Deb*, 9 D.L.R. 27 (1953).

[67] *R.* v. *Sirois*, 27 N.B. 610 (1887).

[68] *R.* v. *Hill*, 7 Can. Crim. Cas. 38 (1901); *R.* v. *Quinn*, 10 Can. Crim. Cas. 412 (1905). Beyond this, the previous charge for the same offense "must have been fully tried and dismissed on the merits and not on any mere point of form" (O'Conner, *An Analysis of and a Guide to the New Criminal Code of Canada* [Toronto, 1955], p. 216).

that on the former trial, if all proper amendments had been made that might have then been made, he might have been convicted of all the offenses of which he may be convicted on the count to which the plea of autrefois acquit or autrefois convict is pleaded.[69]

This rule seems to be an interesting variant of the same evidence rule so popular in America. As stated, it expresses a public policy which is quite generous to the defendant, since the formula forces the prosecution to seek all possible charges on the first trial or run the risk of forfeiting the accusation. But, unfortunately, the courts also employ other, conflicting tests. Recent cases have tended to employ a strict "same act" test, which resembles the "Buller rule" mentioned in Chapter 3,[70] often requiring an exact identity of offenses charged.[71] The latter rule is extremely unfavorable to the defendant. Once again there is an example of the failure of a policy to be sharply defined, an admission of an almost irreconcilable policy conflict, which permits varying solutions to varying situations, even in spite of statutory provisions.

The English law of double jeopardy has been much more influential in the common law world than the American. The English doctrine requiring final judgment before jeopardy can be said to attach is followed in New Zealand [72] and India,[73] for example, although probably not in South Africa.[74] In Kenya, the Code of Criminal Procedure permits the attorney-general to enter a nolle prosequi by stating that the Crown intends to discontinue the proceedings.[75] The defendant is discharged, but the discharge does not operate as a bar to subsequent proceedings. Under this provision, the defendant in

[69] Sec. 518(1), which retains the provisions of the earlier code, Sec. 907(1).

[70] See especially, *R. v. Lamontagne,* 84 Can. Crim. Cas. 225 (1945).

[71] *R. v. Logan,* 81 Can. Crim. Cas. 97 (1944), seems the harshest result obtained under the rule.

[72] *R. v. Hennessey,* 2 C.A. 243 (1873).

[73] *R. v. Nirmal Kanta Roy,* 1 Indian L.R. 41 (Calcutta Ser., 1072; 1914).

[74] *R. v. Kelijana,* 30 Nigeria L.R. 437 (1909); but see *R. v. Twalatunga,* 20 S.C. 425 (1903).

[75] Kenya Code of Criminal Procedure, Sec. 82.

one case was nol-prossed and immediately served with a new information so that two informations (same as indictment, here) existed at the same time. The Privy Council held that there was nothing in the Code which expressly prohibited or authorized the existence at the same time of two informations against the same individual for the same offense based on the same facts. Besides this, such a situation was held not inherently bad at the common law, although the court would not allow an accused to be tried on both indictments.[76]

The short-lived West Indies Federation apparently inherited the law of attachment of jeopardy from the mother country. In a recent case, a jury discharge short of completion of the trial was held no bar to subsequent prosecution.[77] The logic of the English rule asserted:

The jury never as a matter of fact gave their verdict on the first count; they were stopped by the judge before they could do so. . . . The proposition that a jury can be said by virtue of logic or implication to have returned a verdict when in fact they have not done so cannot be supported either by Authority or by principle.[78]

In one respect, Australia's double jeopardy is like our own. Each state has its own penal law, which is codified in three of them.[79] Australia, like the other common law federal states, has raised the federal principle to a higher plane that that of double jeopardy.

As for the problem of the scope of the criminal act, the common law nations seem to prefer some variant of the same evidence test which is utilized in South Africa [80] and Australia.[81] The confusion

[76] *People* v. *Queen*, P. C. on app. from Ct. App. E. Afr., 3 W.L.R. 770, 782 (1960).

[77] *White* v. *R.*, 2 W. I. R. 268 (Fed. Sup. Ct. 1960).

[78] Hallinan, C.J., *ibid.*, p. 269.

[79] See Wagner, *The Federal States and Their Judiciary* ('s-Gravenhage, Neth., 1959), p. 169.

[80] *R.* v. *Levi*, E.D.C. 272 (1906).

[81] *Ex parte Spencer*, 2 Commw. L.R. 250 (1905), where the rule is stated: "the test to be applied . . . is to consider whether the evidence that was necessary to support the second charge would have been sufficient to procure a legal conviction on the first charge."

135

surrounding the test is highlighted by the fact that different results were achieved in Ireland and New Zealand on double jeopardy pleas made after prior acquittals for carnal knowledge followed by subsequent indictments for indecent assault, although both jurisdictions used the same evidence rule.[82] By now, one ought not to be surprised at such uncertainty.

Of those countries influenced by the English law, the most important, in many ways, is India. Unlike England, however, the government of India is based upon a written constitution containing fundamental rights. The Indian Constitution includes a grouping of seven major fundamental rights, among which is the right to freedom, which includes a prohibition against double jeopardy. Article 20(2) of the Indian Constitution provides that "no person shall be prosecuted and punished for the same offense more than once." [83] Despite the language of the clause, Indian courts have adopted the English rule of attachment. The Supreme Court of India declared in 1954:

In order to enable a citizen to invoke the protection of clause (2) of Article 20 of the Constitution, there must have been both prosecution and punishment in respect of the same offense. The words "prosecuted and punished" are to be taken not distributively so as to mean prosecuted "or" punished. Both the factors must coexist in order that the operation of the clauses may be attracted.[84]

But the Indian rule permits the government to appeal from a judgment of acquittal.[85]

In one area of double jeopardy India has departed significantly from the other common law jurisdictions. India has treated the problem of the scope of the criminal act uniquely. Whereas the other

---

[82] *R. v. Burke,* 47 Ir. L.T.R. 111 (1912), plea not good; *R. v. Lemen,* 6 N.Z.L.R. 329 (1888), plea good.

[83] Constitution of India. Like the American system, judicial review is permitted, but is specifically a part of the Constitution itself, Art. 32(1) and Art. 13.

[84] *Venkataraman* v. *Union of India,* All India Reptr. 375, 377 (1954).

[85] *Kalawati* v. *Himachal Pradesh,* 16 Sup. Ct. Jour. 144 (1953).

common law countries have developed conflicting tests of the identity of offenses, India has resorted to a series of devices which seek to curtail the need for such tests. In the Code of Criminal Procedure the provisions concerning the joinder of criminal charges by the prosecution cause many of the central problems of double jeopardy to disappear. Section 235 of the Code permits any number of offense categories to be carved out of one transaction. No matter how many offenses may be constituted by a given act or set of acts, "the person accused of them may be charged with, and tried at one trial for, each of the offenses." [86] Section 240 permits the court or the prosecution to withdraw the charges remaining or stay the inquiry after the conviction has been had on one charge. The effect of the withdrawal is the same as that of an acquittal on such charges. Section 403, unfortunately, detracts somewhat from the full effect of Section 240, since it permits a new trial for a completely distinct event arising out of the original transaction. But the first part of Section 403 declares the policy in clear and ringing tones:

A person who has once been tried by a court of competent jurisdiction for an offense and convicted or acquitted of such offense shall, while such conviction or acquittal remains in force, not be liable to be tried again for the same offense, nor on the same facts for any other offense for which a different charge from the one made against him might have been made.[87]

Part three of the same section excepts from the operation of the policy such offenses as could not have been charged in the original trial because their consequences had not taken place at that time.

The Indian statutory policy is not quite as generous as it might appear, since these quoted sections must be read in conjunction with some others. Nonetheless, it is the best statement of a definite public policy concerning double jeopardy in the entire common law world. If the policy were wholeheartedly applied, the procedure would

---

[86] Indian Code of Criminal Procedure, as Amended and Modified by Act XXVI of 1955, Sec. 235(2).

[87] *Ibid.*, Sec. 403(1). But this should be read with Secs. 236 and 237.

eliminate the need for tests of identity of offenses. The statute is undoubtedly generous to the defendant, which some may find of dubious social value. However, it does remove some of the mystery from double jeopardy, and it places the court back in its position as interpreter, not initiator, of double jeopardy policy.

The common law nations are deeply indebted to English law for their double jeopardy concepts. This accounts for the basic similarity of their approach to double jeopardy problems. Drawing from England the rudiments of this fundamental protection, each common law nation has added some slight nuance to the meaning of double jeopardy.

Double Jeopardy in France

The civil law jurisdictions have tended to borrow from the Roman and the French experiences, and the history of French criminal law has greatly influenced the concepts of the other code nations. Since double jeopardy law is a function of the condition of criminal procedure, it is appropriate to sketch a brief history of French criminal procedure before undertaking an examination of double jeopardy law among the civil law jurisdictions.

The systematization of law began quite late in France. During the reign of Louis XIV, Colbert and his uncle were instrumental in drafting the very important Ordinance of 1670, which was intended as a reform of the unjust judicial system which had prevailed previously. But the Ordinance severely limited the rights of criminal defendants. If a criminal accusation was found baseless three possible alternatives were available to the court: a judgment of acquittal, a "putting out of the court," or a further inquiry. These were all types of acquittal, but were different in degree. The second left the accused still under suspicion, but assumed that he escaped through lack of proof. The further inquiry was merely a provisional acquittal when there were not enough proofs to condemn nor enough to prevent acquittal. It was indefinite in length and permitted the public prosecutor to take up the prosecution at any time, leaving the accused always in a dubious status of perpetual jeopardy.[88] To speak of double jeopardy under such a procedure is obviously impossible. England, in contrast to France, had preserved the accusatory and public procedure, but had also protected the liberty of the accused to a greater degree.[89] With the reforms brought about by the French Revolution, one of the first changes was the suppression of the discretionary powers of the judge in the determination of punishments. However, changes in the nature of jeopardy itself were not made by the Code of 1791 or the Code of Brumaire.[90]

The current French Code of Criminal Procedure clearly indicates that the issuance of a second indictment is precluded where the issue has already been tried by a foreign tribunal,[91] recognizing the generally accepted principle of international law. This has been rationalized by a leading French writer as an attempt,

not only to avoid the conflict of decisions, always unfortunate, but because the principle of *non bis in idem* creates a scandal. Public opinion, at least in countries having a liberal tradition, is even more concerned with respect for individual right than with the efficiency of prosecution.[92]

This generalization is applicable to the entire double jeopardy concept.

As for other provisions of the Code, it is specifically stated that "no person legally acquitted may again be arrested or accused by reason of the same facts." [93] Thus, double jeopardy does exist as an operative principle in France today. It remained in force even dur-

[88] Esmein, *A History of Continental Criminal Procedure* (Boston, 1913), pp. 212–13.

[89] *Ibid.*, p. 289.

[90] Von Bar, *A History of Continental Criminal Law* (Boston, 1916), pp. 320–24.

[91] Code d'Instruction Criminelle, Arts. 5, 7 (Fr. Dalloz, 1958).

[92] De Vabres, *Traité de droit criminel* (3d ed.; Paris, 1947), Sec. 1855. This passage was translated by the author, as were other translations from foreign languages, except when otherwise specifically noted.

[93] Code, Art. 359.

ing the dark days of 1941–1945. But the decisions of French courts "appear singularly to reduce the value of this safeguard, in allowing, for example, a person acquitted in a Court of Assize on a prosecution by the *procureur de la République* before the *tribunal correctionnel* for the *délit* of failing to lay information of the crime or of refusing to render help to a person in danger" to be tried twice.[94] The case law on French double jeopardy is very scarce, the Court of Cassation not having passed on such a question since 1945. Even those few decisions which have been rendered have been severely criticized by professors of law and by some magistrates of the French higher courts.[95] The mere existence of the provision in the Code does not guarantee its uniform application, and in the absence of a large body of case law, it is difficult to comprehend the precise meaning of the general phraseology.

The French criminal procedure, like most of the civil law systems, allows the prosecution a right of appeal from the judgment of the court of the first instance in most cases. This is permitted even though the purpose be to secure a more severe sentence, and "since this procedure is generally alien to common law concepts, there may be a tendency to regard it with suspicion and to ask whether it is not counter to the constitutional right against double jeopardy or to due process of law." [96] There is a clear rejection of the English rule in this matter, although consistent with the practice of some American states. The line between the right of appeal and harassment of an accused is not always easily drawn, but extending the prosecution some right of appeal, at least in controlled situations, would not necessarily endanger the rights of the accused. This phrase, *non bis in idem,* does not bear the same meaning in French procedure, since the trial is usually in separable stages. To evaluate French double jeopardy one must comprehend the criminal procedure.

[94] Vouin, "The Protection of the Accused in French Criminal Procedure," 5 *Int'l. and Comp. L.Q.* 173 (1956).

[95] *Ibid.*, p. 174.

[96] Snee and Pye, "Due Process in Criminal Procedure: A Comparison of Two Systems," 21 *Ohio St. L.J.* 467, 499 (1960).

Double Jeopardy in Other Civil Law Jurisdictions

The examination of the law of the other code nations besides that of France is subject to the same pitfalls. Since it is left to the courts to administer the codes, their precise meanings are left to individual judges. Very little case law has developed around the relevant clauses and not all of it is, as yet, available in the United States.[97] But many of the code provisions are so direct and unequivocal that little room is left for divergent interpretations.

To simplify matters the other civil law jurisdictions will be treated collectively, because the relevant criminal provisions are so similar that some confusion would otherwise be created. The codification of criminal law in those nations can provide some useful alternatives to the familiar common law formulae. Even though the legal environment of the United States is quite different, it is possible that legislative draftsmen might learn from the double jeopardy patterns of these nations.

Few code nations have elevated the double jeopardy clause to a constitutional plane. Japan provides virtually the sole exception. Article 39 of the Japanese Bill of Rights provides that "no person shall be held criminally liable for an act which was lawful at the time it was committed, or of which he has been acquitted, nor shall he be placed in double jeopardy." [98] The use of the phrase "double jeop-

---

[97] The Library of Congress comparative law collection, which is the largest in the nation, does not contain a comprehensive collection of code commentaries and decisions. Even when they are available, these decisions cast little light upon the daily application of the codes. To a large extent, then, one must take the codes at face value. It is only recently that the full texts of the codes themselves have been compiled by a comparative law project which is still in progress, under the auspices of Le Centre Français de Droit Comparé.

[98] 1947 Constitution of Japan. The question of whether Article 39 of the Constitution required complete elimination of all appeals by the state was earnestly considered at the time the temporary law was passed and during the drafting of the code. It was finally decided that there was no double jeopardy in an appeal by the state from an acquittal of the defendant because an appeal is merely a continuation of the original proceeding. See Appleton,

ardy" demonstrates the profound influence of American legal concepts. Apart from the Constitution, the criminal code of Japan is a typical code on the order of the laws of Germany.

Most civil law jurisdictions have treated the double jeopardy concept as a small part of the general criminal law or as part of criminal procedure rules intended to implement the substantive law. A typical example is provided by the Netherlands Penal Code, which deals with the central problem of double jeopardy, the scope of the criminal act:

If several facts, although each one in itself constitutes a felony or a misdemeanor, are so connected that they must be considered as a single continuous action, only one disposition of the criminal law applies; in case of difference, that which fixes the strongest penalty.[99]

Even if several facts which must be considered independent acts constituting several offenses should concur, it is declared to require only one penalty. In such cases, the maximum punishment is not to be raised to more than one-third above the harshest single punishment.[100]

With some variations, this is the pattern of double jeopardy formulation among the code nations.[101] The concept itself is rarely made explicit or substantial.[102] Poland, for example, requires the same

---

"Reforms in Japanese Criminal Procedure under Allied Occupation," 24 *Wash. L. Rev.* 401, 427 (1949).

[99] Art. 56, Title VI, Netherlands Penal Code, in Ancel and Marx, *Les codes penaux européens*, Tome II (Paris, 1957), p. 1394.

[100] Art. 57, in *ibid.*, pp. 1394–95.

[101] The codes of Italy, Belgium, Spain, Germany, Austria, and Poland, among others, provide for cumulative punishments in cases of simultaneous infractions of different parts of the criminal code resulting from a single act. They differ only in the measure of the cumulative punishment. The primary concern of these provisions is with the issue of punishment more than the issue of multiple trials.

[102] It is interesting to observe that even though the principle was not contained in the criminal code, the courts of Weimar Germany employed the double jeopardy concept to bar a second prosecution. It was a weak protection, though, since the prosecutor could demand a review of an acquittal. This acquittal would not necessarily bar further prosecution (Wolff, "German Criminal Justice," 43 *Mich. L. Rev.* 171 [1944]).

treatment for multiple offenses resulting from a single act as the other civil law jurisdictions, but does not expressly recognize a double jeopardy concept. Article 463 of the present Polish Penal Code permits new proceedings after an acquittal in certain circumstances.[103] Thus, Poland and most other code nations have accepted only a portion of the double jeopardy concept as part of their criminal law and procedure. Each code nation differs from every other in the extent of double jeopardy, but none has accepted the extensive American or English view.

In one important respect the code nations have eliminated some of the crucial problems of double jeopardy. Without exception, each has provided some type of compulsory joinder rule, which has had the effect of restricting the state's capacity to divide a single act into a series of separately punishable offenses. When combined with the usual provision requiring a joinder of punishments, the compulsory joinder of trials serves to eliminate the problem of the scope of the criminal act. The code nations do not all agree on the treatment to be accorded multiple violations resulting from connected multiple acts,[104] but that is a rather unusual factual situation.

In some civil law jurisdictions double jeopardy virtually amounts to the common law doctrine of res judicata. The concept has had the effect of extending protection against any subsequent prosecution based upon any fact which has been previously adjudicated.[105] If taken to the extreme, this position contends that an acquittal in a criminal trial should bar a subsequent civil action, as the Columbian Supreme Court has held:

[103] Dobry, in a review of Tadeus Taras, *O nektorych gwarancjach praw oskarzonego w polskum procesir,* in 1 *J. Int'l. Ct. Just.* 140 (1957). This practice was also permitted, although more limitedly, in prewar Poland.

[104] Italy does not require compulsory joinder of diverse violations resulting from several acts (c. III, Art. 81, Italian Penal Code, in Ancel and Marx, *op. cit.,* Tome II, p. 888). Yet, Holland requires joinder of even unrelated acts (Art. 57, Title VI, Netherlands Penal Code, in *ibid.,* pp. 1394–95; a later article excepts separate, independent major offenses from the operation of the principle).

[105] Art. 68, Title VI, Netherlands Penal Code, in *ibid.,* p. 1396. Res judicata has been defined in Chapter 3.

143

Our conclusion is based above all on a supreme reason of public policy represented symbolically in the interest of the state that the unity of its sovereign jurisdiction shall not be impaired by submitting anew to the civil courts a fact the existence or legal significance whereof has already been passed upon by another competent public tribunal. The legal determination that there has been an involuntary, inevitable and purely accidental death rendered in a final decision which is *res adjudicata,* cannot be ignored or refused recognition by a civil court.[106]

Some civil law jurisdictions have made unique contributions to double jeopardy formulation. The Norwegian Code specifically declares that suit cannot be withdrawn once the accusation has taken place,[107] expressing a policy which greatly limits the state's power of prosecution. The Japanese Criminal Code now permits state appeal from prior acquittals but requires a preliminary application to the Supreme Court.[108] Both of these unusual facets of criminal procedure are unknown to the common law. Both could, if adopted by common law nations, help to eliminate some double jeopardy problems.

It cannot be maintained that the principle of double jeopardy is recognized by all code nations. Some have accepted portions of the common law principle. Others have completely rejected or ignored double jeopardy. The doctrine was virtually unknown to the criminal law of mainland Nationalist China.[109] Turkey, influenced by both Moslem and Western legal concepts, permits retrial long after

[106] *Carrizo de Crespo* v. *Laserna Pinzon,* 52 Gaceta Judicial 796, 798 (Colo. 1941), as quoted and translated in P. Eder, *A Comparative Study of Anglo-American and Latin-American Law* (New York, 1950), p. 6.

[107] C. VII, Art. 82, Norwegian Criminal Code, in Ancel and Marx, *op. cit.,* Tome II, p. 1301. Some limited exceptions to this policy are permitted.

[108] Abe, "Criminal Procedure in Japan," 48 *J. Crim. L.C. & P.S.* 365 (1957).

[109] Nationalist China retained private rights to institute criminal suits, but this often conflicted with public prosecution. This situation, which parallels the condition of early English criminal procedure, precludes the existence of any double jeopardy concept. See Wang, "Chinese and American Criminal Law: Some Comparisons," 46 *J Crim. L.C. & P.S.* 798 (1955).

a prior acquital, so that a person who has been tried and found not guilty may be subjected to subsequent trials even after the judgment has become final.[110] The universal character of the concept of double jeopardy cannot be demonstrated.

Double Jeopardy in Authoritarian Nations

Ideological considerations may become determinative in matters of criminal policy. Perhaps a distinction should be made between authoritarian penal systems and the rest, since authoritarian concepts "of criminal justice must not have anything in common with social policy," and "its very essence is punitive, not protective." [111] Fascist Italy, for example, did not even recognize commonly accepted principles of international law respecting double jeopardy. Article 11 of the *Progretto definitivo* provided that where an offense is committed in Italian territory, the offender, whether citizen or foreigner, would be tried again in Italy, even if he had already been tried abroad. If the crime had been committed abroad, he could still be tried again at the request of the Minister of Justice.[112] Such a provision was a very useful political weapon and was used repeatedly for that purpose. In Nazi Germany the criminal procedure, when it was settled, placed the accused on a level which made him subservient to the state and its instrumentalities of prosecution,

[110] The Turkish Criminal Code permits retrial after "final" acquittal where: a document used as proof during the trial which had an effect on the judgment is later proved to be false; it appears that a witness or an expert who gave testimony under oath either intentionally or negligently gave false testimony on behalf of the accused if it had effect on the judgment; a member of the court who took part in the judgment has shown a dereliction of duty; the accused makes a reliable confession relative to the offense after his acquittal (Turkish Code of Criminal Procedure, Art. 308, Art. 310, as translated in "Constitutional Rights in the United States and the Criminal Laws of Turkey" [anon. unpub. MS, 1950, Library of Congress]).

[111] Radzinowicz, in an address appearing in Radzinowicz and Turner, *The Modern Approach to Criminal Law* (London, 1941), p. 314.

[112] Stallybrass, "A Comparison of the General Principles of Criminal Law in England with the 'Progretto Definitivo' of Alfredo Rocco," in *ibid.*, pp. 452–53.

while the Nazi criminal law was only dimly related to the needs of the German people.[113]

If one examines the laws of the Soviet Union, it is not easy to classify the system of criminal law as being authoritarian per se, so far as announced criminal rights are concerned. The most recent criminal law revisions in Russia demonstrate an awareness, at least, of the concept of double jeopardy. In that nation, the statutes provide, "criminal proceedings may not be brought and, if brought, must be discontinued . . . against persons who have already been tried on the same charge, the judgment having become final." [114] The previous law, the Code of 1926, had provided that "where a person is found guilty of an act which comes within the scope of several provisions of the criminal law, and where a person has committed more than one crime and has not yet been sentenced for one of them, the court after having determined the measure of social protection for each crime ultimately imposes the measure of social protection in accordance with the provision which treats the most severe crime of those committed and which provides the most extreme measure of social protection." [115] This provision gave the Soviet Union's judicial officials control over double jeopardy policy, to be resolved in terms of their notions of the needs of the society. On paper, this is not so different from the tendency which can be observed in American double jeopardy law, in which the courts play a significant role in setting double jeopardy policy.

Soviet criminal law has changed drastically, a development which has had a corresponding impact upon double jeopardy. The Code of 1926 of the Russian Soviet Federated Socialist Republic and the cor-

[113] See Wolff, *op. cit.*, p. 1076. Nazi laws and Nazi courts were often only a thin façade for mass terrorism when political matters were involved. Some semblance of legality was retained when nonpolitical (or nonracist) cases were being decided.

[114] Law enacting the Basic Principles of Criminal Procedure of the U.S.S.R. and of the Union Republics, Sec. 5, Pt. 9, published in *Izvestia*, Dec. 26, 1958, and translated by Feldbrugge in Szirmai (ed.), *The Federal Criminal Law in the Soviet Union* (Leyden, Neth., 1959), p. 111.

[115] Sec. 48, quoted by Van Bemmelen in Szirmai, *op. cit.*, p. 22, in the introduction to the work.

responding articles found in the other republic codes permitted the imposition of criminal punishment for a socially dangerous act, even though it may not have been expressly proscribed by a criminal statute. Criminal liability could be imposed by analogy to that article of the criminal law which most closely resembled the alleged infraction.[116] This rule was effectively reversed in the 1958 reforms, which now require the violation of an act specified by some criminal statute.[117] Obviously under the former laws double jeopardy would have been meaningless, since the state had almost unlimited opportunities to incriminate an individual virtually at will and without real restriction. It remains to be seen whether this current reform will really liberalize Soviet criminal concepts and protect the accused.[118]

The international law of double jeopardy is recognized by the Soviet Union to some extent. The new code provides that Soviet citizens who have committed crimes abroad are subject to criminal prosecution according to the laws in force in that union republic in which they are called to appear for trial. If they have already been sentenced abroad, the court is empowered to mitigate the sentence or to decide that it shall not be served.[119] But since this is entirely a matter within the discretion of the court, the international law on the matter of double jeopardy is apparently not strictly applied in the Soviet courts.

In one respect, the law of the Soviet Union bears some resemblance to that of the code nations. The provisions of the 1958 reform law permit a merger of punishments similar to those noted in the code nations for violations of separate articles of the criminal law, so that the court may pass a cumulative sentence for all the crimes

[116] Grzybowski, "Soviet Criminal Law Reform of 1958," 35 *Ind. L.J.* 129 (1960), cites Art. 16 of the R.S.F.S.R. code to that effect.

[117] Art. 3, Basic Principles of Criminal Legislation of the U.S.S.R. of 1958, in *ibid.*, p. 130.

[118] See Kline, "New Principles of Criminal Law in the U.S.S.R.," *Rev. Contemp. L.* (1959), p. 114. This journal is dominated by lawyers friendly to the Comminist point of view.

[119] Art. 5, Sec. I, Basic Principles, in *ibid.*, p. 169.

taken together.[120] On the basis of these and other provisions of the Soviet law, it is difficult to type the Soviet law in the spectrum of legal systems. It can be said that the Soviet concept of double jeopardy is identifiable and is given some content.

But double jeopardy in a Communist state must have a very different meaning from that which it bears in America, England, or France. In Hungary, employee's courts must be set up in all large industries with jurisdiction in matters of labor discipline, damage to personal or social property, and the like. The conviction of an offense by a court of law for a criminal offense committed within the plant is defined as a disciplinary offense, which entails additional disciplinary punishment and automatically places the defendant in double jeopardy.[121] The legal basis of responsibility for an attempted crime is the same as that for a completed crime because of the social danger to the socialist legal order.[122] However, Hungary, having a concise criminal code, also provides for the merging of punishments for the violations of different portions of the code.[123] Hungarian criminal provisions, like those of the Soviet Union and of Poland, have some appearance of liberality, although no certain evidence exists to describe the implementation of these provisions.

Any comparative analysis of legal systems runs the risk of employing arbitrary classifications. Some legal systems are not easy to categorize, especially the more primitive systems. For example, in the former English Somaliland Protectorate the laws permitted whole villages, districts, and tribes to be punished by the governor whenever "any serious offense has been committed against the interests of the Protectorate." [124] Obviously, such primitive criminal law does not reach the same level of sophistication as that of the common

---

[120] Art. 35, Sec. IV, Basic Principles, in *ibid.,* p. 177.

[121] Gsovski and Grzybowski (eds.), *The Laws and Courts in the Soviet Union and Eastern Europe,* II (London, 1959), 1519–20. The same courts exist in the Soviet Union, although their powers are not the same.

[122] Schafer, "Hungarian Criminal Law," 22 *Mod. L. Rev.* 172 (1959).

[123] Ancel and Marx, *op. cit.,* Tome II, p. 811, contains the Hungarian Penal Code of 1950, Art. 57, which is relevant here.

[124] The Laws of the Somaliland Protectorate (1950), II, c. 71, p. 673.

law, code, or totalitarian legal systems. Clearly, the concept of double jeopardy is not likely to be found where criminal procedure is in an immature stage of development.

Comparative Systems of Criminal Prosecution

No consideration of foreign double jeopardy law would be complete without some attention being given to the criminal procedure of those nations which employ some kind of double jeopardy concept. Double jeopardy cannot be understood if treated merely as an isolated doctrine. As the next chapter will describe for the United States, the concept of double jeopardy is a part of the legal framework in terms of which the prosecution operates, and its significance is a function of the condition of the criminal procedure. Besides, it would be deceptive to accept double jeopardy formulations of other nations at face value. The doctrine is intended to control and delimit the role of the prosecutor as a state functionary, and to the extent that it serves this purpose, the accused is protected from state harassment.

In France, during most of the period from the thirteenth century through the seventeenth century, when some act had come to light which either the judge or the public prosecutor regarded as calling for some punishment, the machinery of judicial investigation was set in motion. After completing this stage, the prosecutor formulated his complaint, specifying thereon the particular punishment which he sought to have inflicted. After that, the court considered the complaint and decided the matter according to its individual discretion, "and it was this individual discretion, and this alone, which determined the manner and measure of punishment." [125] Before such an imposing structure of state prosecution, the accused was almost helpless.

This procedure was changed by the Ordonnance Criminelle of 1670, which governed French criminal procedure down to the Revolution. Under this newer procedure, the king's prosecutor on the complaint of a private individual instituted the investigation before

[125] Von Bar, *op. cit.*, p. 263.

the magistrate in charge of that function. He conducted secret interrogations, inspections, and inquiries, after which he could order the accused to be brought before him for interrogations which were secret and without the benefit of counsel. The trial was in secret before seven judges, the accused being interrogated by the presiding judge, and then the whole report of the preliminary investigation was read. If all this was not efficacious, torture was permissible.[126]

As previously noted, the French Revolutionary reforms changed much of this. However, the basic outline of the so-called inquisitorial system remained. The *enquête officieuse*, for example, was an "invitation" to appear for questioning before the *police judiciaire*, which procedure was undertaken in addition to preliminary searches and seizures. During these interrogations the suspect was not informed of the charge, nor did he have the advantage of counsel, and he could be subjected to the third degree. The harshness of these rules was considerably mitigated by the passage of the present code in 1957.[127] But in its approach, the French procedure, like the German, must be classified as inquisitorial. Of the German, it has been said:

In criminal procedure the state, represented by the state's attorney, and the accused do not oppose one another as equals pursuing their mutual claims. The criminal proceeding is the method, prescribed and regulated by law, in which the state exercises its power to investigate and inflict punishment on such of its subjects as disturb the public order.[128]

Yet the German prosecutor's role is different from the French, especially in the matter of institution of suit.[129]

The Anglo-American criminal procedure, by contrast, must be classified as "accusatorial." Under this system, a functionary, usually

---

[126] See Berg, "Criminal Procedure: France, England and the United States," 8 *DePaul L. Rev.* 256, 262 (1958).

[127] Code de Procédure Penale, Arts, 75–78, especially.

[128] Wolff, *op. cit.*, p. 1076.

[129] Each court has a public prosecutor's office attached in Germany. The senior official instructs the junior prosecutors, and all prosecutors are bound to comply with the official instructions of his superior (Eichler, "German Criminal Jurisdiction," 5 *Int'l. and Comp. L.J.* 545 [1956]).

called the prosecutor, formulates a charge and presents it on behalf of the state against the accused, who answers the charge before a court of law. In England, the sole right and power to accuse, to collect evidence, and to manage prosecutions has traditionally rested with the individual and the police.[130] All prosecutions are nominally at the suit of the Crown, though in most cases any member of the public may prosecute. So, "though there is a Director of Public Prosecutions who prosecutes the more serious cases, the majority of cases are prosecuted by 'private persons.'"[131] Such a procedure is virtually unknown to the American practice. The nearest modern English counterpart to the American district attorney is the director of public prosecution, whose office was not created until 1879. This official prosecutes all offenses punishable by death or those of a peculiar public interest, although Parliament never intended that he should be a prosecutor of the American type.[132] Some writers have said that the American prosecuting system is more related to the continental civil law prosecutor and that the office may well have originated in the "schout" of New Netherlands, a position found in the Dutch legal system.[133]

Summary

In the first chapter it was noted that most jurists and legal writers consider the double jeopardy principle to be as fundamental as almost any other in the law of civilized nations. This claim reappears

[130] Stephen, *A History of the Criminal Law of England* (London, 1883), I, 493–95.

[131] Berg, *op. cit.*, p. 298. Most of these private prosecutions are police prosecutions, instituted by police officials, who decide, upon their own knowledge, that a charge should be made. Private prosecutors must usually pay for the hire of their own solicitors unless the case falls under the jurisdiction of the director of the public prosecutions.

[132] Stephen, *op. cit.*, I, 501.

[133] See Van Alystyne, "The District Attorney—Historical Puzzle," *Wis. L. Rev.* (1952), p. 126. It can be said that "the office of the district attorney lies outside the tradition of English prosecution" (*ibid.*, p. 128). Research is very scanty upon the question of the historical origins of the office of the public prosecutor in the United States.

throughout the body of the case law of the United States, appearing with much less frequency in other nations. Whether derived from Roman law, canon law, or common law, the principle is supposed to be embodied in all legal systems which lay claim to respect for the individual.

A search through the case law and codes of many nations reveals that, indeed, some such concept is usually recognized, whether in the language of the anglicized Norman French (as in Engand) or in the Latin phrase *non bis in idem* (as in most of the code nations). But it would be superficial to stop at that point and be satisfied that the principle has actually become universally accepted. A closer inspection reveals that some modern nations have no double jeopardy concept at all. In the code nations the concept has not been fully accepted, and even those provisions which do protect defendants against repeated prosecutions are not upon a constitutional plane. Even England has not raised the concept to the level of certain other fundamental protections. Only Japan, India, and the United States have incorporated the concept into their constitutions.[134] The concept of double jeopardy is used most frequently in common law nations and has reached its most complicated development there.

The main interest of a study of comparative double jeopardy law must be reformative. Looked at from the point of view of the development of public policy, the code law nations have apparently developed an approach to the problem of the scope of the criminal offense which is different from, and possibly superior to, that of the common law nations. It is probably inherent in a true code law that overlapping criminal offense categories would be eliminated and that provisions would be made for those fewer offenses which might, in a particular case, happen to conjoin. Perhaps some of the central difficulties in American and English double jeopardy law are not really capable of solution in terms of artificial tests, but a more sweeping clarification of criminal law may be needed. Without some movement towards codification of criminal law, the courts must con-

[134] The Japanese were under American influence and even duress during the drafting of their constitution, according to Appleton, *op. cit.*, p. 426.

tinue to guess at the legislative intent in creating new offense categories.

Several other points can be made on the basis of the comparative study of double jeopardy. First, in those nations which have a federal system, no definite solution to the problem of overlapping federal and state jurisdictions seems (despite Grant's observations) to have developed. The Canadian and American federal systems, though mirror opposites in most ways, have settled on a policy of multiple prosecution because of the significance of jurisdictional lines. Second, the American view of the attachment of jeopardy before the conclusion of a trial is probably without parallel anywhere else in the world, lending support to the argument that the American doctrine is quite faulty as a matter of logic and public policy. Third, the question of the right of the prosecution to appeal from an acquittal of the defendant is not handled in any unanimously agreed upon fashion, although most code nations appear to be free to grant that right. Here, the English and American (federal) law could both be benefited by a reconsideration of the basis of their policy. Both systems have barred state appeal, for the most part, but have quite different views of the nature and effect of an appeal.

Some specific double jeopardy provisions call for more intensive study if a thorough-going improvement of double jeopardy law is desired. For those trained in the common law, the blend of common law tradition with some code law advantages, such as the system to be found in India, should be instructive. The provisions regarding joinder of criminal charges are not unlike those proposed recently by the American Law Institute, which were intended to improve the American formulation of double jeopardy. Since most code nations have tried to solve the problem of multiple punishments flowing from multiple convictions, it is quite possible that the law of a particular code nation—the Netherlands might be suggested—would repay further study to improve that aspect of American double jeopardy law. The laws of the totalitarian nations, so far as they affect double jeopardy, should serve to remind us that not all totalitarian regimes have the same view of law. It is interesting to note, however, that the totalitarian nations prefer to disregard the international law of double jeopardy, which is otherwise generally accepted, for internal political or ideological reasons.

The generalized concept of double jeopardy is accepted by most civilized nations, although some may disagree as to its importance. The significance of double jeopardy varies greatly from nation to nation depending, to a large extent, upon the criminal procedure of the nation. Americans should not be surprised to find so many differences in double jeopardy when we reflect upon the different interpretations of double jeopardy that exist within the American states. In fact, it is surprising that most of the world's legal systems agree, even to the extent that they do agree, on the concept of double jeopardy.

« 5 »

The Policy Issue:
The Power of the Prosecutor

Beneath the surface of doctrinal development in the United States and abroad lie some profound policy considerations. The history of double jeopardy is a long one and an explanation must be given for the persistence of the doctrine. In order to do so, it is necessary to examine the implementation of double jeopardy by concentrating upon the function of the official toward whom the doctrine is pointed—the public prosecutor. The primary policy issue resolves around the decision whether the community is well served by a restriction upon the prosecutor's powers to initiate and pursue the prosecution of criminal suspects. Seen in this light, double jeopardy is discerned as a principle employed by the state to control one of its own officials in the interest of a greater community concern, which is the protection of the liberties of the criminal defendant.

Double jeopardy is an important limitation upon the discretion of the prosecutor because it determines the number of times that a criminal action can be instituted. Moreover, double jeopardy issues precede all questions of substantive criminal law. Complications in the resolution of double jeopardy policy have arisen because double jeopardy policy operates in the interstitial area between criminal procedure and substantive criminal law. In order to resolve many of the problems of double jeopardy policy it is necessary to decide whether it is necessary to restrain the prosecution in its most fundamental function, that is, the power to initiate criminal suits.

In speaking of the fourteenth amendment in 1959, Chief Justice Warren stated:

As in all such cases we are forced to resolve a conflict between two fundamental interests of society; its interest in prompt and efficient law enforcement, and its interest in preventing the rights of its individual members from being abridged by unconstitutional methods of law enforcement.[1]

The specific purposes of the protection are the avoidance of unnecessary harassment, the avoidance of social stigma, the economy of time and money, and the interest in psychologial security. Each has been discussed in an earlier chapter. Now these claims must be explored in depth.

The critical question of double jeopardy concerns the number of times that the defendant may be brought to trial. The question has become more difficult to resolve as an increasing number of criminal statutes have been created, a development which has weakened the significance of double jeopardy as it has increased the power of the prosecutor. According to one judge, "the definition of offenses is a matter of legislative authority, and the determination of whether and when to prosecute for more than one offense growing out of the same transaction is a matter of policy for the prosecuting officer and not for the courts." [2] But if the courts do not perform the task, how is

---

[1] *Spano* v. *New York,* 360 U.S. 315 (1959).

[2] *District of Columbia* v. *Buckley,* 128 F.2d 17 (D.C. Cir. 1942). In his concurring opinion to this significant case, Associate Justice Rutledge indicated the fragility of the double jeopardy protection: "But in some instances legislative refinement has defined generically identical offenses with narrow differences in intent or in the means or methods of perpetration, e.g. assault with various specific intents and with variously specified weapons. Some of these differences are substantial, others too slender for, in effect, nullifying the constitutional protection against double jeopardy. When they are so or the question is doubtful, the second step should be taken consciously and deliberately, not ignored or taken automatically as is done when the process stops with applying the 'same or different evidence' test. . . . [And] on narrow, technical distinctions of method, means, and specific intent, men may be convicted of the same offense once, twice, or as many times, simultaneously or successively, as the prosecuting officials determine in their discretion" (*ibid.,* pp. 21–22).

double jeopardy to serve as a meaningful restriction upon the prosecution?

The Prosecutor's Office

The prosecutor's office is one of the least understood of the decision-making functions of the American political system. Of all public officials, "the prosecutor has more control over life, liberty and reputation than any other person in America," said Former Attorney General Jackson.[3] The prosecutor can cause a citizen to be indicted or not to be indicted. He may decide to try a case or to dismiss it before the defense is given a chance to present its case. If he secures a conviction, he may make recommendations as to the nature of the sentence. But there has been very little research into the nature of the office, and "of the function of the rule of law in relation to the exercise of the prosecutor's discretion, a dominant practice of bargaining for pleas of guilty, and the entire process of sentencing and correctional treatment."[4] It is at those points that double jeopardy questions arise. While it is beyond the scope of this discussion to engage in a full-dress disquisition upon the prosecutor's office, some sound understanding of that office is indispensable.

The federal attorney general has far more power to oversee the functions of the district attorney's than have the various state attorneys general. It is directed by federal statute that each United States attorney must make reports to the attorney general as he shall direct and that the attorney general "shall have supervision over all litigation to which the United States or any agency thereof is a party."[5]

[3] Jackson, "The Federal Prosecutor," 31 *J. Crim. L.* 3 (1940). For a political view, see Jacob, "Politics and Criminal Prosecution in New Orleans," 8 *Tul. Studies in Pol. Sci.* 77–98 (1963).

[4] Remington, "Criminal Justice Research," 51 *J. Crim. L.S. & P.S.* 12 (1960). However, two excellent papers on the subject were delivered at the 1968 annual meeting of the American Political Science Association in Washington, D.C. They are entitled "The Decision to Prosecute," by George F. Cole, and "The Federal Prosecutor and His Environment," by James Eisenstein.

[5] 28 U.S.C.A. Sec. 507 (1954). "There is no express authority vested in the Attorney General to institute suit in any of the numerous cases in which the United States is plaintiff; and yet he is invested with the general superin-

Unlike the county prosecutor in most states, the United States district attorney is appointed to his post.

Despite the statutes, the United States attorney is vested with considerable discretion in the daily conduct of his office, especially in the decision to institute criminal actions. He may decide many important matters without consulting the attorney general's office, such as when and where to institute criminal suits and whether to submit them to the grand jury.[6] Only in unusual cases will the attorney general's office intervene in the normal process of the institution of a criminal suit.[7]

But since the general police power still rests with the several states, the powers of the state prosecutors are of even greater importance to criminal procedure generally, and to the problem of double jeopardy specifically, if only because of the far greater volume of criminal suits which are instituted by state prosecutors. Accordingly, the role of the local prosecutor in the states is of unusual significance for double jeopardy law.

The position of the state attorney general vis-à-vis the local prosecutors is usually quite different from that of the federal attorney general. An attorney general of Ohio has stated a not unusual situation as follows:

The office of the Attorney-General is almost exclusively a civil law office, involved on behalf of the state in cases in which no criminal statutes are usually involved. In Ohio the prosecution of cases is left, except in very

---

tendence of all such suits" (*United States* v. *San Jacinto Tin Co.*, 125 U.S. 278 [1888]). The assistant attorney general in charge of the Criminal Division has responsibility for, and supervision over, the enforcement of federal criminal laws and has general direction and supervision over United States attorneys with respect to the conduct of criminal prosecutions (*United States Government Organization Manual* [Washington, 1961], p. 217).

[6] His discretion is not subject to the control of the federal district court (*United States* v. *Segelman*, 86 F. Supp. 114 [D.C. Pa. 1949]).

[7] See Williams, "Through the Looking Glass: The Office of the United States Attorney," 3 *Prac. Law.* 49 (1957). Occasionally, the Attorney General issues directives to serve as a policy guide for the United States attorneys. As mentioned at a latter point in this chapter, Attorney General Rogers did issue a directive concerning one area of double jeopardy.

rare instances, to the prosecuting attorneys in our 88 counties, and to municipal officials. They are, of course, elected by the people in their respective areas, and are not subject to the jurisdiction of our Office. They may be required to file reports with us, and they may turn to us for opinions on matters involving interpretation of statutes. In addition the Governor and the legislature may call upon the Office from time to time to exercise investigative and law enforcement functions. This does not, however, change the basic function of the office, which is the practice of the civil side of the law.[8]

From time to time a local prosecutor inquires of the state attorney general as to the meaning of a criminal statute or as to the significance of the double jeopardy clause. In such instances it is customary for the attorney general to refer to case precedents informing his interpretation. On occasion, though, the attorney general will indicate his personal view of the proper course of action.[9] Many observers have reached the conclusion, however, that uniform statewide criminal prosecution policies are frequently lacking.[10]

In the United States, the constitutional provisions and statutes which describe the powers and duties of the prosecuting attorney of the various states do not depict the office as it actually functions, "for the habits and routine of administration often—perhaps usually —make the practical picture far different from the legal outline upon which it is built." [11] Nonetheless, some understanding of the role of the prosecutor may be obtained through a glance at the relevant legal provisions.

Commonly, the prosecuting attorney must be a member of the bar, but beyond this no qualifications are prescribed. The office is

[8] Saxbe, "Functions of the Office of Attorney General of Ohio," 6 *Clev.-Mar. L. Rev.* 323, 335 (1957).

[9] See *Opin. of the Attny. Gen. of Ohio,* III (1927), 1990, for a rare example of advice extended by the attorney general concerning a double jeopardy situation.

[10] A keen analysis is presented by Ploscowe, "The Significance of Recent Investigations for the Criminal Law and Administration of Criminal Justice," 100 *U. Pa. L. Rev.* 805 (1952).

[11] Baker and De Long, "The Prosecuting Attorney: Powers and Duties in Criminal Prosecution," 24 *J. Crim. L.* 1025 (1934).

almost always elective.[12] The attorney general's authority to conduct criminal prosecutions does vary among the states, sometimes being based upon the common law, occasionally on statute, more rarely upon a constitutional provision.[13]

Control of the Prosecutor

One of the powers and duties of the local prosecutor is to prosecute all violations of the law within his jurisdiction, even when the laws are looked upon with disfavor by local citizens.[14] The local prosecutor is under the general supervision of the state attorney general,[15] but he is not carefully supervised by the attorney general. The prosecutor is left to his own conscience or to political considerations in the choice of alternative actions. The desire to make a record may control his choices to the neglect of legitimate interests secured by law.[16] The prosecutor may issue statements to display his

[12] There are no locally elected prosecuting attorneys in Delaware or Rhode Island. All prosecuting officers are appointed by the attorney general in those states.

[13] At common law, according to Blackstone, the attorney general prossessed the authority to prosecute upon the complaint of a citizen for "gross and notorious misdemeanors, riots, batteries, libels, and other immoralities of an atrocious kind" (Blackstone, *Commentaries on the Laws of England* [Worcester, Mass., 1790], Vol. IV, Secs. 308–10).

[14] It is debatable whether the prosecutor may refuse to enforce a law which does not have the support of public sentiment, but the usual rule is that he may not do so, at the risk of breaching his oath of office (*State* ex. rel. *Johnston* v. *Foster,* 32 Kan. 14, 3 P. 534 [1883]; affirmed, 112 U.S. 201 [1884]). For double jeopardy, the problem is created in the reverse situation where the prosecutor is being overly zealous.

[15] See Arizona, Revised Statutes, Sec. 41–193 (4); Alabama, Code, Title 55, Sec. 236 (West, 1954); Iowa Code Annotated, Sec. 13.2 (7) (1949); Michigan Statutes Annotated, Sec. 3.183 (1952); South Dakota, Code, Sec. 55.1501 (1939)—each are examples of different administrative patterns. There are twenty-two other state provisions, but none really attempt to centralize or to control the prosecutor's discretion.

[16] See Pound, *Criminal Justice in America* (New York, 1930), p. 187. It must be remembered that the prosecutor is usually an elected official and that his office is often a stepping stone to more exalted political positions. Accordingly, questions of political expediency may intrude upon the diligence with which he carries out his functions.

record of "convictions." Yet more than 90 per cent of these "convictions" are really guilty pleas which are made on so-called "bargain days" in the expectation of a lighter punishment.[17]

The most frequent reason why the attorney general is reluctant to insist upon prosecution is that he is unaware of conditions in the local prosecutor's office. If the attorney general is to be effective as the supervisor of the prosecutor, if he is to exercise his power to suppress, he must know something about the particular activities and functions of the prosecutor. But present reporting systems, where they do exist, are inadequate for the purpose of control because they probably come too late to enable the attorney general to halt inadequate prosecution or to intervene before a case is terminated.[18] To remedy many of the objections to the loosely controlled prosecution process, a useful article suggests the enactment of a model act which would "restore accountability to a single coordinating official and some measure of administrative responsibility for acts of discretion." [19] Lacking such an act, the current state of criminal procedure permits no central control of either investigation or prosecution.[20] Currently there is a trend toward greater centralization of the machinery of law enforcement and prosecution and even toward the abolishing of the elective office of the prosecutor. Some of these new approaches would authorize the attorney general to appoint the

[17] *Ibid.*, p. 184. In debating the abuses resulting from "bargaining" for lesser charges, the Bronx district attorney once claimed that there were no such abuses or, if there were, all that would be necessary was for "the judge and the district attorney to do their duty," since "if they are not conscientious men, that is something that the public must observe and no rule of law will change" (Foley, to the Roundtable on Prosecution and the Courts, in Marcus, *Proceedings of the Governor's Conference on Crime, the Criminal and Society* [Albany, 1935], p. 64). This observation carries a ring of resignation to the abuses. After all, not all prosecutors are guided by the highest motives.

[18] Sunderland, "Circumventing the Corrupt Prosecutor," 48 *J. Crim. L.C. & P.S.* 537 (1958).

[19] See Nedrud, "The Career Prosecutor, Part III," 51 *J. Crim. L.C. & P.S.* 649 (1961).

[20] Perhaps annual reporting could be supplemented by entirely appointive career prosecutors who could be shuffled about to prevent local alliances.

local prosecutors.[21] Such a proposal does not solve the problem of making law enforcement more mandatory than discretionary or of preventing local alliances or local sentiments from obstructing the enforcement of state laws.

The courts are understandably reluctant to issue a writ of mandamus to compel the prosecutor to perform his duties. In any event, the writ would be difficult to enforce.[22] The only situation in which the elective prosecutor need fear ouster is for criminal activity of his own, and even where such conduct exists, ouster proceedings are very rare.[23] Some states require a preliminary hearing as a check upon the abuse of the prosecutor's powers, a provision which does afford some protection,[24] but the accused himself has no civil recourse against the prosecutor. The prosecutor is generally immune from civil suit for malicious prosecution.[25] Since the prosecutor is not subject to control by state officials or by private citizens, one wonders that such a powerful individual does not more frequently abuse his office. But to trust in the ultimate good faith of the prosecutor is a danger to civil liberties, since the prosecutor's bias is rarely favorable to individual rights. One trenchant comment on the status of the prosecutor is that "if he is merely lazy or utterly incompetent, his position is simply impregnable." [26]

The temptation of the prosecutor to exploit his fullest powers to bring criminal accusations would seem to be especially great in Kentucky, Louisiana, Arkansas, and Florida, because these states pay part of the salaries of some prosecutors on the basis of fines levied as a result of convictions. Under such a provision, a Louisiana district attorney received an estimated $18,622.50 in fees in 1954.[27] Conflict

[21] See Warren, "A State Department of Justice," 21 A.B.A.J. 495 (1935).

[22] See, for example, Board of Supervisors v. Simpson, 107 Cal. 2d 402, 227 P.2d 14 (1951).

[23] See 65 Yale L.J. 212 (1955), n.

[24] See "Prosecutor's Discretion," 103 U. Pa. L. Rev. 1057, 1064 (1955), n.

[25] Anderson v. Bishop, 304 Mass. 396, 23 N.E.2d 1103 (1939).

[26] Binkley, "The Prosecuting Attorney in Ohio—an Obsolete Office," 18 Nat'l. Mun. Rev. 572 (1929).

[27] Nedrud, "The Career Prosecutor, Part I," 51 J. Crim. L.C. & P.S. 348–49 (1960).

of interest on the part of the prosecutor is common, too, since only a few states have statutes prohibiting the prosecutor from conducting a private practice.[28]

The prosecutor's role is peculiarly important for double jeopardy law because of the increasing discretion granted the prosecutor and the increase in the number of crimes for which an accused may be charged. It has been estimated that "the number of crimes for which one may be prosecuted has at least doubled since the turn of the century." [29] Whether one accepts this particular estimate or not, the lawbooks have begun to bulge with potentiality for prosecution presented by the rapidly multiplying number of offense categories: the prosecutor "stands a fair chance of finding at least a technical violation of some act on the part of almost anyone." [30] On the other hand, the crime rate in the United States has risen alarmingly during the same period, so that it might be argued that the prosecutor is not sufficiently zealous, that society has little need of hamstringing him at a time when it is under stress from the criminal element within the society, and that double jeopardy itself should be curbed for the greater interest of society.

The policy of double jeopardy has been established by the courts, with minimal cooperation from the legislatures. As a result of many judicial interpretations of the clause, one observer concludes that:

A prosecutor, by carving up what is essentially one criminal transaction into a great number of offenses, may prosecute a person until the statute of limitations has run its course. This is true even though each trial may result in an acquittal and the only reason for the cumulative prosecutions is the prosecutor's subjective evaluation of the guilt of the individual. This possibility leaves the door open to vexatious litigation with its consequential nervous strain upon the mind and body of the individual as well as the inevitable drain upon his finances.[31]

[28] Arizona, Statutes Annotated, Sec. 12–128 (1956), which applies in countries over 100,000 population, is typical of provisions found in seven other states.

[29] Laws, "Criminal Courts and Adult Probation," 3 *N.P.P.A.J.* 354 (1957).

[30] Jackson, *op. cit.*, p. 5.

[31] Knowlton, "Criminal Law and Procedure," 11 *Rutg. L. Rev.* 94 (1957).

Although this judgment may be colored by the author's experience in defending the *Hoag* case, it presents a true picture of the interaction of double jeopardy formulation between the functionings of the prosecutor and the courts.

Some appellate courts have seen fit to condemn the prosecutor's zeal and the occasional abuses of the trial court's discretion. Especially criticized has been the addition of conspiracy counts to those for the substantive crime, for "as the law now stands," one jurist asserted, "we have no power to prevent the cumulation of sentences even though the substantive crime is the one which the conspiracy contemplated," and "this practice seems to us [the court] plainly improper." [32] Some courts have called upon the legislature to prevent this kind of abuse.[33] It would seem that, to a large extent, the punishment may be fitted to the criminal by the practices of the prosecutor.

To a considerable extent, American criminal procedures permit the prosecution to decide upon the quality of the punishment, depending upon the type of offense. Narcotics dealers are frequently punished by cumulative sentences, as are white slavers.[34] A court may refuse to regard as error the possible unfairness of imposing cumulative sentences for a false income tax return and the perjury which might have accompanied it where the "obvious real purpose" of the prosecution was to punish violators of the Volstead Act.[35] In such situations, double jeopardy may be a slim reed for the defense. As noted above, the state legislatures have occasionally stepped in to limit the discretion of the prosecution in certain areas. The United States Congress has sometimes done the same. In specific instances Congress has placed provisions in statutes to prevent federal prosecution after a state prosecution based upon similar conduct has taken place.[36] Besides this, Section 682 of the Criminal Code of Sec-

[32] *Hartson* v. *United States*, 14 F.2d 561, 562 (2d Cir. 1926).

[33] See *Westfall* v. *United States*, 20 F.2d 604, 606, 607 (6th Cir. 1927).

[34] *Roark* v. *United States*, 17 F.2d 570 (8th Cir. 1927).

[35] *Steinberg* v. *United States*, 14 F.2d 564 (2d Cir. 1926).

[36] See, for example, 18 U.S.C. Sec. 2117 concerning burglary of a vehicle carrying interstate or foreign shipments.

tion 12(b)2 of the Rules of Criminal Procedure almost forecloses the right of appeal by federal attorneys from adverse rulings. For the most part, however, the prosecutor is relatively free from restraint in instituting suit, except for double jeopardy considerations.

The prosecutor's role has changed considerably from that which he enjoyed in the eighteenth century. The legally sanctioned area of discretion has increased considerably. The uses of this discretion are now directed primarily toward individual cases and offenders, rather than toward the statutes and rules in their general operation. Most significantly, "the discretion exercised by the eighteenth-century jury has shifted very largely to the modern prosecutor." [37] The administration of criminal law has become concentrated in the courts and "even more in the prosecuting attorneys." [38] The police magistrate and the prosecuting attorney have become the most powerful officials in our system of criminal justice.[39] Whether this tendency is a necessary product of the growing scope of state activities or whether it has been a random growth, it is now a fixed point in the American legal universe.

The critical role of the prosecutor in double jeopardy matters is not often recognized by the judiciary, so obscured are the policy considerations of criminal prosecution by the dogma of constitutional development. But the opinion of the Supreme Court of New Jersey in *State* v. *Hoag* "is significant for its conscious recognition that the ultimate issue involved is that of the proper scope of the prosecutor's discretion to formulate charges." [40] In that case, after argument was made in the Appellate Division, Judge Jayne wrote, with some concern: "Assuredly our prosecutors are aware that the concept of double jeopardy is designed to prevent the government

[37] Hall, *Theft, Law and Society* (2d ed.; Indianapolis, 1952), p. 142.

[38] See *Patton* v. *United States*, 281 U.S. 276 (1930), which holds that the defendant, with the persuasion of the prosecutor, could waive the constitutional right of trial by jury.

[39] Hall, *op. cit.* p. 144.

[40] Ferguson, "Formulation of Enforcement Policy: An Anatomy of the Prosecutor's Discretion Prior to Accusation," 11 *Rutg. L. Rev.* 511 (1957), n. 20.

from unduly harassing an accused, and we are confident that they will not resort unfairly to multiple indictments and successive trials in order to accomplish indirectly that which the constitutional interdiction precludes." [41] The real issue, the vice, had been isolated. It was the injection of the prosecutor's "private notion of criminal policy into the public policy of the state." [42] This public official has more control over an individual's liberty than any other,[43] yet his discretion is broadly tolerated by the courts and the legislatures.

The easier it is made for the prosecutor to prove guilt, the more difficult it becomes for the defendant to prove his innocence. This reciprocal effect is inherent in the dual character of our criminal procedure, but the fact has gone unnoticed in the criminological reform movement, "which reflects hardly any suspicion that police and prosecutors are not omniscient." [44] The problem is of crucial importance since it concerns a challenge to those values which are contained within the Bill of Rights, which is, in any event, largely a document of criminal procedure.[45] Here are contained the safeguards against oppression, but many members of the bar are ignorant of, or unconcerned with, the problem of the infringement of these protections. Thus, it is not easy to resolve the double jeopardy dilemma. It is wisely observed:

The formula is simple: logic and science must be limited by policy; but the application is difficult and calls for the nicest integration of experience in actual criminal administration with the subtlest comprehension of the ethical implications of criminal procedure.[46]

[41] *State* v. *Hoag*, 21 N.J. 496, 114 A.2d 573 (1955).

[42] Ferguson, *op. cit.*, p. 515.

[43] See "Prosecutor's Discretion," p. 1057 n. As was said in *Freeland* v. *People*, 16 Ill. 380, 383 (1855): "In all such cases, the attorney for the people may and should refuse to prosecute beyond the exigencies of public policy, the objects of punishment being example and reformation."

[44] J. Hall, "Objectives of Federal Criminal Procedural Revision," 51 *Yale L.J.* 728 (1942).

[45] *Ibid.*, pp. 728–29.

[46] *Ibid.*, p. 732. A brilliant sociologist suggests the balancing interests: "On

Even when criminal statistics are taken into consideration, the problem remains, *au fond,* in the area of ethics, an area in which jurists tread gingerly.

In a few states it is provided that the plea of former jeopardy must be passed upon by the jury unless the plea is insufficient as a matter of law.[47] The right to have the issue tried by a jury may be waived, however.[48] This attempt to control the prosecutor through the jury system is occasionally codified in a statute.[49] In the last analysis, though, most courts have held that whether it is a proper practice to harass and annoy the accused by successive prosecutions growing out of the same transaction is a matter which addresses itself to the sound discretion of the prosecuting attorney, who will be governed by the circumstances. It is doubtful that jury consideration of the nature of the defense and its merits is much of a protection to the defendant, since it occurs so late in the criminal process. The protection would be more helpful at a much earlier stage, particularly during the grand jury investigation.

Under current practice, the grand jury is only a theoretical check upon unjustified prosecutions. In many instances the grand jury merely adopts the suggestions of the prosecutor and permits him to make the real determination of who will be formally accused. Even

---

the one hand we must strive to maintain the social interest in the individual's freedom as guaranteed in our constitutions and as the mass of the population and the offender himself conceive that freedom; on the other we must try to absorb into our procedure that principle of individualized diagnosis and treatment that is the essence of all social case work and that is apparently inconsistent with what the prisoner himself and the public at large regard as 'justice' " (Glueck, *Crime and Correction: Selected Papers* [Cambridge, 1952], p. 57).

[47] See *Hourigan* v. *State,* 38 Okla. Crim. 11, 258 P. 1057 (1927).

[48] *Thomas* v. *State,* 76 Ga. App. 637, 67 S.E. 894 (1910), and *Taylor* v. *State,* 4 Tex. Crim. 29 (1898); *contra: State* v. *Phillips,* 27 Ariz. 349, 223 P. 586 (1925).

[49] Ohio Criminal Code of 1930, Secs. 13440–45, permits the prosecuting attorney to place the issue before the jury by denying the validity of the defendant's plea of double jeopardy.

if a grand jury should refuse to indict, many jurisdictions permit a resubmission of the charge to a subsequent grand jury.[50] Many other jurisdictions permit the resubmission of an ignored charge,[51] if the proper order of the criminal court is obtained. Despite these facts, there are writers who have concluded that "in criminal proceedings in the United States the law shows a distinct partiality toward the accused." [52] If this is true at the point when trial has already begun, it may not be true of the earlier stages in the criminal proceeding.

It can happen that in a situation of political importance a skillful prosecutor may continue a long series of harassing trials. An example of such a case is the prosecution of William Remington for perjury in denying membership in the Communist Party. Similar examples of prosecution persistence may be found in the cases involving Harry Bridges and R. Stanley Dollar.[53] Many state courts permit

---

[50] United States v. Thomas, 251 U.S. 407 (1920), and see 69 U. Pa. L. Rev. 80 (1920); contra: State v. Green, 111 Mo. 585, 20 S.W. 304 (1892). "The prosecuting attorney has very great powers, both de facto and de jure. It has already been pointed out that in the list of the de facto powers must be included a great share in deciding whom the grand jury will indict. Where informations may be filed, he even has de jure the power to launch criminal proceedings" (F. Puttkammer, Administration of Criminal Law [Chicago, 1953], pp. 190–91). In the late 1920's and early 1930's there came to be increasing feeling, manifested most clearly in the report of the Wickersham Commission, that the grand jury was an inefficient "rubber stamp" for the prosecutor, who actually conceived its investigations, directed its secret proceedings, and drafted its indictment. The grand jury was considered to be virtually useless as a check upon the prosecutor (National Commission on Law Observance and Enforcement, Report on Prosecution (Chicago, 1931), pp. 34–37, 124. See also United States v. Costello, 350 U.S. 359 (1956), which reflects the same attitude toward the grand jury.

[51] Washington, Revised Code, Sec. 10.28.180 (1951), and eleven other states.

[52] Hobbs, "Prosecutor's Bias, an Occupational Disease," 2 Ala. L. Rev. 51 (1949).

[53] "Trial by Persistence," 4 Stan. L. Rev. 537 (1952), n.: "The prosecution of William Walter Remington is well on the way to becoming another marathon of sovereign persistence. It may rank with the long war of the United States against R. Stanley Dollar or the controversial proceedings against Harry Bridges. The causes of such persistencies entice political speculation."

the prosecution to prove any offense of which the indictment may be said to give notice, even if the indictment indicates on its face that it is dealing with another, similar offense, as in the trial of Al Capone.[54] One wonders whether these defendants have been much consoled by the existence of the double jeopardy clause.

The prosecutor's decisions have usually been shielded from judicial inquiry by the magical invocation of the formula "within the prosecutor's discretion,"[55] which seems to imply almost carte blanche so far as the initiation of proceedings is concerned. In New Jersey, the statutory provision that "each prosecutor . . . shall use all reasonable and lawful diligence for the detection, arrest, indictment and conviction of offenders against the laws"[56] was not judicially tested until fifty-four years after its enactment.[57] The prosecutor's discretion in formulating charges gives rise to at least three problem consequences: repeated or successive trials (double jeopardy), the cumulation of sentences (which is not usually treated as double jeopardy by the courts), and compromises of criminal liability by the exchange of a guilty plea for an easier disposition of other counts.[58]

The history of the rise of the prosecutor's office is directly related to the English struggle for the recognition of civil liberties. It is out of this historical fabric that today's anomalies in criminal justice have been torn. The fact that the prosecutor has been granted such sweeping powers in the United States has its causation in matters unique to the American situation.

Procedural Powers of the Prosecutor

In England, the courts had battled with the Crown in the name of the "immemorial rights of Englishmen," which placed the common law in the position of intercessor between the state and the individ-

---

[54] See *Capone* v. *United States*, 51 F.2d 604, 616 (7th Cir. 1931).

[55] See *Giuseppe* v. *Walling*, 144 F.2d 608, 620 (2d Cir. 1944); *Brack* v. *Wells*, 184 Md. 86, 40 A.2d 319 (1944).

[56] New Jersey, Stat. Ann. 2A, 158–55 (1952).

[57] *State* v. *Winne*, 12 N.J. 152, 96 A.2d 63 (1953).

[58] See Ferguson, *op. cit.*, p. 524.

ual. This conceptualization of law has been greatly influential in the United States, where colonials at the time of the Revolution were concerned with putting checks on royal power.[59]

But conditions in the United States were quite different, and the geography of the new nation created unusual problems. The federal system and the breadth of the country were instrumental in preventing the growth of a coordinated, unified attack on the problem of criminal procedures. Extreme decentralization resulted in a lack of organization and the hypertrophy of procedure.[60] Today, lack of cooperation between states may be added to a lack of cooperation between the agencies of criminal investigation to explain the weaknesses of the procedural system.

In the conduct of prosecutions, the United States departed radically from the English system. In the early, formative years, the states provided an independent public prosecutor for each local circuit of county, using as the model the federal district attorney of the Judiciary Act of 1789. The federal office was based upon a combination of the French *procureur du roi* of the old regime and the English attorney general.[61]

Once the indictment is drawn up by the prosecutor, his powers are still considerable, particularly under modern criminal procedure permitted by court rules. The indictment formerly had to be drawn with precision and could neither be amended nor would any variance be permitted.[62] This safeguard to the defendant is now gone, for "the pleadings have lost their rigidity, and their specificity with it." [63] The former common law rigidity permitted the defendant to avail himself of his prior conviction or acquittal in a subsequent prosecution, but now much of the protection afforded by these rules has been lost in the general trend toward simpler pleading. The Federal Rules now allows the prosecutor great latitude.[64]

---

[59] See Pound, *op. cit.*, p. 105. [60] *Ibid.*, p. 175. [61] *Ibid.*, p. 150.

[62] *Ex parte Bain*, 121 U.S. 1 (1887).

[63] Goldstein, "The State and the Accused: Balance of Advantage in Criminal Procedure," 69 *Yale L.J.* 1173 (1960).

[64] See especially, Federal Rules of Criminal Procedure, 7(c).

The effect of this liberalization of criminal pleading rules is to weaken the double jeopardy defense which might otherwise be available to the defendant. The permissiveness of the court with respect to the use of variances in pleading makes it difficult, since the charge is fluid, to determine just what offense has actually be litigated.[65] The effect of pleading rule changes is, then, to upset the balance of the advantage between the prosecutor and the accused—in this case, to weaken a constitutional plea. It may be concluded:

However much he can be said to benefit from the widely publicized decisions in certain areas of constitutional law, the hypothetical "Accused" can find little to please him in current developments in the criminal trial process. These developments reflect entirely too little concern about the inherent inequality of litigating position between the expanding state and even the most resourceful individual, much less the vast majority of resourceless ones. And even more fundamentally, they reflect the subtle erosion of the accusatorial system, relieving police and prosecutor in many instances of the pressures necessary to maintain their actions at the optimum level of responsibility.[66]

There has been a tendency to water down double jeopardy, to berate its importance, or to question whether it may not be little more than an antique, but to take such a position is to lose sight of the tendency to arm the prosecutor with more and more power, which double jeopardy is intended to limit. The meaning and the content of double jeopardy may shift from place to place and from time to time, but the doctrine still contains a right of fundamental importance, particularly in a system of criminal procedure such as ours.

Although the drafting of the indictment is extremely important,[67] it is especially significant when conspiracy charges are added to other substantive counts. Federal attorneys have been most adept in

[65] *Short* v. *United States,* 91 F.2d 614, 622 (4th Cir. 1937), shows this.

[66] Goldstein, *op. cit.,* p. 1199.

[67] Slovenko, "The Law on Double Jeopardy," 30 *Tul. L. Rev.* 428, 429 (1955), says, "The [double jeopardy] provision protects against multiple punishments of a convicted person for the same offense by successive prosecutions or by the recently developed multiple count indictment."

the use of conspiracy charges to secure more ease in utilizing evidence, to avoid the statute of limitations, to obtain more and easier double convictions, and to bolster their personal reputation for diligence. This attitude led District Judge Holt to say, more than fifty years ago:

> There seems to be an increasing tendency in recent years for public prosecutors to indict for conspiracies when crimes have been committed. A conspiracy to commit a crime may be a sufficiently serious offense to be properly punished; but when a crime has actually been committed by two or more persons, there is usually no proper reason why they should be indicted for the agreement to commit the crime instead of for the crime itself. . . . Prosecutors seem to think that by this practice all statutes of limitations and many of the rules of evidence established for the protection of persons charged with crime can be disregarded.[68]

The use of conspiracy indictments to convert a joint misdemeanor into a felony has resulted in abuses of the conspiracy statue.[69] As a matter of double jeopardy law, acquittal or conspiracy does not bar a subsequent conviction of substantive crimes based on the same events charged.[70] In the converse situation, as well, double jeopardy is no bar.[71] Thus, prosecutors are provided with an easy device for a double prosecution at two separate trials. In addition, as a matter of evidence law, a conspiracy to commit an act is much easier to prove than the actual commission of that act.[72]

One more important power of the prosecutor is worthy of stress—that is, the power to dismiss or to nol-pros a suit before it reaches its conclusion. Questions of the attachment of jeopardy arise as a result of the use of this broad power of the prosecutor. It is a general rule that once jeopardy has attached, the entry of nolle prosequi without the consent of the defendant bars further prosecution on the same

[68] *United States* v. *Kissel,* 173 F. 823, 828 (C.C.N.Y. 1909).

[69] See report of the 1925 Conference of Circuit Judges, *Reports of the Attorney General* (Washington, 1925), pp. 5–6.

[70] *Woodbury Corp.* v. *Pick,* 41 F.2d 148 (1st Cir. 1930).

[71] *Dunn* v. *United States,* 284 U.S. 390 (1931).

[72] See *United States* v. *Baker,* 61 F.2d 469 (2d Cir. 1932); *United States* v. *Speed,* 78 F. Supp. 366 (D.C.D.C., 1948).

charge.[73] But the defendant will usually agree to nolle prosequi, since it frequently is a part of a negotiated agreement between the prosecutor and the defendant, an agreement in which the accused is not on very strong bargaining terms.

At common law, the attorney general could dismiss a prosecution on his own official responsibility,[74] and in a few states the prosecutor still has the sole power to do so.[75] Other states place the supposed authority within the discretion of the court.[76] With respect to the power to dismiss a case, there are no statutory limitations upon the prosecutor's choice.[77] The reasons for the dismissal may vary, but failure of witnesses to appear is a common justification. Of course, the defendant's consent is not needed. Another common occurrence is that the complaining witness may withdraw his complaint. Of indictments nol-prossed by the Philadelphia district attorney's office from May 1, 1953, to January 31, 1954, 31.49 per cent were nol-prossed because the prosecution was withdrawn and 26.07 per cent because of lack of prosecution.[78]

[73] *Mount* v. *State*, 14 Ohio 295 (1846); *State* v. *Richardson*, 45 S.C. 106, 25 S.E. 220 (1896); Georgia, Code Annotated, Sec. 27-1801 (1948). But "when a *nolle prosequi* is entered before a trial, there may be another prosecution on the basis of a new indictment" (*People* ex rel. *Hoyne*, 284 Ill. 315, 120 N.E. 244 [1948]).

[74] See 33 *Corn L.Q.* 407 (1948), n.

[75] *People* v. *Newcomer*, 284 Ill. 315, 120 N.E. 244 (1918); *Denham* v. *Robinson*, 72 W. Va. 243, 77 S.E. 970 (1913); Louisiana, Revised Statutes Annotated, Sec. 15:329 (1951).

[76] California, Penal Code, Sec. 1385 (Supp., 1953); Idaho Code Annotated, Sec. 19-3504 (1948); Utah Code Annotated, Sec. 77-51-4 (1953), and eleven other states.

[77] Statutes do not prescribe the conditions and the situations in which the device may be used. Even those states in which the prosecutor must secure the permission of the court do not, in practice, limit the prosecutor's decision to terminate the case, since his justifications will usually suffice.

[78] "Prosecutor's Discretion," p. 1068 n. Table I contains this material. Data of this type is very scarce and is not usually made publicly available. In 1950, of the 7,897 cases beginning as felonies in the felony branch of the municipal court of Chicago, 2,494 were nol-prossed, 874 were discharged, 443 were dismissed for want of prosecution, 1,226 were sent to the grand jury, and 2,860 were reduced at preliminary hearing from a felony to a misdemeanor (Dash, "Cracks in the Foundation of Criminal Justice," 46 *Ill. L. Rev.* 385, 392 [1951], n. 16).

There can be no doubt that some sort of "bargain system" of justice exists which influences the actions of the prosecutor as enforcer of public policy. Looked at hopefully, the system aids in clearing the court calendar of work which would otherwise clog the court's business. Cooperation between successful criminal lawyers and the prosecution is a common pattern and helps condition the defendant's procedural rights. In one survey, it was found that 57 per cent of criminal lawyers questioned believed that personal connections with the district attorney were helpful. Besides this, half admitted friendly contacts with police and district attorneys.[79] Thus, cliques are formed which help to maintain the formal basis but which are separate from it. The bargain system can be explained, and perhaps justified:

The development, in recent times, of tremendous urban communities, the increase in criminal activity and the consequent increase in the congestion of the criminal court calendars throughout the country, made it apparent that in many cases it was sensible to permit a defendant to plead guilty to an offense lesser than that with which he was charged.[80]

But such an attempt ignores the issue of whether the courts or the prosecutor is the proper agency to discover and to determine guilt. The powers of the prosecutor are so great that he is beginning to act as a judge.[81]

Of the nineteenth century, the great English legal historian Holdsworth concluded that the prosecution had "all the advantages it could wish for." [82] Since then the office, always more powerful in

[79] Wood, "Informal Relations in the Practice of Criminal Law," 62 *Am. J. Soc.* 54 (1956).

[80] Marcus, in *Proceedings of the Governor's Conference*, (Albany, 1935), p. 602.

[81] In the Soviet Union, the dual system of investigation gives the procuracy (the prosecution) joint responsibility with the police in the preparation of criminal trials. The procuracy, which underwent mild reforms in 1955, has the treble duty of conducting criminal prosecution, overseeing criminal and civil proceedings through the right of protest to higher tribunals, and, to an extent, supervising the legality of minor executive action. See Lipson, "The New Face of 'Socialist Legality,'" 7 *Problems of Communism* 25 (1959).

[82] Holdsworth, *A History of English Law* (London, 1903), IX, 229.

the United States than in England, seems to have increased in its powers. For double jeopardy, the result of this increase is clear: either the prosecution must be curbed by the use of the clause (or some procedural alternative) or double jeopardy will be further weakened. The existence of conflicting and confused court interpretations of double jeopardy may, of course, continue into the indefinite future; but even this choice is one which continues the slow erosion of the meaning of double jeopardy. A fundamental reordering of the position of the prosecutor's office in the administration of criminal justice might eliminate some of the need for the protection of the defendant, but lacking this, double jeopardy continues to be necessary.

In the last analysis, it must be admitted:

The evasion and nullification of the Fifth Amendment is not the result of generations of community habit, as violations of the Fourteenth may by some be said to be, but is the self-serving production of a small class of office-holders which could be immediately and effectively terminated by a firm order, meant to be obeyed, from their common chief, the Attorney-General of the United States, or from his single superior in the governmental world.[83]

It is doubtful, however, that a simple order from the Attorney General would really solve the problem, or, indeed, whether it is the proper constitutional way to increase the significance of double jeopardy.

Administrative Restraints upon the Prosecutor

Some observers hold out the hope that the prosecutor may restrain or control himself in the use of his potential powers, or that the higher officials in criminal administration may apply a curb to the prosecutor's power.[84] For example, it has been suggested that

---

[83] Ireland, "Double Jeopardy and Conspiracy in the Federal Courts," 40 *J. Crim. L.C. & P.S.* 447, 457 (1949).

[84] Paul Williams, the United States attorney for the Southern District of New York, finds the prosecutor already quite limited: "From the moment that a defendant is apprehended until the rendering of the verdict, the prosecutor

articulation by the Justice Department of a complete set of standards for the exercise of the discretion to withhold federal prosecution would be helpful. One of the first examples of this approach was in the administration and enforcement of the Mann Act. Federal district attorneys were told to ask themselves, on order of the Attorney General: "What reasons exist, if any, for thinking the ends of justice will be better served by a prosecution under federal law than under the law of the state having jurisdiction." [85] Obviously, the intent of this suggestion is to reduce the likelihood of multiple prosecution and to limit the possibility of double jeopardy situations.

This policy to avoid double jeopardy was pursued by the Department of the Army in 1958. In that year the Department issued a policy statement to all commands asserting that it is the policy of the Department that an individual who has been tried in a state court, though subject to military law, should not be tried again by courts-martial under the Uniform Code of Military Justice for the same act or acts. An exception to the policy requires the personal determination of a commander exercising general court-martial jurisdiction. The Navy and the Air Force now have similar policies.[86]

The import of these policy declarations is to forswear the powers available to the prosecution, despite court permission in the form of double jeopardy decisions sanctioning the exercise of state power or the power of the prosecutor. In the most controversial area, that of concurrent state and federal jurisdiction over criminal matters, the most interesting developments have taken place. As indicated in Chapter 3, many states have voluntarily relinquished their power to prosecute after a federal conviction, although this practice is permit-

---

is limited by the rules of procedure which exist to safeguard the freedom of the defendant and insure him a fair and speedy trial" ("The Prosecutor and Civil Rights, 13 Record of N.Y.C.B.A. 129 [1958]). The prosecutor frequently feels hampered by procedural limitations.

[85] As noted in Schwartz, "Federal Criminal Jurisdiction and Prosecutor's Discretion," 13 Law & Contemp. Prob. 73 (1948).

[86] American Bar Association, Section on Criminal Law, Proceedings, ed. Hickman (Chicago, 1959), p. 52.

ted by the Supreme Court. On the federal level the restraint has occasionally resulted from the prosecution's own order, usually by the chief of a department.

Some doubt was cast upon the propriety of federal prosecution following that of the state in *Pennsylvania* v. *Nelson*,[87] but the *Bartkus* case made clear that the practice was constitutionally permissible. Many people were upset by this decision, including Justice Brennan. In his dissent, Brennan said that the extent of participation by the federal authorities constituted a second federal prosecution of Bartkus and that what happened "was simply that the federal effort which failed in the federal courthouse was renewed a second time in the state courthouse across the street."[88]

Generally, duplicating prosecutions do not take place, although they are technically possible, and the choice between federal and state action is made by the prosecuting attorney.[89] On April 6, 1959, United States Attorney General William Rogers issued a directive to federal attorneys which was intended to have the effect of restricting the federal government's use of its constitutional power to try a defendant already tried by a state court (permitted under *United States* v. *Lanza*). In this directive, the Attorney General noted the decision in the *Bartkus* case, rendered a week previously by the Supreme Court, and indicated that it was the policy of the Department of Justice not to try a defendant for the same act in a federal court

[87] Warren wrote: "We are not unmindful of the risk of compounding punishments which would be created by finding concurrent state power. In our view of the case, we do not reach the question whether double or multiple punishment for the same act directed against the United States has constitutional sanction" (350 U.S. 509, 510 [1955]).

[88] 359 U.S. 121, 169 (1959).

[89] Schwartz, *op. cit.*, p. 71. The author goes on to point out that neither has a choice involving the federal system since each proceeds in his own tribunal for an offense committed against his own sovereign. He proposed as an alternative to the *Bartkus* solution that, for certain purposes, the federal and state prosecutors be regarded as "auxiliary" one to the other, since there is a common American legal community for the purpose of deterring certain types of antisocial conduct, and the community may act either through its state organizations or, when that is not feasible, through the federal (p. 73).

after he had been tried in a state court unless the reasons were compelling. The Attorney General stated that it was the duty of the Justice Department to observe not only the ruling of the court "but the spirit of the rulings as well," [90] even though the rulings did permit the very thing which Rogers was seeking to minimize. He declined to set forth any detailed rules to deal with overlapping federal and state criminal jurisdiction, but required that before the institution of a federal case following state prosecution, the United States district attorney had to submit a recommendation to the appropriate assistant attorney general in the Justice Department, who would have the duty of bringing it to the attention of the Attorney General.[91]

The policy of the Attorney General was given its first real test on December 3, 1959, when the Solicitor General, J. Lee Rankin, asked the Supreme Court to vacate a judgment in the case of George B. Petite, a Baltimore lawyer who had already been convicted before both federal and state tribunals. This was an extremely unusual procedure because, though the Solicitor General may occasionally "confess error," the case went beyond such a confession of error since the Government sought to rectify a violation of its own policy.[92]

The defendant had been convicted, in the United States District Court for the Eastern District of Pennsylvania, of conspiring to make false statements to an agency of the United States at deportation hearings. Subsequently, he was indicted in the District Court of Maryland for suborning the perjury of two witnesses at the hearings. Among the overt acts relied upon in the first indictment was the testimony of the same two witnesses. The defendant moved to dismiss the Maryland indictment on the ground of double jeopardy, but his motion was denied by the United States District Court for the District of Maryland.[93] The resulting conviction was affirmed by the Court of Appeals for the Fourth Circuit.[94] There is one unusual fea-

[90] Department of Justice Press Release, April 6, 1959.

[91] Presumably, this procedure is mandatory, but there is no evidence of any fixed practice.

[92] See Department of Justice Press Release, Dec. 3, 1959.

[93] *Petite* v. *United States,* 147 F. Supp. 791 (1959).

[94] *Petite* v. *United States* 262 F.2d 788 (D.C. Cir. 1959).

ture of this situation: these facts are not those of the *Lanza* or *Bart-kus* cases, or indeed of the Attorney General's announced policy. Both cases involved in the *Petite* case had been tried in the federal courts.

After certiorari had been granted by the Supreme Court of the United States, the Government filed its motion in the Supreme Court for an order vacating the judgment below and remanding the case to the District Court with instructions to dismiss the indictment on the ground that "it is the general policy of the Federal government that several offenses arising out of a single transaction should be alleged and tried together and should not be made the basis of multiple prosecutions, a policy dictated by considerations both of fairness to defendants and of efficient and orderly law enforcement." [95] The Solicitor General indicated, on behalf of the Government, that the policy was closely related to that against duplicating federal-state prosecutions, which had been declared earlier by the Attorney General. The Supreme Court complied with the Government's request and remanded the case to the Court of Appeals with orders to vacate its judgment and dismiss the case. [96]

Some members of the Court who had not agreed with the *Bartkus* case, also failed to agree with the import of this decision, which granted considerable discretionary powers to the prosecution in the double jeopardy area. In a separate opinion, Justice Brennan praised the Government for doing the just and proper thing in requesting the Court to wipe the slate clean of the second federal conviction for the same criminal conduct. But Brennan took the occasion to upbraid the Court itself:

With all deference, I do not see how our duty can be fully performed in this case if our action stops with simply giving effect to a "policy" of the Government—a policy whose only written expression does not even cover the case at bar. . . . The Government has reserved the right to apply or not apply its "policy" in its discretion. [97]

[95] *Petite* v. *United States*, 361 U.S. 529 (1960).   [96] *Ibid.*, p. 530.
[97] *Ibid.*, p. 531.

The objection is a fundamental one. It is a doubtful practice to permit a constitutional right to be shaped by the very officers of the state whom it is intended to control. Yet, because of the decisions of the courts, the prosecution is given a broad discretion and now may be in a position to set the policy of double jeopardy which the courts and the legislatures seem unwilling or unable to do.[98]

The prosecutor is not the sole law enforcement official with whom the defendant has contact. The police agencies work closely with the prosecutor, even more in the federal criminal system than in the states.[99] The prosecutor, who sometimes is seeking to compile a record, "will be seen leading in many man hunts," [100] bringing the full weight of the state to bear upon a criminal suspect. When he goes into the courtroom, the prosecutor is armed with all the information the state can provide him. He is opposed, most often, by an ill-paid criminal lawyer. If, under these circumstances, the prosecution is to be permitted to apply its own notion of double jeopardy policy, criminal justice begins to lose its significance. Of course, at times and in some areas the prosecution is ill-prepared or even incompetent, but it would seem more proper to improve the quality of the prosecution rather than to diminish the defendant's rights.

[98] The central problem of double jeopardy law is that of the scope of the criminal act, or how many criminal accusations may be carved out of one offense. It is this problem with which the *Petite* case attempted to deal, although without any written rule to that effect. Yet, "if overzealously applied by the undue fragmentation of conduct into a series of minutiae, such an approach would threaten the underlying content of the Constitutional proscription," since "the practice of atomizing what is essentially a single criminal act into a series of separate crimes . . . can hardly be accepted as consistent with the spirit and intent of our system of criminal justice" (editorial, *N.J.L.J.*, April 25, 1957, p. 4, cols. 1 and 2). This practice can be remedied in many ways, but this particular writer calls for a "rule of reason" unless there is judicial clarification of the principles operative in this area. Until then a "common sense administration of the criminal laws by law enforcement officials had best be heeded." One wonders whether this is much help to those seeking the use of the double jeopardy protection.

[99] American Bar Foundation, *The Administration of Criminal Justice* (Chicago, 1959), p. 88.

[100] Pound, *op. cit.*, p. 187.

Some fundamental problems of social policy are involved in the implementation of double jeopardy, whether administered by the courts,[101] the legislatures, the prosecutor, or all three in conjunction. On the highest level of analysis, the issue is that of the direct confrontation of the individual by the organized force of the state. On the one hand, since the crime rates have been growing by leaps and bounds in the United States, perhaps the prosecution function should not be hampered if the society is to be protected. On the other hand, the history and tradition of individual liberties would seem to require that only questions of grave social danger should be held to outweigh those rights.

In response to what is felt to be an expanding crime problem, the state legislatures, as well as Congress, have increased the number of offenses described on the statute books. In 1931, 76 per cent of all the inmates of federal and state prisons had been incarcerated for the commission of acts which had not even been crimes fifteen years earlier. Since 1900, approximately 500,000 new state laws have been enacted to control criminality, leading to a situation of antiquated and absurd penal codes, often in conflict with one another.[102] The situation indicates that a drastic amendment of our penal codes may be necessary in order to avoid overlapping crime categories,[103] as will be suggested in the following chapter. By way of comparison, England has also increased the number of crimes in response to a

---

[101] See *United States* v. *Candalaria,* 131 F. Supp. 797 (S.D. Cal. 1955), in which the court reduced a sentence because the prosecutor indicated an intention to charge the defendant with another offense at a later date—unusual judicial policy-making.

[102] Barnes and Teeters, "Defects in Our Criminal Law," from *New Horizons in Criminology* (Englewood Cliffs, N.J., 1951), pp. 77–78. This problem has been referred to repeatedly, but is basic to double jeopardy.

[103] See *ibid.:* "No significant change in the philosophy of penal treatment can be consummated until our penal codes are drastically amended and a rational system of criminal procedure developed. This radical suggestion is not made by dreamers or sentimentalists. Insistence upon a regressive philosophy is outmoded." Chapter 6 will treat the matter in some detail, but it should be noted that this increase in criminal categories has created hosts of double jeopardy evasion techniques for the prosecutor.

supposed crime wave.[104] The civil law nations, on the other hand, have not responded by increasing the number of criminal categories. Legislative creation of new punishment categories has more than counterbalanced the limited use of administrative restraints.

The prosecutor's power may be exercised on a selective basis. He may use it to advance his political fortunes or to penalize minority groups. The official policies for dealing with law-breaking are not as significant as the informal factors, including the age, sex, wealth, education, political prestige, color, or nationality of the offender.[105] Controlling the prosecutor is difficult unless it is firmly decided that the theory of criminal punishment requires some devices to place him in restraint. Even if there is a crime wave,[106] and even if the legislatures should decide to multiply the number of criminal categories, the question remains whether the prosecutor is the proper official to choose punishment alternatives or whether that choice should not be proscribed in some other manner, as the double jeopardy clause, for one device, would provide.

The Basic Policy Issues

There are very few sources to which one may turn to discern the prosecutor's own image of his role and function. As though to remedy this deficiency, a diary or set of recollections has recently appeared, written by the former Bronx County, New York, district attorney. Although written for popular consumption, it is a highly literate statement of the viewpoint of the public prosecutor.[107]

[104] The number of persons found guilty of indictable offenses in England has doubled within the twenty-year period from 1938 to 1958, forging ahead of the population increase. The data may indicate a minor crime wave, and the courts' response seems to have been to increase the length of sentence while decreasing the number sent to prison (Mannheim, "Developments in Criminal Law and Criminology in Post-War Britain," 51 *J. Crim. L.C. & P.S.* 600 [1961]).

[105] See Sutherland and Cressey, *Principles of Criminology* (New York, 1955), p. 285.

[106] The existence of a crime wave is questioned by Daniel Bell in *The End of Ideology* (Glencoe, Ill., 1960), p. 137. Bell feels that crime rate statistics are unreliable and deceptive.

[107] Frank, *Diary of a D.A.* (New York, 1957).

182

Justice Martin M. Frank concedes that as Bronx County prosecutor he possessed broad discretionary powers. He asserts that the states have granted the prosecutor sweeping powers based on the theory that more precisely described duties would tend to confine his permissible activities and hamper vigorous, effective law enforcement. Consequently, "an overzealous prosecutor is as great a menace to public safety and tranquillity as is a deficient, slothful, or corrupt one." [108]

Judge Frank admits that it is the duty of the courts to protect the rights of an accused against the inordinate zeal of a district attorney, although the public prosecutor is a quasi-judicial officer himself. The district attorney frequently hopes to occupy a seat on the bench, a fact which often tempts a young practitioner to become a prosecutor. Judge Frank states that nearly every assistant district attorney on his staff "was spurred by the hope of becoming a judge, and he knew that its realization rested largely upon the reputation he made." [109] In forty years, forty men from the Bronx district attorney's office were elevated to the judiciary. Frequently, ex-prosecutors passed judgment upon the actions of the incumbents. The Bronx pattern of judicial advancement may not be typical, but it does help explain the willingness of young lawyers to serve at low pay in the prosecutor's office, and also explains the zeal they often display.

Judge Frank heartily endorses the grand jury system on the ground that "uncontrolled power in the hands of an ambitious, unscrupulous, or overzealous individual is open to abuse." [110] In his opinion, the grand jury is an adequate check upon that danger. On the other hand, Frank complains about the rigidity of inflexible statutory punishment standards which force the prosecutor to bargain for pleas of guilty to offenses less than those specified in the indictment.[111]

[108] *Ibid.*, p. 44.
[109] *Ibid.*, pp. 45, 72. The author is now a New York Supreme Court justice, having been elected to that office on the nomination of both major political parties.
[110] *Ibid.*, p. 87.   [111] *Ibid.*, p. 272.

Even a dedicated public prosecutor cannot deny the existence of his broad, discretionary powers. If he expects the court to restrain his errant fellow prosecutors, then he should recognize the need for formal constitutional protections such as that provided by the double jeopardy clause. The grand jury is rarely concerned that a defendant may have been previously tried for the same offense, nor is this fact likely to be brought to their attention. When the potential power of the district attorney is combined with the power of the police to make arrests, the need for the protection of accused persons becomes even more apparent.[112]

The essentials of the criminal law in the United States are contained in the judicially enforced Bill of Rights, which sets some limitations upon the efficiency of criminal administration in the name of justice. Efficiency cannot be the primary criterion, for if power is to be curbed, this can only be done by making the law inefficient. Every limitation upon the exercise of political power has been a recognition of the undesirability of legal efficiency, for the purpose of protecting the weak against the strong and the individual against the state.[113] If efficiency is not to be the criterion, the compilation of criminal statistics and the proliferation of criminal penalties are beside the point. On the other hand, it can be decided, as a matter of policy, to sacrifice some individual rights in the name of the efficiency of the criminal process. This should be a matter for the conscious and deliberate consideration of the official policy-makers rather than being relegated, by default, to the prosecutor, who is only the administrator of criminal policy. There has been a tendency in the United Staes to cede power to the prosecutor. This tendency

[112] Alan Barth's book effectively stresses the incipient dangers to civil liberties; see *The Price of Liberty* (New York, 1961), pp. 210–11.

[113] Seagle, *Law, the Science of Inefficiency* (New York, 1952), takes this thesis as its major contention. Mill's *On Liberty* is quite relevant in this regard, except that Mill adds that there must be a protection against the majority as well as the state. Unfortunately, it can be shown that minority groups, especially Negroes, are peculiarly subject to the practice of discrimination by prosecutors (see Sutherland and Cressey, *op. cit.*, p. 286, which is drawn from W. Turner, "Differential Punishment in a Bi-racial Community" (unpub. M.A. thesis, Indiana University).

threatens to undermine the double jeopardy protection. The general attitude of the courts has been well expressed as follows:

This court is powerless to exercise its discretion but must determine the issues solely upon the discretion of the District Attorney, regardless of whether or not it may believe such discretion proper. . . . The prosecution or the dismissal of all criminal cases rests in the honest discretion of the United States District Attorney.[114]

Sometimes it is argued that the historical basis for double jeopardy has disappeared, but this view contains the fallacy of assuming that because the accused had so few rights in the sixteenth and seventeenth centuries, he has too many rights now.[115] It should be remembered that "one of the commonest arguments against allowing prisoners to be defended by counsel always was, that rogues had too many chances of escape already." [116] All this need not imply an impending threat of curtailment of the basic guarantees of the Bill of Rights, but, instead, a decline in the significance of principles of protection like the double jeopardy clause, which are less dramatic than the self-incrimination clause or the right of counsel.

It is to be hoped that criminal policy will be based on the conclusions of the most scientific investigation of the policy alternatives, through the use of the newer techniques of criminology.[117] As yet, no thorough study of criminal administration and its control has been made available to us by criminologists. This makes it difficult to consider objectively the merits or demerits of a strengthened double jeopardy policy. Perhaps a future study of the impact of the institutions of criminal administration, particularly of the prosecutor's office, will reveal a more empirical basis for policy-making.

114 *United States* v. *Brokan et al.,* 60 Fed. Supp. 100, 103 (S.D. Ill. 1945).
115 Hall, 51 *Yale L.J.* 729.
116 L. Stephen, *A General View of the Criminal Law of England* (London, 1863), p. 175.
117 See Radzinowicz and Turner, "The Meaning and Scope of Criminal Science," in Radzinowicz and Turner (eds.), *The Modern Approach to Criminal Law* (London, 1941), pp. 22–23. However, criminology has not felt the full impact of the survey techniques of sociology.

Whatever unconscious psychological forces may be at play, a rational prosecution and punishment policy can be constructed to which double jeopardy may make a contribution. The "sense of injustice" is stressed by Edmond Cahn, the eminent jurisprudent, as underlying the common desire to restrict the abuse of public authority. Whenever officials misuse their power, or oppress the innocent and the unoffending, they provoke our sense of injustice.[118] This "sense of injustice" may underscore the necessity of restricting the arbitrary decisions of the prosecutor. Certainly, the layman when confronted with the state of double jeopardy law frequently displays some shock which the lawyer has ceased to feel. This may imply that a strengthening of double jeopardy law could meet common expectations more than a harsh policy. Occasionally, some courts have been moved merely by considerations of fair play in their interpretation of double jeopardy.[119] In a complicated society, our goals may have shifted from the protection of the innocent to the administrative goal of insuring the proper treatment of the guilty.[120] This tendency must be reconsidered, for double jeopardy is only one of a group of important liberties. It may be necessary to weigh competing social interests:

[118] Cahn, "The Consumers of Injustice," 34 *N.Y.U. L. Rev.* 1166, 1179 (1959).

[119] In Pennsylvania, the Supreme Court in one of its decisions has adduced an interesting justification for extending double jeopardy protection: "The double prosecution would also be unjust because it would force the defendant to reveal on his trial for involuntary manslaughter what his defense was, and then when he was tried for murder, the Commonwealth would know how to meet the defendant's evidence and also how to strengthen any part of its case which had proved to be weak at the first trial. Such a procedure is not in accordance with the American idea of fair play and it would be contrary to established standards of just procedure" (*Commonwealth* v. *Thatcher*, 364 Pa. 326, 69 A.2d 619, 625 [1950]). This rationale is another example of the play, or game, element in legal thinking.

[120] See 57 *Yale L.J.* 133 (1947), n. Many courts have tended to confuse penological questions with questions of double jeopardy, especially in the sentencing process (see *United States* v. *Michener*, 332 U.S. 784 [1947]). This demonstrates a concern with the more rehabilitative aspects of criminal law.

A law or procedure, which, in the general opinion, unnecessarily or arbitrarily overemphasizes the social interest in the general security to the undue interference with the social and individual interests in the life and well-being of each person, is unjust, for it unnecessarily enslaves human beings.[121]

Such a policy involves a rational calculation even though some of the factors may be irrational.

As with most policy judgments, the ultimate questions in double jeopardy policy are ethical ones. Although the choice cannot be made here, it may be suggested that some of the factors which have been mentioned should be brought to the attention of the makers of policy. The American prosecutor has broad discretionary powers which have been expanding with the passage of numerous criminal statutes. If it is felt that society is best served by this virtually unchecked power, or that it can trust in the self-restraint of the prosecutor, then double jeopardy law may not be unsatisfactory. But if it is felt that the double jeopardy protection is to be accorded some significance in its modern context of criminal procedure, then there is a desperate need for clarification and definitive choice.

[121] Glueck, *op. cit.*, p. 75.

» 6 «

Conclusions:
Criticism and Reform

There are many legal restrictions upon the federal and state prosecutors besides the double jeopardy clause. These limitations are contained in constitutions, statutes, evidentiary rules, and rules of criminal procedure. The presumption of innocence until guilt is proven is certainly very important. The grand jury, the petit jury, the privilege against self-incrimination, guarantees of speedy trial and due process are each formidable protections for accused persons. More recently, preliminary hearings and pretrial discovery techniques have been added to the array of protective techniques. Yet double jeopardy is a different kind of protection because it determines the number of times that a person may be tried, not merely the way in which he may be tried. Double jeopardy is unlike all other restraints upon the power of the prosecution in that it can prevent the initiation of suit and also determine the point at which a criminal action is ended.

The largest number of double jeopardy situations are caused by poor legislative drafting:

In any case it must be remembered that the underlying cause of the conflict is the failure of the criminal statute in question to state clearly what should be the allowable unit of prosecution. In such a situation it is up to the court to decide whether each individual act is to be punished separately or whether the entire course of conduct embracing a series of acts should be treated as one crime.[1]

[1] Einstein, "Allowable Unit of Criminal Prosecution," 16 *Intra. L. Rev.* 139 (1961).

188

Basic reforms in double jeopardy policy will require some changes in established criminal policy. If changes are not made in substantive or procedural criminal rules, the significance of double jeopardy as a constitutional protection will continue to be vague. These changes, because they will have a profound impact upon the entire criminal law, should be made by the legislatures, which are charged with the task of determining general policy. Perhaps, as with the passage of the Federal Compulsory Testimony Act, the legislature may desire to reduce the importance of the constitutional protection.[2] But whatever the final policy resolution may be, it ought to be made by the Congress and the respective state legislatures.

Double jeopardy is an established part of the legal universe of American law. Sometimes praised, sometimes attacked, frequently neglected, it has, nonetheless, begun to attract the concern of more and more writers and jurists as a constitutional principle under stress. Its seeming clarity has obscured the social problems at its center, problems which threaten to overwhelm the judges who are charged with interpreting its meaning. Perhaps the day has passed when the nation needs this kind of protection against its own law enforcement machinery. If so, that fact should be faced. But if, as seems more likely, the need is even more critical, then some more adequate devices to strengthen double jeopardy are necessary. On the lowest level, the least that can be done is to separate the tangled meanings of the clause to make a more precise policy. On the highest, a reconsideration of the impact on double jeopardy of American criminal procedure and of substantive criminal law may be necessary.

[2] Because the fifth amendment privilege against self-incrimination had been invoked with great frequency by witnesses seeking to avoid disclosing information to congressional investigating committees, Congress passed an immunity statute, described heretofore, for the purpose of coercing testimony. The protection of the fifth amendment claim can be removed by a court order. The court which issues the order need only consider the effect of the immunity statute upon the constitutional clause which it modifies (*Ullman* v. *United States,* 350 U.S. 422 [1956]).

Criticism

The criticism of double jeopardy law in the United States began almost as soon as the contours of that law were being determined. An article appearing in 1883 bemoaned the judicial corruption of double jeopardy:

If it were not a matter of such importance it would be laughable to see a court very gravely state the principle of former jeopardy, call it a great and fundamental maxim, and then proceed, with unchanged countenance, to violate the principle deciding the case before them. Nobody disputes the justice or the obligation of the rule of former jeopardy in the abstract, the difficulty is in deciding where it shall be applied.[3]

In 1906 the clause was praised as the "beacon light of modern civilization." [4] The principle is supposed to be embedded in all systems of jurisprudence [5] and to have been placed in the American constitutions to ensure a "stricter vigilance over the rights of the citizens against the state." [6] In the early years of double jeopardy law, a general optimism as to its meaning and importance seems to have prevailed, an optimism which may have dimmed with the passage of time.

By the close of the last century, some voices of disapproval could be heard. Justice Hammersly of Connecticut, writing in *State* v. *Lee,* said that double jeopardy, which could be traced to a dictum of Coke, was a rule of procedure in the seventeenth-century criminal law and could not be held to dominate the settled principles of nineteenth-century jurisprudence.[7] With this pronouncement begins the modern criticism of double jeopardy, which, for the first time in

---

[3] Batchelder, "Former Jeopardy," 17 *Am. L. Rev.* 748, 749 (1883).

[4] Payne, "The Doctrine of Previous Jeopardy," 62 *Cent. L.J.* 295 (1906).

[5] *State* v. *Lee,* 65 Conn. 265, 30 A. 1110 (1894).

[6] *State* v. *Jones,* 7 Ga. 422, 424 (1849).

[7] 65 Conn. 265, 275, 30 A. 1110, 1120 (1894). Hammersly concludes: "It is, however, immaterial to the defendant what the practice at common law may have been" (p. 277). To say that double jeopardy is a rule of procedure merely confuses the issue. Double jeopardy operates between the areas of substantive criminal law and procedure.

several centuries, has called into question the fundamental nature of the protection.

Those who adhere to a negative view of double jeopardy indicate that the doctrine arose at a time when the death penalty was imposed for at least a hundred crimes, and the criminal procedure had placed the criminal defendant at a decided disadvantage. It is pointed out that the defendant appeared without counsel, without witnesses, and without the right to be sworn in his own behalf. Although "this was our inheritance," because "the bases for the view have long since disappeared, inquiry is invited as to whether under present day trial procedure the rule is still sound." [8] Those who apply this historical criticism stress that the state constitutional double jeopardy provisions were inserted without much discussion or any fixed ideas of their technical meaning, usually in emulation of the federal constitution or those of sister states.[9]

Perhaps the most devastating criticism of double jeopardy has been made by William Comley of Yale, who has accused the judges of setting at liberty men guilty of the most atrocious crimes because of "slavish devotion to an erroneous interpretation of a quaint and curious phrase extracted from the old records of medieval lawyers." [10] With great consistency, Comley maintains that the regrettable escape of the guilty from criminal punishment has been aided by the use of the double jeopardy clause. He calls for an abandonment of the notion that there can be no swift and certain pursuit and punishment of offenders consistent with civil liberties, an attitude which reflects a fear that persists long after the cause has been removed.[11] Comley proceeds to demolish the American concept of attachment of jeopardy, which, he claims, is guided by concepts derived from

[8] Slovenko, "The Law on Double Jeopardy," 30 *Tul. L. Rev.* 428, 429 (1955).

[9] See opinion of Justice Robinson in *State* v. *Brunn,* 22 Wash. 2d 120, 154 P.2d 826 (1945).

[10] Comley, "Former Jeopardy," 35 *Yale L.J.* 678 (1926).

[11] *Ibid.*, p. 686. This attitude indicates a fear of judicial usurpation of legislative power to determine criminal policy, a singularly ill-founded emotion in this context.

the Middle Ages, thus permitting a man to escape trial because of a preceding trial in which he has not been in "any jeopardy either of his life or limbs." [12] Echoing this analysis, a more recent article declares that improved trial procedure and the diminished likelihood of governmental tyranny have obviated the danger of repeated prosecutions for the same crime so that the original basis for the double jeopardy doctrine has disappeared.[13] These judgments are not supported in the accompanying notes by any empirical data and are the results of intuitive evaluation of the utility of double jeopardy. The motive force for the evaluations seems to be the feeling that people must be protected from criminals who seek to misuse double jeopardy in order to "jeopardize the public." [14]

There are those critics who agree with the general purpose of the double jeopardy clause but wish to see it treated as a matter of flexible public policy and not as a fundamental principle of jurisprudence.[15] They claim that double jeopardy is not a rule of law, but that it is nothing more than the declaration of an ancient and well-established public policy which may be disregarded when some overruling consideration of policy intervenes.[16] Whenever a court employing this approach fears that a defendant may escape punishment, it should be more willing to relax the protection of double jeopardy, perhaps permitting more than one prosecution for the same criminal transaction.[17] As the doctrine has developed, these critics would insist, instead of being a protection of hapless victims against multiple prosecution, double jeopardy has been warped by attempts to compensate for other mistakes in law enforcement and criminal procedure. To take the place of a formal double jeopardy policy, a flexible rule which would balance the protection of the individual against the state's interest in securing punishments is fre-

---

[12] *Ibid.*, pp. 615–16.   [13] 57 *Yale L.J.* 133 (1947), n.

[14] 14 *U. Pitt. L. Rev.* 538, 589 (1953), n.

[15] See *State* v. *Brunn*, 22 Wash. 2d 120, 127, 154 P.2d 826, 832 (1945).

[16] "Double Jeopardy," 24 *Minn. L. Rev.* 561 (1940), ed. n.

[17] The most notable case of this is *State* v. *Hoag*, especially the Superior Court opinion in 21 N.J. 496, 114 A.2d 573 (1955).

quently proposed.[18] Thus, in states which do not permit appeal by the prosecution, the state should be allowed more leniency in the application of double jeopardy.

Another school of thought would require a redefinition of double jeopardy in order to clarify and strengthen those portions of the principle which still have validity. The need for a clarification of double jeopardy is indubitable.[19] One necessary distinction is that between double prosecution and double punishment. In determining this question, inquiry should be concentrated upon the nature of the defendant's conduct, the physical character of the criminal transaction, rather than upon the number of offenses arising from the transaction.[20] The protection against multiple punishment has as its rationale the belief that the defendant's punishment should be commensurate with but not greater than his criminal liability. The legislature, as the law now stands, may create as many offenses as it desires out of a transaction or activity and can cause punishment to be meted out for any of them without regard to the others.

The impulse which moves this last group of critics is the feeling that the number of punishable offenses committed, not the number of statutes violated, should determine the amount of punishment.[21] The problem of overlapping offenses created by the multiplication of criminal statutes is usually considered to be the central area of concern. Accordingly, most reformers of double jeopardy make the criticism that the traditional tests for the meaning of the "same offense" are inadequate. Judge Bigelow concludes:

[18] See Mayers and Yarbrough, "*Bis Vexari:* New Trials and Successive Prosecutions," 74 *Harv. L. Rev.* 14 (1960).

[19] Jones, "What Constitutes Double Jeopardy?" 38 *J. Crim. L.C. & P.S.* 379, 389 (1947).

[20] *People* v. *Devlin,* 143 Cal. 128, 76 P. 900 (1904), dictum: "in each case where two or more statutes are violated the court must decide on the basis of its particular facts and the legislative intent whether . . . one or more punishments can be inflicted" (*People* v. *Moore,* 143 Cal. App. 2d 333, 299 P.2d 691, 700, 757 [1956]). This problem has been noted in Chapter 2.

[21] See 11 *Stan. L. Rev.* 721 (1959).

Most of the troublesome questions relating to former acquittal would be avoided by a rule which required the state to charge in a single indictment or accusation all the offenses that were part of the same transaction or occurrence; and which precluded the state from thereafter pressing any charge against the defendant which it should have advanced on the first prosecution.[22]

This reform has been the fruit of that form of criticism which seeks to give double jeopardy a more modern significance to meet the experience of contemporary criminal procedure in the United States.

This last approach to double jeopardy, which calls for its redefinition, seems the most appealing. It merely carries into double jeopardy law an attitude which has begun to influence the interpretation of all law, a vision of a changing law to meet changing social needs. The policy of double jeopardy, or of any other basic principle, ought to be reviewed from time to time in order to determine whether the need which gave initiative to that principle has disappeared. In the case of double jeopardy protection that need remains. Those who hold the contrary position may at some future time present evidence to support their stand, but in the absence of such evidence it seems safer to adhere to a view which would protect the individual against the prosecutory power of the state.

---

[22] Bigelow, "Former Conviction and Former Acquittal," 11 *Rutg. L. Rev.* 490, 500 (1957). Bigelow also says: "I believe that questions of former acquittal can be satisfactorily answered by a procedure requiring all charges against a defendant growing out of one occurrence to be joined in a single indictment, and by a liberal application of the principle of collateral estoppel by judgment" (*ibid.*, p. 505). Bigelow also stresses what he considers to be a fundamental difference between a former acquittal and a former conviction, which he feels have different bases. The multiple count indictment is the primary villain because it tends to "minimize the likelihood of unwarranted acquittal but also greatly enhances the potential penalty for any given criminal transaction. In opposition the double jeopardy inhibition against successive prosecutions is frequently invoked to limit the amount of permissible punishment" (57 *Yale L.J.* 133 [1947], n.). In this latter article, he calls for sentencing at the trial level to be final rather than permitting appellate courts to consider the specific amount of punishment in a case. Ultimately, a sentencing board could be established to help separate the disparate functions of fact-finding and determining punishment.

Walter T. Fischer, the attorney who argued for the defendant in the *Bartkus* case, has recently offered a novel interpretation of the double jeopardy concept. Fischer maintains that double jeopardy has a basis in the common law as well as in the American Constitution. He contends that the constitutional protection is considerably narrower than the common law rule, from which he concludes that the double jeopardy concept contained in the common law is still fully operative to protect a defendant in the absence of a statute to the contrary.[23]

Codification of Substantive Criminal Law

The primary reason for the heightened need for double jeopardy protection is found in the system by which public policy in the criminal law area is made. Substantive provisions are adopted piecemeal into the statute books to be digested, by some mysterious process of assimilation, into the body of the law itself. The legislatures transmit the criminal code from one generation to another without bothering to weed out obsolete portions or to harmonize the old with the new.[24] Possibilities for punishment multiply, and the scene is set for a double jeopardy situation. Courts have struggled vainly in an effort to make order where none was intended, deriving "tests" which are little more than apologies for legislative negligence. The criminal defendant cannot be certain which of the tests will be applied, or of the meaning of double jeopardy generally.[25]

What may be needed is a genuine recodification of the criminal law which could serve the purpose of removing the gaps and the overlapping penalties. Such a drastic solution would remove most of

[23] Fischer, "Double Jeopardy," 28 *U. Chi. L. Rev.* 592 (1961).

[24] See Kirchheimer, "The Act, the Offense, and Double Jeopardy," 58 *Yale L.J.* 513 (1949).

[25] See Parker, "Some Aspects of Double Jeopardy," 25 *St. Johns L. Rev.* 188, 202 (1951): "The authorities show that the double jeopardy clause, like the other clauses of the fifth amendment, was designed to afford an accused a maximum amount of security from arbitrary or tyrannical acts of government. It was not meant as a suit of armor which might be indiscriminately used to clothe a wrongdoer and thereby prevent just and proper punishment for his crime."

the causes of double jeopardy situations. The nations which have adopted the code system of law seem to have less necessity for the double jeopardy principle, probably because the peculiar legal configuration which must present itself rarely arises. Codification would have an impact far beyond the area of double jeopardy law and must be considered in the light of general criminal policy. However, it must be weighed together with other available methods of double jeopardy reform.

A few extremist reformers demand a fundamental re-examination of the foundations of criminal law and procedure in the light of modern knowledge of psychiatry, psychology, and social casework. The re-examination would go "more deeply than the drafting of logically articulated but wrongly premised penal codes" and "cannot be satisfied by 'speeding up justice' when nobody has a clear idea of what justice is." [26] This contention seems visionary at the present stage of development of those sciences, although they may throw some light upon criminal policy. There is little enough agreement among various wings of psychiatry and psychology as it is, so that to impose these disciplines upon the criminal law might add to the confusion. Perhaps the most useful contribution of these sciences could be made at the stage of the imposition of sentence, as it is occasionally today; the drafting of provisions of substantive criminal law in terms of psychiatry or psychology is unlikely. For double jeopardy, this approach would be fruitful only if the psychological impact of multiple punishment were capable of calculation.

The need for a comprehensive criminal code is readily apparent. In some jurisdictions there is almost exact duplication in several statutes. Sometimes two statutes will prescribe different penalties for exactly the same transaction, with the defendant's fate hanging upon the accident of which one is chosen by the prosecutor. Even

[26] Glueck, *Crime and Correction: Selected Papers* (Cambridge, Eng., 1952), pp. 72–73. Glueck says that "the legal and institutional provisions for the protection of society must be based not so much upon the gravity of this particular act . . . as upon his personality, that is his dangerousness, his personal assets" (p. 88). Of course, this drastic approach would revamp all criminal law, not merely the double jeopardy area.

when existing statutes are redrafted, the rewriting is based upon the understanding that "though the drafting style is new, the existing structure of the statutes remains intact," and no substantial changes are made.[27] An exception can be found in Wisconsin, where, as stated in a 1953 bill, an objective of codification was "codification by stating in one chapter general principles applicable to all crimes and classifying crimes as nearly as possible according to the social interest protected." [28] Another goal was the maintenance of a fair balance between the societal interest in speedy and efficient law enforcement and its interest in protecting accused persons from unwarranted deprivation of liberty because of the operation of the criminal process. These tensions, between a true codification and a mere reassembly of old provisions, have marked American codification movements, which have been, until recently, very feeble indeed.

The propensity for random creation of new criminal statutes can be found in eighteenth-century English practice. Private members of Parliament frequently sponsored the creation of new criminal offenses by statute. Many members lacked legal education and the necessary experience and concentrated only on their particular measure, paying little or no heed to the general state of the criminal law. The relationship between the newly drafted act and the body of law was rarely examined.[29] Jeremy Bentham, in particular, was outraged by these parliamentary habits. He was always the enemy of the confusion, inconsistency, and clumsiness of the statute law. Bentham coupled a desire for consistency with a contempt for lawyers who benefited from the unnecessary intricacy of the law. He proposed the most radical idea in the movement towards codifica-

[27] Remington, "Criminal Law Revision: Codification vs. Piecemeal Appeal," 38 *Neb. L. Rev.* 400, 403–4 (1954).

[28] Platz, "The Criminal Code," *Wis. L. Rev.* 353 (1956). This purpose was stated in the 1953 bill.

[29] Radzinowicz, *A History of English Criminal Law and Its Administration since 1880*, I (New York, 1948) 20. See also contemporary criticisms, such as Lord Hardwick's 1756 speech in 14 *Reports from the Committees of the House of Commons* 34–35 (1793–1802).

tion in the English-speaking world, the appointment of a "Legislation Minister" who had the task of supervising the clarity and consistency of the law. In addition, there would be a "Legislative Inquiry Judiciary," a supreme investigating committee to investigate the newly proposed laws as to their utility and their consistency with other laws. The committee was to have far-reaching powers to call witnesses, both public and private, in order to conduct a sort of grand inquest.[30] Thus, Bentham foresaw the problems which were to become much greater in our own day than in his own—problems which pervade all criminal law as well as the area of double jeopardy.

Despite Bentham's writings and those of subsequent reformers, there has been no comprehensive treatment of the criminal law in the United States. The best-trained lawyers have had little involvement with the law of crimes, and there has been no legal theorist willing or able to undertake the charting of the contours of the subject, to order its doctrines, its rules and practices, in the light of underlying policies.[31] It would be necessary to canvass the existing law and practice, articulate the issues, and appraise the competing values, so that the choice of substantive criminal laws could be rationalized. This would largely eliminate the overlapping which creates double jeopardy situations.

When and if the changes are made, they would have to be a product of legislative mandate.[32] The greatest justification of codification, if there is any at all, is the intricacy of criminal law.[33] Laws not of the same age are now retained side by side. Old laws no longer enforced go unrepealed, and others have been so frequently

---

[30] Greaves, "Bentham on Legislative Procedure," 33 *Economica*, No. 35, 308–37 (1931). The codification idea was one of Bentham's most important contributions to the growth of Anglo-American law.

[31] Wechsler, "The Challenge of a Model Penal Code," 65 *Harv. L. Rev.* 1097, 1098 (1952).

[32] This was part of the rationale for the *Hoag* case—that is, that fundamental changes in policy were not for the judiciary to make.

[33] Calvert, "The Vitality of Case-Law under a Criminal Code," 22 *Mod. L. Rev.* 638 (1959), should be consulted.

amended as to be difficult to find or understand. The result has been the encrusting of statutes with a growth of exceptions, with debilitating effects.[34] So far as double jeopardy is concerned, the problem of multiple punishment has become one of guessing at legislative intent. Although a complete revision of the criminal law might not be possible, at least some general propositions of interpretation with specific mention of the effect of overlapping in a new statute, such as are found in the code law nations, would prove helpful.

Some writers anticipate a growing approval in the United States of the continental approach to reform of law by codification.[35] There have been some codification movements in this country, the most notable of which resulted in the adoption of the Field Code of civil procedure in New York State, a model for procedural reform. But American codification movements have been limited in aims and limited in point of time. It may be hoped that, with the disappearance of the distrust of the legislature, codes and legislative reforms generally will play a larger role than ever before. The institutional barriers are not great, but the tradition of the common law represents a formidable inhibition. Whatever the obstacles, "the persistent judicial application of unrealistic double jeopardy doctrines calls for legislative reform . . . and because of double jeopardy's constitutional basis, even more than in civil cases the goals of trial convenience and avoidance of multiplicity of suits deserve prompt and effective implementation." [36]

---

[34] See Stone, "A Primer on Codification," 29 *Tul. L. Rev.* 304 (1955).

[35] See Wagner, "Codification in Europe and the Codification Movement in the Middle of the 19th Century in the United States," 2 *St. Louis U.L.J.* 359 (1953).

[36] "Statutory Implementation of Double Jeopardy Clauses: New Life For a Moribund Constitutional Guarantee," 65 *Yale L.J.* 344, 350, 351 (1956), n. As the note points out, the fact that by a single muscular contraction a man violates several provisions of substantive law may, possibly, justify cumulative imposition of sentences, but it does not follow that a new trial is justified for each such offense. The confusion, the weakness, of the double jeopardy law must be ascribed to judicial failure to recognize that new rules must be devised to cope with the fact that a single fact situation may, today, give rise to a number of substantive offenses.

Two states, Louisiana and Wisconsin, have attempted thorough revisions of their substantive criminal codes. Illinois, Minnesota, and New Mexico are also progressing toward some sort of codification.[37] In 1942, Louisiana adopted a comprehensive criminal code, codification being a part of the tradition of that state, since "on the civil law side Louisiana had never known anything but codification." [38] The intention to codify the criminal law was deeply rooted in the history of the drafting of the civil code, but it was brought to a head by the growing incomprehensibility of the Louisiana criminal law, and especially by numerous instances of overlapping and duplicating criminal statutes.[39] However, the Louisiana codification was not so sweeping that double jeopardy problems have been removed or even much diminished. Some states have enacted statutes in the double jeopardy area, often expanding constitutional protection where it had been narrowed by the courts.[40] But there has been no attempt to make a general codification of double jeopardy law.

The best example of the inadequacy of codification in the United States is to be found in the United States Criminal Code itself. As announced by the Senate Judiciary Committee reporting the Revision of Title 18 to the Eightieth Congress in 1948, the purpose of the codification of the criminal law was to revise the laws relating to federal crimes and criminal procedure, making it easy to find the criminal statutes "because of the arrangement, numbering and classification" so that "the original intent of Congress is preserved." [41] The so-called "revision" was supposed to eliminate obsolete and executed provisions and to end uncertainty and to make it unnecessary to examine the many volumes of the statutes at large. The revi-

[37] Remington, "Criminal Justice Research," 51 *J. Crim. L.C. & P.S.* 9 (1960).

[38] Smith, "How Louisiana Prepared and Adopted a Criminal Code," 41 *J. Crim. L.C. & P.S.* 126 (1950).

[39] See 5 *La. L. Rev.* 1 (1942) for a complete survey of the attempt.

[40] For example, the state of New York has taken this step. See *People* v. *Savarese*, 201 App. Div. 401, 114 N.Y.S.2d 816 (1952).

[41] Judiciary Comm., Revision of Title 18, U.S.C., S. Rep. No. 1620, 80th Cong., 2d Sess., April 24, 1947, p. 1. Senator Wiley reported the bill from committee.

sion was intended to substitute plain language for awkward terms, to reconcile conflicting laws, omit superseded sections, and consolidate similar provisions.[42] The last revision had been in 1909 as a result of a commission study begun in 1897. However, no sweeping changes were made at that time, although twenty-one new sections were added in the current code, ten of which created new offenses.[43]

The results of the revision were not startling. Many sections were consolidated where they overlapped, but supposedly without making any changes. In one instance, eleven sections were consolidated into a single section, which resulted in a great saving of space and notable improvement in the style of the language. As Representative Eugene J. Keough, member of the Committee on the Revision of the Laws, stated before the House Judiciary Committee: "We proceed upon the hypothesis that since [the Code revision] was primarily a restatement of existing law, we should not endanger its accomplishment by the inclusion in the work of any highly controversial changes in laws." [44] This statement indicates the generally conservative attitude toward codification which seems to prevail.

Obviously, the United States Code is not a true codification. More precisely it is a "consolidation," because it merely rearranges the laws on particular subjects according to the subject matter and tries to show their current status. Codification entails the elimination of needless verbosity, of fruitless distinctions and duplication, and especially of irrational penalty variations.[45] The redrafting of existing statutes upon the understanding that no substantial changes are to

[42] Judiciary Comm., Revision of Title 18, U.S.C., H.R. Rep. No. 304, 80th Cong., 1st Sess., April 24, 1947, p. 1. Representative Robison reported the bill from committee.

[43] *Ibid.*, pp. 2–3.

[44] Hearing before Subcommittee No. 1 of the House Judiciary Committee, March 7, 1947. Keough was a member of the Committee on the Revision of the Laws.

[45] See Remington, 33 *Neb. L. Rev.* 400, 405. The few "codes" which were enacted in the nineteenth century cannot be compared with continental codes, which are far more inclusive in scope. American codification has always fallen far short of the goals of comprehensiveness and elimination of duplication.

be made is the usual American pattern of criminal reform in the substantive area.

A rational system of criminal justice may await the construction of a comprehensive criminal code. There will always be a gap between community standards, as enunciated, and the actual standards of behavior. If the social process were completely successful, every member of the community would possess the will and the ability to abstain from acts which injure commonly shared values. As an ultimate kind of criminal law, it may be hoped that a corrective code which concentrates upon situations of damage to community values caused by those having "destructive intent" may be produced.[46] Such a code would specify the measures appropriate to the destructive situation caused partly by community failures. But, short of this goal, it is possible to eliminate much of the duplication of criminal law by a codification of greater scope than those which have heretofore taken place in the United States, thus reducing the likelihood of the occurrence of double jeopardy. If a comprehensive criminal code were adopted, however, the state should get a right of appeal from the acquittal of a defendant in order to compensate for the loss of the opportunity to split offenses into separate prosecutions, while the defendant would have less opportunity to escape punishment because of an error of law.

There are certain shortcomings of codification which should be mentioned. The primary fault is that such sweeping changes in criminal law presume the existence of an agreed criminal policy. Since no uniform approach has as yet been advanced, the current multiplicity is likely to continue. A more fundamental fault of codification is that it imposes an artificial and somewhat inflexible symmetry upon the many forms of criminal conduct. A thorough codification

[46] Dession and Lasswell, "Public Order under Law: The Role of the Advisor-Draftsman in the Formation of Code or Constitution," 65 *Yale L.J.* 192 (1955). Moran proposes a single substantive act which would require a determination of all ripe criminal charges at one joint trial. The state would have to charge at one time all possible accusations unless it had an excuse for its failure ("The Future of the Criminal Law: Criminal Law in Its Modern Public Law Context," 11 *Rutg. L. Rev.* 587 [1957]).

of substantive criminal law, might remove potential double jeopardy situations, but it would probably be inconsistent with American legal traditions. However tempting, the reform of substantive law seems an unlikely solution to problems of double jeopardy. Hence, whatever reforms there may be must appear in the realm of criminal procedure.

The Model Code of Criminal Procedure

For almost twenty years the American Law Institute had on its agenda of unfinished business a proposal to prepare a model penal code, similar to other codes it has prepared (especially in the commercial law area). The penal code project was launched in 1931 by a proposal of the American Bar Association, the American Law School Association, and the American Law Institute, through representatives to a Joint Committee on Improvement of Criminal Justice.[47] Double jeopardy was one of the proposed areas of scrutiny. In 1930, the American Law Institute completed a proposed model code of criminal procedure, but no penal code resulted. In 1951, the penal code project was renewed, utilizing the assistance of an advisory committee of lawyers and others from related social science disciplines. In 1952 the Rockefeller Foundation granted funds to permit the undertaking to proceed.[48]

The official final draft of the model penal code is now available. The object of the drafters was to canvass the existing law and practice, "articulating legislative issues, analyzing possible solutions, and appraising the competing values and considerations which a legislative choice should weigh.[49] The penal code is not a comprehensive,

[47] See American Bar Association Report No. 25, LVI, 494, 513 (1931).

[48] Wechsler, *op. cit.*, p. 1097.

[49] *Ibid.*, p. 1130. Professor Wechsler has been among the most active persons seeking criminal law reform and codification. He believes the current penal laws to be ineffective (the high rate of recidivism could be cited), inhumane, and unscientific (*ibid.*, p. 1103). The preparation of the United States criminal code would seem to bear out Wechsler's judgment of being unscientific.

concise statement of basic penal principles, but an attempt at clarification of some of the major problems.

The original American Law Institute commentary on the Administration of the Criminal Law resulted in an official draft on double jeopardy which appeared on August 15, 1935. This commentary did not accept the status quo in double jeopardy law. It was the first critical analysis of double jeopardy to be made in depth. The commentary rejects the American rule of attachment of jeopardy on the grounds of logic and history. The draft finds that there was no plea of "double jeopardy" known to the common law (although the plea was known by other names) and that no principle of the common law existed which permitted anything short of a final conviction or acquittal to serve as a bar to a second prosecution for the same offense.[50]

Accordingly, the draft proposes a model code of criminal law administration to remedy some of the defects of double jeopardy. Section 6 requires a final judgment in order for a defendant to be able to claim former jeopardy, while Section 7 makes an exception for the discharge of the jury without the defendant's consent and without a showing of mainfest injustice to the state or the defendant if there were no discharge. The commentary to Section 6 demonstrates a reliance upon persuasive cases which are not of the majority view as to the attachment of jeopardy.[51]

The draft suggests other striking departures from the usual American double jeopardy rules. Section 13 would permit the state to appeal from a judgment of acquittal, although, at the time, only one state permitted appeal from a judgment of acquittal on the ground of error at the trial level. Section 15 would make a conviction for a violation of the criminal law of the United States or of another state or country a bar to any subsequent prosecution, reversing the *Lanza*

[50] American Law Institute, "Double Jeopardy," *Commentaries on the Administration of the Criminal Law—Official Draft* (Chicago, 1935), Aug. 15, 1935, pp. 7–8.

[51] It has been held in two well-considered English cases and in a United States case that the rule that a jury must be kept together in a criminal case is a rule of practice and not of law" (*ibid.*, p. 61).

case rule. Section 18 seems to adopt a same evidence rule in order to interpret the meaning of the phrase "same offense":

Where proof of the same facts is sufficient to convict a person of either of two offenses, a conviction of acquittal of such a person of one of such offenses is a bar to a prosecution of such person for the other of such offenses based on the same facts.

Another section permits as many criminal accusations as there are people or property injured by the defendant's conduct.[52]

The 1935 draft represents the fruit of a widespread concern with the adequacy of double jeopardy law. It is an attempt to redefine that law, to select those principles from the best reasoned cases which might be useful in clarifying the meaning of double jeopardy. The draft is best described as a restatement of existing case law, although there are some departures of substance. It tends to treat multiplicity of convictions, multiplicity of trials, and cumulation of punishment as a single problem. The current American Law Insti-

[52] Sec. 13: *ibid.*, p. 13 and the commentary at p. 111.

Sec. 15: *ibid.*, p. 15. The commentary on page 128 cites the *Lanza* case rule as the majority position, points out that the English case law is to the contrary, and attempts no further explanation. The proposed rule would, however, be in accord with the statutory rule of about twenty jurisdictions. One must assume that the drafters believed their rule to be self-evidently superior.

Sec. 18: *ibid.*, p. 15. Section 18 has a self-contained exception which seems to destroy its effectiveness. It states that the section does not apply to cases where by a single act "a person offends against two statutes," giving as an example an act which violates a statute forbidding the sale of liquor to a minor and the sale of liquor on Sunday. The futility of this rule is but an echo of the same difficulty with interpretative double jeopardy rules generally, which seems to have plagued the courts as well. It is doubtful whether the the problem is capable of solution on this basis.

Sec. 22: *ibid.*, p. 18. This rule would cover cases such as a larceny of fifteen articles belonging to the same person, permitting as many prosecutions as there were articles stolen. It was felt by the drafters that the rule merely stated the majority position (see commentary at *ibid.*, pp. 148–73). Few more troublesome problems exist in double jeopardy law, but the draft's proposal is not especially helpful in resolving the problem. Sections 25 and 26 try to develop a rule for cases in which two offenses have a third offense as a necessary common element. It seems to flow from the lack of adequate protection left by the preceding rules.

tute model code is supposed to be an improvement, not merely "the perpetuating of inconsistencies existing in the case law." [53]

The Model Penal Code

The final draft of the Model Penal Code, which, in part, deals with double jeopardy, appeared in 1962. The double jeopardy section of the Code is an attempt to reach the substantive problems which lie at the root of double jeopardy. The Code does not consider the question of the right of the state to appeal from an acquittal, because it was felt that the matter might better be dealt with in a procedural code. On the other hand, the Code, unlike the original 1935 draft, now extends the principle of res judicata into the double jeopardy area.

The greatest single innovation of the Model Penal Code is the requirement that "a defendant shall not be subject to separate trials for multiple offenses based on the same conduct or arising from the same criminal episode, if such offenses are known to the appropriate prosecuting officer at the time of the commencement of the first trial and are within the jurisdiction of a single court." [54] This is a notable narrowing of the language of the 1956 draft. Under that proposal a second trial was barred for all offenses "based on a series of acts or omissions motivated by a purpose to accomplish a single criminal objective" or if "the offenses are based on a series of acts or omissions motivated by a common purpose or plan." [55] This change from 1956 to 1962 is a major concession to the opponents of a broader double jeopardy concept. Even so, it rejects the currently prevailing view.[56] The policy resolution which has been made in this section is

[53] American Law Institute, *Model Penal Code, Tentative Draft No. 5* (Chicago, 1956), April 27, 1956, p. 66.

[54] Sec. 1.07(2).

[55] Sec. 1.08-2(b) and (c) (1956 draft). This approach is close to that employed in the state of California, as described below.

[56] *Pinkerton* v. *United States,* 328 U.S. 640 (1946); *State* v. *Blackledge,* 215 Iowa 199, 243 N.W. 534 (1932). The "same offense" problem, treated at length in earlier chapters, is overcome, somewhat, by the current Model Penal Code provision.

that which underlies the whole Code, that the defendant should be confronted but once in a complete accusation, while, on the other hand, the defendant ought not to benefit because facts concerning his criminal activity have been concealed from law enforcement officials.[57]

The most important double jeopardy feature of the 1956 Code, the provision which requires joinder of all available accusations in one trial,[58] was really procedural, since it insisted on the entire matter being litigated at one time. It did not require that they all be treated as the same legal offense, which is a substantive matter. The provision seemed, at first glance, much more sweeping than it really was. Section 1.08(1) permitted prosecution for each offense established by the same conduct, although prohibiting conviction of more than one offense in certain situations. This was the point closest to a substantive change which could be found in the 1956 Code. The current (1962) Code retains the compulsory joinder feature, but it now prevents the prosecution from instituting second trials for "multiple offenses based on the same conduct or arising from the same criminal episode." [59] The 1956 provision seems the most revolutionary, since it would have the effect of interpreting statutory language according to a rule highly favorable to the defendant. The force of the provision would be limited to proscribing multiple convictions, however, and would not serve as a protection against multiple trials, except as provided by Section 1.10 (1956 draft).

The Code recognized the need for some tests against the possibility of undue multiple trials to replace those which have been evolved by the courts, asserting that "the weakness of most current tests is . . . that they are so narrowly drawn as not to afford any real protection against the cumulation of the number of prosecu-

---

[57] American Law Institute, *Model Penal Code, Tentative Draft* (1956), p. 36.

[58] Sec. 1.08-2(c). This contradicts the ruling cases *Morgan* v. *Devine*, 237 U.S. 632 (1914), and *Oddo* v. *United States*, 171 F.2d 854 (1949).

[59] American Law Institute, *Model Penal Code, Proposed Official Draft* (Philadelphia, 1962), Sec. 1.07(2).

tions, the number of convictions, or the amount of punishment." [60] The final draft, which is similarly worded, may not cure the existing deficiencies. Section 1.09 attempts to list situations in which new trials will be barred. Former acquittal, former conviction, and improper termination would have this effect. The excuses for termination are much the same as those now existing in the form of exceptions to the attachment of jeopardy. The section replaces the usual judicial tests for the identity of an offense with a narrow test requiring a violation of the same statute based upon the same facts.[61] As one of the excuses for proper termination of a trial, the Code includes the finding of a legal defect in the proceedings which would make any judgment entered upon a verdict reversible as a matter of law. This provision has the effect of permitting appeal by the state from an acquittal on the grounds of legal error only. The commentary to this section points out that in no jurisdiction may the state appeal from an acquittal if there is no error of law, asserting that to go so far would probably violate the federal constitution.[62] If this provision of the Code were adopted, a constitutional change would be required in those states which prohibit the prosecutor's appeal.

Subsection (4) of Section 1.08 has as one of its purposes the specific listing of the "manifest necessity" exception to the attachment of double jeopardy. The virtue of clear presentation may be offset by the vice of continuing a curious, outworn feature of double jeopardy law. In this respect, at least, the 1935 draft was more radical and more logical, simply abandoning the concept of attachment of jeopardy and replacing it with the English final judgment rule. The

[60] *Tentative Draft* (1956), p. 35. *State* v. *Hoag,* 21 N.J. 496, 114 A.2d 575 (1956), is cited as an illustration of the inadequacy of the usual tests. Of course, it should be recalled that *Hoag* ignored the previous New Jersey precedents to a large extent.

[61] Sec. 1.09, para. 1. Subsection (1) retains the lesser-included offense doctrine, so that a person found guilty of a lesser-included offense may be tried again for the greater.

[62] Sec. 1.09(4)(b)(2) and p. 48.

attachment doctrine is retained, the commentary informs us, because it is "based upon the premise that it is undesirable to allow the state to withdraw from a poorly received case and to start once again with the hope of better success the second time." [63] The Code does eliminate the distinction now made between trial before a judge and trial before a jury, which is usually made in attachment situations.[64]

In one major respect the Penal Code extends protection to a defendant far beyond that which is usually accorded him. Contrary to the rule in most states, the Code extends the principle of res judicata into the criminal law, asserting that the 1932 American Law Institute reporter was wrong on principle in refusing to make this reform.[65] How can this provision be said to be consistent with the narrow test for the identity of a former offense contained in the same section? The process of limiting protection in one subsection while extending it in another may merely add another source of confusion to double jeopardy law.

The Code attempts to protect the defendant with the test for the identity of offenses in Section 1.09. This section is the heart of the double jeopardy provisions found in the Penal Code. It bars prosecution for a different statutory violation after a former prosecution has been completed, even if based on different facts in certain situations. Most importantly, the section prohibits prosecution where a former prosecution had resulted in an acquittal or conviction and the subsequent prosecution is for an offense of which the defendant could have been convicted on the first prosecution, or for an offense with which the defendant should have been charged under the compulsory joinder provision (Section 1.07). This provision would be a

[63] *Ibid.*, p. 53.

[64] Compare *Correro* v. *United States*, 48 F.2d 69 (9th Cir. 1931), with *Rosser* v. *State*, 159 Va. 128, 167 S.E. 257 (1933).

[65] See American Law Institute, *Model Penal Code, Tentative Draft* (1956), p. 49, which cites *United States* v. *Oppenheimer*, 242 U.S. 85 (1916), as a useful precedent. The difficulties inherent in this view have been commented upon earlier.

formidable protection for the defendant were it not for the proviso extending double jeopardy to a subsequent prosecution for the same conduct "unless the offenses charged in the former and subsequent prosecutions each requires proof of a fact not required by the other." [66] The compulsory joinder innovation, for which the Penal Code is most noted (so far as double jeopardy is concerned) seems to extend to offenses of which the defendant could have been initially charged, but not to cases involving the same conduct if different proof of facts is needed to differentiate the charges. Unless subsequent interpretation should clarify the meaning, an apparently hopeless incongruity seems to exist within the Code. It would always be possible for a skillful prosecutor against whom the compulsory joinder provision is asserted to claim that although the same conduct is involved, and though he could have made the same charge in the first trial, the offense charged in the first trial requires proof of a different fact from those charged in the subsequent proceeding.[67]

The compulsory joinder concept, which is reinforced by Section 1.09, has the interesting feature of shifting the burden of showing a former jeopardy to the prosecution. Subsection (1)(c) would permit the prosecutor to raise as a defense to a claim of double jeopardy the fact that the offense now being charged was not consummated at the time of the first trial or was not known to the police or the prosecutor when the former trial began. In this situation, the defen-

[66] Sec. 109(1)(c).

[67] The Illinois compulsory joinder statute has been read in this way (*People v. Calloway*, 74 Ill. App. 2d 418, 221 N.E.2nd 73 [1966]); so has the Missouri statute (*State v. Osborne*, 413 S.W.2nd 571 [Mo. 1967]). But the California joinder rules, which are much stricter than those of the Model Penal Code rest upon the defendant's dominant intent and purpose, making the criminal transaction indivisible and preventing continual trials, even if there should be multiple victims (*Neal v. State of California*, 55 Cal. 2d 11, 19, 357 P.2d 839, 843–44 [1960], based rather loosely upon Calif. Pen. Code, Secs. 1023 and 654). The California rules are the greatest protection available against multiple trials available anywhere in the United States. Minnesota is slightly less generous (see Minn. St. 609.035).

dant's claim of double jeopardy would be unsuccessful if the prosecutor could demonstrate his ignorance of the commission of the offense. The provision would seem to place a premium upon the inefficiency or ineptitude of the police or the prosecutor.[68]

If the trial judge improperly terminates the former prosecution, the subsequent trial is barred. The reasons for this policy are explained:

Improper termination results, almost without exception, from erroneous but good faith rulings by the trial judge. Under these circumstances, giving the defendant immunity from the burden of subsequent prosecution for the same offense, or one of which he might have been convicted, is warranted. To go further and grant him immunity for any offense arising out of his conduct seems disproportionate to the trouble caused him.[69]

[68] It is important to understand the 1956 joinder proposal itself if the limitation upon the prosecutor is to be comprehended. Section 1.08(2) required a single prosecution if the offenses are known to the proper officer of the police or prosecution and: "(a) the offenses are based on the same conduct; or (b) the offenses are based on a series of acts or omissions motivated by a single criminal objective, and necessary or incidental to the accomplishing of that objective; or (c) the offenses are based on a series of acts or omissions motivated by a common purpose or plan and which result in the repeated commission of the same offense or affect the same person or the same persons or the property thereof." Since the double jeopardy clause has as its purport the control of the prosecutor's discretion, this reform would seem to accomplish that purpose most admirably. The comments indicated that the phrase "'same conduct' meant a single act or single instance of negligence or recklessness which resulted in the commission of more than one offense," giving as an example the case in which a single shot results in the death of two persons, requiring both homicides to be joined in a single trial (ibid., p. 36). If this were the effect of Code Section 1.08, why did Section 1.10 state that a subsequent prosecution for the same conduct is barred "unless the offenses charged in the former and subsequent prosecutions each required proof of a fact not required by the other"? (Sec. 1.10[1][c]). Would not the proof of the death of one person be different from the proof of death of another in the case illustration? Would the proof of the fact of one death resulting from negligence be necessary to the proof of the other? The prosecutor could easily work within the limits of 1.10 and not feel hampered by the compulsory joinder provision. The 1962 changes did not repair this difficulty.

[69] Ibid., p. 59.

Accordingly, the protection to the defendant only extends to the same charges, in cases of improper termination. The ambiguity in the policy statement is the same as that which seems to prevail throughout the Code's double jeopardy provisions. The question of how far the defendant's protection extends to similar offense categories is never definitely resolved.

The Penal Code also undertakes to settle the question of former prosecution in another jurisdiction. The Code provides that if an offense falls within the jurisdiction of the states or of the United States, the first prosecution acts as a bar if it results in a conviction, acquittal, or final order for the defendant. In order to fall under this provision, the subsequent prosecution must be based upon the "same conduct" or "the same series of acts or omissions, unless . . . each requires proof of a fact required by the other or the second offense was not consummated when the former prosecution was initiated." [70] The provision would essentially reverse the case law of most states and of the federal government.[71] However, it would be subject to the same fault which can be seen in the interpretation of similar state statutes. The difficulty is in deciding whether the state and federal prosecutions are for the "same offense." Curiously, the Penal Code would prevent a former prosecution in a foreign country from serving as a bar to subsequent state and federal prosecution, contrary to the federal rule, fifteen state statutes, the 1935 draft, and the generally held view of international law. The Code drafters explain their position by saying that the matter "is best dealt with, in our view, by international agreement." [72]

The final section which has bearing on double jeopardy concerns former prosecutions before courts lacking jurisdiction or whose jurisdiction has been fraudulently procured by the defendant. Section 1.11 is essentially a codification of well-accepted principles of the

[70] Sec. 1.10(1)(b).

[71] Besides reversing the *Lanza* and *Bartkus* cases, it would reverse many state cases, such as *State* v. *O'Brien,* 106 Vt. 97, 170 A. 98 (1934), and *State* v. *Simpson,* 78 N.D. 360, 49 N.W.2d 777 (1951).

[72] American Law Institute, *Model Penal Code, Tentative Draft* (1956), p. 61.

common law of double jeopardy. The problem has not been considered at all in this work because it is no longer an area of contention.[73] The principles at stake are similar to the principles of "equitable estoppel" and the "clean hands" doctrine of equity law.

The Penal Code has been a significant undertaking in criminal law reform generally, as well as in the reform of double jeopardy law. For double jeopardy, the major innovation is the compulsory joinder feature, which would seem to eliminate many double jeopardy problems by forcing the prosecutor to join all his charges in one accusation. Professor Wechsler has said of this device:

[It is] designed to cast the balance in favor of cleaning up the charges against a particular man at one time, in the view that he is only one man, and that however many things he has done the slate ought so far as possible to be cleared so that he may be dealt with as the one man that he is, and appropriately disposed of.[74]

Despite this observation, Sections 1.07, 1.08, 1.09 and 1.10 do not appear to force such a joinder as Wechsler envisions. The Code seems to alternate between a complete compulsory joinder provision (which would be most salutary) and a rigid "same fact" test, which would have the opposite effect. The Code may have been the product of too many draftsmen.

The Code has segregated the concept of double jeopardy into three divisions: prevention of multiplicity of trials, prevention of multiplicity of convictions, and prevention of cumulation of punishment. These three divisions are represented by each of the first three double jeopardy sections. The drafters knew, however, that some aspects of double jeopardy cut across these lines, creating the need for considerable cross-reference between the sections. This Code style has the effect of simplifying double jeopardy only to complicate it.

[73] However, the rule would have been useful in *Martinis* v. *Supreme Court*, 15 N.Y.2d 246, 206 N.E.2d 165 (1965), in which the defendant rushed into a local court in order to avoid a later, more serious charge in a higher court.

[74] Wechsler, in American Law Institute, *Proceedings* (Chicago, 1956), p. 139.

Several matters remain at loose ends after one reads the Penal Code's double jeopardy sections. First, if codification is the best way to reform double jeopardy, would not an indispensable step be the reversal of *Palko* v. *Connecticut*, [75] since only a consistent nationwide policy would insure a uniform interpretation of the Code. Second, how could a procedural change overcome constitutional objections? The Code drafters, by extending res judicata and collateral estoppel, have fundamentally changed the character of double jeopardy. It becomes the criminal law analogue to the usual civil rules. But in New York, as in many other states, "the right to assert the claim of former jeopardy is guaranteed by the constitution" and *"res judicata* . . . does not rest upon any constitutional provision," being "merely a rule of evidence." [76] To mistake double jeopardy for res judicata or collateral estoppel is to forget that double jeopardy is a doctrine with a long and definite history, a history which bears little relationship to the civil law.[77] Finally, it may be asked whether the whole scheme would be constitutional, since it would drastically change the meaning of a constitutional clause without the usual steps towards amendment of the Constitution.[78]

The Penal Code drafters have presented a definite, if arbitrary, scheme of double jeopardy law, as they admit.[79] The Code would provide a fairly logical system of judgment standards, but that

[75] 302 U.S. 319 (1937).

[76] *United States* v. *Carlisi*, 32 F. Supp. 479, 482 (E.D.N.Y. 1940).

[77] "While former jeopardy has its roots deep in our common law system, collateral estoppel has for its basis mere policy considerations" (Currie, "Multiple Prosecutions, Collateral Estoppel, and the Constitution," 16 *Wash. & Lee L. Rev.* 61 [1959]).

[78] Then, too, the concept of collateral estoppel and, to some degree, res judicata are themselves quite confused. The concepts have been called "estoppel by record" (*United States* v. *Accardo*, 113 F. Supp. 783, 786 [D.N.J. 1953]); "estoppel by verdict" (*Goodman* v. *McLennan*, 334 Ill. App. 405, 80 N.E.2d 396, 420 [1948]); and "estoppel by judgment" (*Gordon* v. *Gordon*, 190 Fla. 73, 59 S.2d 40, 43 [1952]), among other things. See Miller, "The Historical Relation of Estoppel by Record to Res Judicata," 35 *Ill. L. Rev.* 41 (1940). These terms are defined elsewhere in this study.

[79] American Law Institute, *Model Penal Code, Tentative Draft* (1956), p. 60.

should not imply that the Code would be applied in a consistent fashion. It has been said that the compulsory joinder rule would be a "novel principle in criminal prosecution." [80] But the adoption of a compulsory joinder procedure might call forth a liberal procedure for the amendment of indictments and other responses which could change the nature of double jeopardy completely.

Current Procedural Rules

A change such as that proposed by the drafters of the Model Penal Code would bear some resemblance to the present joinder requirements of the Federal Rules of Criminal Procedure. By the Act of May 8, 1792, the Supreme Court was given the power to regulate equity pleading and practice.[81] Until June 29, 1940, there was no legislation permitting the Supreme Court to regulate federal criminal procedure by the rule-making power.[82] The Federal Rules of Criminal Procedure were an attempt to follow the pattern of the highly successful Federal Rules of Civil Procedure. Attorney General Cummings had been instrumental in securing the enabling act of 1934, which had resulted in the 1938 Civil Rules. Cummings also suggested that similar rules in the criminal area would be desirable, which suggestion, after review by President Roosevelt and his advisers, was recommended to the Congress.[83]

The rule of joinder of offenses contained in the Federal Rules is largely permissive, granting the prosecution the right to join two or more offenses in one indictment as several counts of the same indictment. The offenses charged may be felonies, misdemeanors, or both, as long as they are based on the "same act or transaction" or constitute "parts of a common scheme or plan." [84] Another rule permits the court to order two or more indictments to be tried together if the

---

[80] See Orfield, "Joinder in Federal Criminal Procedure," 26 *F.R.D.* 23, 76 (1960).

[81] 30 Stat. 554 (1792).   [82] 54 Stat. 688 (1940).

[83] Holtzoff, "A Criminal Case in the Federal Courts," in *Federal Rules of Criminal Procedure—1955* (St. Paul, Minn., 1955), p. 3. The Federal Rules have been adopted by many states, usually without significant modification.

[84] *Federal Rules of Criminal Procedure,* Rule S(a).

offenses could have been joined in a single indictment, the procedure remaining the same as if the prosecution were under a single indictment.[85] This latter rule is rarely used, since judges hesitate to instruct the prosecutor how to perform his tasks. If used more freely the rule would achieve some of the ends sought for by the drafters of the Model Penal Code.

Federal Rule 8(a), the permissive joinder rule, merely codified existing law.[86] It is "substantially a restatement of existing and familiar law." [87] The due process question, which would also involve double jeopardy, has never really been decided. For example, in *Brandenburg* v. *Steele,* the defendant was charged with eleven counts in one indictment which stated eleven separate offenses. The defendant, seeking release on habeas corpus, asserted that to charge him with eleven separate offenses in a single indictment and to try him before one jury amounted to a denial of due process of law. This claim was dismissed, *per curiam,* by the Court of Appeals, with the following rationale:

In view of the statute and rules prescribed by the Supreme Court above referred to, which authorized the procedure which resulted in the appellant's conviction, it is obvious that he is entirely mistaken in his assertion about denial of due process. He was dealt with in accordance with long established practice and conventional federal procedure.[88]

The case might be used to justify a compulsory joinder rule as an extension of the Federal Rules. At the least, it is an illustration of the fact that some defendants may feel that such a joinder rule would work to their disadvantage.

If a mandatory joinder rule is adopted, it would be necessary to alter other provisions which bear on the joinder provision. These changes would be necessitated by the desire to balance the advantages between the state and the accused. Currently, for example,

85 *Ibid.,* Rule 13.
86 *United States* v. *Sherman,* 84 F. Supp. 130, 131 (D.E.N.Y. 1947), and *Ingram* v. *United States,* 272 F.2d 567, 568 (4th Cir. 1959).
87 *Rakes* v. *United States,* 169 F.2d 739, 743 (7th Cir. 1946).
88 177 F.2d 279, 281 (8th Cir. 1949).

Federal Rule 7(e) permits the amendment of an indictment at any time only if no additional or different offense is charged. If a compulsory joinder rule were adopted, amendment would have to be easier in order to insure the prosecution a hearing for all its potential charges. Similarly, Federal Rule 48 permits the United States Attorney to dismiss an indictment, but the dismissal may not be filed during the trial unless the defendant consents. A compulsory joinder rule would require that dismissal be easier to obtain, since the prosecution must be given every chance to prove its best case.[89]

One other change, which has been mentioned previously, might be made necessary because of an adoption of a compulsory joinder rule. This would be a change in federal government appeal rules so that the United States Attorney might be permitted the same right of appeal which the defendant now has available to him. Under the current law, the federal attorney may appeal from all district courts directly to the Supreme Court "from the decision or judgment sustaining a motion in bar, when the defendant has not been put in jeopardy," and in special cases where the invalidity of a statute or the insufficiency of an indictment are involved.[90] Perhaps if the prosecution is to have but one good opportunity to try the defendant, that try should be a complete one, including the entire right of appeal. After all, it is a slight inconvenience to the defendant, since he need not appear at his appeal, and the mental discomfort caused him is still preferable to the situation presented him by current pro-

---

[89] Rule 7(c) requires a "plain, concise statement . . . of the essential facts constituting the offense charged." This need not be changed, since it merely eliminates the need for technical forms. Rule 31(c) states: "The defendant may be found guilty of an offense necessarily included in the offense charged or of an attempt necessarily included therein if the attempt is an offense." This fits in admirably with the Code scheme, indeed the drafters of the Code may have had the Federal Rules in the forefront of their consideration when making their studies. The changes proposed by the drafters would fit within the purpose of the Federal Rules: "These rules are intended to provide for the just determination of every criminal proceeding. They shall be construed to secure simplicity in procedure, fairness in administration, and the elimination of unjustifiable expense and delay (Rule 2).

[90] U.S. Code Annotated, Title 18, Sec. 3731.

cedure, which permits multiple trials. One fact cannot be denied, that is, that the defendant has often taken undue advantage of his right to appeal, especially under the Federal Rule requiring a full statement of all defenses and objections.[91]

Dession's Code of Correction

Professor George H. Dession attempted to complete a code of correction. His death cut short the completion of his task, but the Code, which remains as an unpublished and uncompleted manuscript in the Yale Law Library, contains some of the most interesting suggestions toward double jeopardy reform. Part of this work appeared in a note in the *Yale Law Journal*.[92] Dession's suggestions provide some of the most profound ideas ever advanced for the reform of double jeopardy.

Dession's draft requires that "an act, omission, practice or transaction, or two or more such connected together, or constituting parts of a common scheme or plan," must "be joined in a single trial." [93] The provision includes the "laws of another jurisdiction," thus effectually reversing the *Lanza* and *Bartkus* cases. This brief section expands the concept of a compulsory trial to permit of no such exceptions as contemplated by the Model Code—a distinct improvement, at least from the point of view of clarity.

More radically, Dession's draft also requires that civil tort claims, or, as he said, "claims for reparations arising out of the situation,

[91] This is Federal Rule 12(b)(2), which would seem to require the defendant to present all his defenses before the trial. In actual practice, this is not done. Instead, "it is obvious tactics for the defense counsel to save most doubtful questions of law for the trial. Their function is not to see that the laws of the land are enforced, but to get their clients out of the so-called clutches of the prosecutor. Why raise a disputed question of law in advance of trial, when an erroneous ruling can be corrected, if the whole matter can be saved until the evidence is in, when there is no possibility of correcting errors adverse to the prosecution?" (Steffen, "Concerning Double Jeopardy and the New Rules," 7 *Fed. B.J.* 92 [1945]).

[92] See 65 *Yale L.J.* 354 (1955).

[93] Dession, "Code of Correction" (unpub. MS, Yale Law School, 1955), Sec. 64.

shall so far as possible be determined in a single proceeding." [94] Behind this radical reform is Dession's basic philosophy of double jeopardy: "that a situation subject to correction or any combination or series of related situations shall be evaluated in context, as a whole, and with finality within a reasonable time." [95] Obviously, Dession's concept of joinder is far broader than present rules would permit, and broader, too, than the proposal of the American Law Institute.

Dession also suggests that the right of appeal by the Commonwealth "from any rulings thought to involve material errors of law prejudicial to the Commonwealth" ought to be broadly granted.[96] His logic is clear. A new trial is a continuation of the original proceeding "whether on application of the respondent or of the Commonwealth." [97] He has adopted the view of Justice Holmes's dissent in the *Kepner* case, carrying it to its logical conclusion. One other minor change is suggested which would extend the lesser included offense doctrine to cover assaults in situations involving rape or robbery.[98] Beyond this, Dession's Code is silent. He never considers the question of attachment of jeopardy, of the effect of dismissals, of the import of overlapping punishment categories, or other significant matters. One can only assume that in time he would have turned his interest to those problems.

The multiple joinder concept, which Dession applies more rigorously than have the drafters of the Model Penal Code, would have the effect of solving some of the most pressing procedural aspects of double jeopardy. The procedural question deals with the policy of preventing undue harassment to an accused, so that his life need not be disrupted in order to defend himself against a set of criminal accusations. Then, too, the expenditure in time and money by both the prosecution and the defense might be appreciably reduced by such a multiple joinder provision. However, more than procedural matters underlie double jeopardy policy. There are real substantive issues at stake which require careful restudying before a satisfac-

---

[94] *Ibid.*, Sec. 62. [95] *Ibid.*, Pt 2. [96] *Ibid.*, Sec. 67.
[97] *Ibid.*, Sec. 68. [98] *Ibid.*, Sec. 65(5).

tory solution can be reached on the question of the contemporary meaning of the double jeopardy clause. The adoption of a compulsory joinder procedure would be a great step forward in this direction, but it would help solve only the question of multiple prosecution, not the issue of multiple punishment, nor would it, of itself, be sufficient to meet the host of other problems which fall under the general heading "double jeopardy."

Furthermore, new double jeopardy problems are arising as new rights are discovered in other clauses of the Bill of Rights or in state constitutions. The status of probation hearings and of rehabilitation commitments of narcotics addicts is thrown into doubt by recent decisions regarding juvenile court hearings. Are all these matters quasi-criminal in character? If they are, double jeopardy would probably apply to them.[99]

Summary and Conclusion

As we have seen, two broad approaches to the reform of double jeopardy law in the United States have been suggested: one, a general codification of the criminal law itself, which would eliminate overlapping and duplicating provisions as much as possible, and, two, a reconstruction of double jeopardy, either through a procedural codification or through a redefinition of the elements of double jeopardy. Each of these methods has its drawbacks, but any attempt to consider double jeopardy apart from the context of the entire body of criminal law and procedure must fall short of success because, as has been noted previously, the significance of double jeopardy is a function of the substantive criminal law and of criminal procedure. Nevertheless, it is encouraging to realize that, for the

[99] The basic decision is *Re Gault,* 387 U.S. 1 (1967). Although juvenile proceedings had not previously been regarded as penal in nature, there may be a hidden second punishment or a second trial possible in many states (see *Hulton* v. *State,* 171 Tex. Crim. 420, 351 S.W.2d 248 [1961]). The states have not regarded probation hearings as double jeopardy (*Settles* v. *State,* 403 S.W. 2d 417 [Tex. 1966]), but, then, commitment of narcotics addicts has not even been deemed penal (*People* v. *Reynoso,* 50 Cal. Reptr. 46, 412 P. 2d 812 [1966]).

first time in the United States, double jeopardy problems are undergoing a period of rational re-examination under the pressure of widespread dissatisfaction with the current state of that body of law.

How successful have the various suggested reforms been in achieving the goal of clarifying double jeopardy? Each of the suggested reforms would, if adopted, represent some improvement over the status quo. From the point of view of brevity, the Model Penal Code is highly commendable and a distinct improvement over the rather rambling 1935 draft. Dession's Code is even more succinct, if relatively incomplete. There is a genuine advantage in having double jeopardy law reduced to as short a statement as possible. Much of the confusion surrounding double jeopardy law is due to the multifarious precedents, which tend to obscure the outcome of a double jeopardy claim. From the point of view of brevity, then, each of the proposed solutions has some advantages worthy of mention.

But conciseness is not the sole concern of the law. Primarily, the law attempts to resolve disputes while safeguarding the interests of the individual as well as of society at large. The policy questions which underlie double jeopardy have not been solved by any single reform suggested. Each has failed, at a different point, to meet the issues raised in the earlier survey of double jeopardy law. The 1935 draft eliminates the concept of attachment of jeopardy, for example, which seems an imaginative step forward. But the draft retains all the old "tests" for the identity of offenses. The Model Penal Code, on the other hand, eliminates the need for some of the "tests," but retains the concept of the attachment of jeopardy. Similarly, the 1935 draft meets the demand of many reformers in extending the right of appeal to the prosecution, while the Model Penal Code would withhold that right. Dession's Code ignores the problem of attachment entirely. All these reform proposals retain the doctrine of lesser-included offenses without examining its foundations. Since all the proposals seem to possess some lapses, it is difficult to choose among them. If one may suggest a single reason for the weaknesses in the proposals it would be that each of them fails to proceed from a consistent policy viewpoint. Various reforms strengthen the defendant's position, others, that of the states. The final product is inconsistent. This factor demonstrates the advantage of Dession's Code, which proceeds from a single, definite view of the relationship between the prosecutor and the accused.

The phrase "double jeopardy" was unknown to English law. The pleas of autrefois acquit and autrefois convict are probably attributable to Blackstone, although the concepts existed before his time. Although many writers have maintained that the policy of double jeopardy is to make certain that "a case once terminated upon its merits would not be reopened and tried again," [100] this is assuredly not an explanation of the goals of double jeopardy policy. The various Latin maxims from which the concept may have been derived demonstrate the different policy aims which are contained in double jeopardy.[101] Much of the confusion which surrounds the implementation of the clause stems from the conflicting policies which it represents.[102] In modern criminal procedure, the primary goal should be a single complete trial including all possible charges. This simple achievement would satisfy the basic needs of double jeopardy policy while assuring the state a complete hearing.

Of all the reform suggestions, that of a compulsory joinder provision would be most helpful. If rigorously applied, it would eliminate the need for tests of identity of offenses in cases of successive trials. In order not to reward the ineffectiveness of the prosecutor's office,

---

[100] J. Miller, *Handbook of Criminal Law* (St. Paul, Minn., 1934), p. 534.

[101] *Nemo debet bis vexari pro una et eadem causa* means that no man shall be twice *vexed* for one and the same offense. This phrase is often used to justify the doctrine of res judicata. But another maxim states: *Nemo debet bis puniri pro uno delicto* (no man should be punished but for one offense), which constitutes a different policy goal.

[102] David Fellman, in reviewing the law of double jeopardy, concludes: "It cannot be denied that the double jeopardy guaranty doctrine is now in a state of considerable confusion" (*The Defendant's Rights* [New York, 1958], p. 202). Professor Fellman agrees that reform is long overdue and that a good start would be a statutory compulsory joinder requirement. Fellman also regards the potential power of the prosecutor as inconsistent with the spirit and purpose of double jeopardy.

however, the defense should bar a second trial for crimes whose commission would have been known to an alert prosecutor. This would place the burden for inefficiency where it belongs—on the shoulders of the state's attorney and not upon the defendant.

The adoption of a compulsory joinder procedure would only touch upon the problem of multiple trials, not of multiple punishment. Assuming that the prosecution is forced to bring all its charges against the defendant in one proceeding, the number of charges and the amount of possible theories of punishment are only limited by the number of statutes actually on the books. It is probably desirable to adopt a solution similar to that employed by almost all the civil law nations, that is, a fixed formula for calculating the maximum punishment to be meted out for the commission of a related series of crimes. The specific formula should be established by each respective legislature. Of course, unrelated crimes and unrelated conduct would not fall under these provisions. The advantage of the civil law system of meting out punishment is that it eliminates the need for tests to determine legislative intent or to create presumptions regarding intent.

The problem of attachment of jeopardy can be eliminated by adopting the English rule requiring final judgment of acquittal or conviction. To do so would destroy some of the protection now available to the defendant, but in the name of insuring a full hearing for both the state and the accused. If procedural limitations are increased so that it is made difficult for the prosecution to withdraw a case once it is begun, much of the justification for this rule would disappear. If the elimination of the attachment doctrine were combined with the compulsory joinder procedure, the basis for a logical and just system of double jeopardy law would be laid. That would make double jeopardy a protection against being tried twice, in a context in which the word "trial" meant a full and fair hearing for the state and the accused.

If the attachment doctrine is retained, it would be necessary to substitute an "extrinsic-intrinsic" test for the exceptions to attachment. The need for exceptions is apparent. Those exceptions should

223

be made on considerations of public policy, so that events extrinsic to the trial and not caused by the defendant should be treated differently from those events which are caused by the defendant, or are procured by him, if they are "intrinsic" to the trial. If an event is beyond the causation of anyone at the trial (extrinsic) and prevents the normal conclusion of the trial, it should not bar a retrial. If the events are "intrinsic," an inquiry should be made to determine whether the defendant was at fault in preventing the normal conclusion of the trial. To continue the current exceptions to the attachment doctrine, as the Model Penal Code provides, would be to perpetuate the inadequacies of many centuries.

In a scheme such as that advanced here, which would eliminate attachment of jeopardy and combine it with a compulsory joinder procedure (for trials and punishments), it is logical to abolish the doctrine which forbids appeal by the state from the acquittal of the defendant. The policy is to insure that the defendant is protected against harassment by the state while insuring a complete and final determination of all matters which flow from a single course of unlawful conduct caused by a particular defendant. Such a policy requires that the right of appeal be employed until all legal matters surrounding that course of conduct be resolved, whether on the intitiative of the state or of the defendant.

It is difficult to justify a duplication of trials on the state and federal levels if the defendant has received a full and fair trial on one or the other level. Since the federal system is an important feature of the American government, however, a reversal of the *Lanza* and *Bartkus* cases might not serve a useful purpose, although it would secure a single complete trial for the defendant in accordance with the literal meaning of the concept. There is no reason, consistent with the policy of a single complete hearing of all criminal offenses flowing out of a single course of conduct, for continuing the institution of multiple trials and multiple punishment except for the existence of the federal system. Many states have already recognized this fact and have reversed the *Lanza* and *Bartkus* cases by statute. Of course, there is less justification for permitting multiple trials for the violation of municipal ordinance and state statutes, since, even as a technical matter, the municipality is a creature of the state.

Because of the currently widespread view of international law on the question, it seems necessary to retain the rule which holds that criminal judgments in foreign courts serve as a bar to subsequent proceedings in the United States. The Model Penal Code is probably in error here on the grounds both of consistency and of international law. There is no reason for the United States to depart from a generally held rule of international law in this instance.

The current meaning of double jeopardy as a criminal doctrine should be retained rather than extending the doctrine into the area of tort law (as Dession would do) or applying the civil doctrine of res judicata (as the Model Code would do). Double jeopardy arose out of the civil law as an answer to specific criminal problems. Its history has always been part of a development separate from the civil law. In fact, the concept arose to meet inadequacies in criminal law and procedure. For this and other reasons already stated, double jeopardy should retain its criminal character together with other fifth amendment rights.

To insure a uniformity of application, the *Palko* decision should be reversed, federal concepts extended. Admittedly, uniformity of double jeopardy law is not an overwhelming necessity, but if a codification of double jeopardy were to take place, this step would help to insure a consistent interpretation of double jeopardy law. On the other hand, such a decision might overburden the federal courts, since double jeopardy is a commonly claimed defense in criminal cases. Currently, the protection of double jeopardy is sometimes restricted to capital cases only, as in Pennsylvania, or made to extend to all minor offenses, as several other states hold.

Assuming that the reform of double jeopardy is necessary, improvements could be achieved in several different ways. Statutory formulas might be prescribed by the legislatures; rule changes by the courts or administrative orders by the executive department could be employed. Of the three, statutory reform would be the most proper channel, since the problem arises, in part, because of statutory punishment alternatives. Changes by court rule could not reach substantive questions, and since the prosecutor is a member of the executive arm of government, it may not be politic, aside from legal questions, to resort to self-restraint. Statutory reform would force public debate of the double jeopardy issue, assuring some popular contribution to resolution of the policy issues.

Double jeopardy is in danger of becoming a meaningless phrase. Almost sixty years ago, one writer noted that the boundaries of double jeopardy were being obscured:

> What are the boundaries within which there is jeopardy, and without which there is no jeopardy? These questions are difficult of solution, and but little help is given either by text-writers or by adjudications of the courts. The cases are mainly confined to the facts at issue, and the textbooks to an enumeration of these facts and cases. No general rule applicable as a test has been given which has not been so cumbered with exceptions as to render the rule useless and unreliable. Yet nothing within the whole domain of the criminal law is of more importance.[103]

This statement is still valid, but could be further amplified to account for twentieth-century additions to the confusion.

Little has been done in the United States to clarify this constitutional concept. Few portions of the Bill of Rights are as litigated, but the significance of double jeopardy remains shrouded in doubt. In some areas of double jeopardy law, the outcome of the defendant's plea is highly unpredictable and the effectiveness of this great liberty is accordingly diminished.

The historical meaning of double jeopardy is also unclear. Although similar to the civil res judicata rule in some ways, its history is more complex because the concept requires the existence of a relatively sophisticated criminal law and criminal procedure. The great English law writers are most responsible for the creation of the principle, although their colonial students in America were the first to raise the concept to constitutional dignity.

Similar double jeopardy rules abound among the common law na-

[103] Harvey, "Former Jeopardy," 10 *Va. L. Rev.* 411 (1904).

tions, providing evidence of the dependency of double jeopardy upon the Anglo-Saxon criminal law and procedure. The problem of double jeopardy is not important in those legal systems which have developed criminal law systems unlike the common law model. This fact throws light upon the possibilities for cure, indicating that codification could be a salutary remedy in England and America.

In American criminal procedure, the outstanding fact is the predominant role of the public prosecutor. This has made the double jeopardy problem more acute in this country, raising some fundamental issues of civil liberties. The direct confrontation of a criminal defendant by the powerful office of the prosecutor requires the development of restraints upon the possible abuses of power. Apart from double jeopardy, there are no restrictions upon the number of times that a person may be tried by the states. With the increase in the number of criminal statutes, double jeopardy protection has become virtually indispensable.

Those differences which exist between English and American versions of double jeopardy can be traced, in part, to the different modes of criminal prosecution. The English prosecution is circumscribed by many legal and customary rules. The need of double jeopardy is not so acute in Great Britain, accounting for the lack of stress placed upon the protection. The American law has, conversely, tended to develop the double jeopardy concept to its fullest extent, as a reaction to the expansion of the powers of the prosecution.

American double jeopardy law has its source in the federal constitution. The divergencies among the states are complicated variations upon the federal theme. As a result, American double jeopardy is rich in legal fictions which surround the protection. But if the concept is to retain its importance as a part of the Bill of Rights, some radical reconsideration is in order.

Double jeopardy law is not esoteric. It is not removed from the pressures and stresses which affect other legal concepts. From time to time certain concepts decay while others may take on a new and heightened meaning. From this vantage point it seems that double jeopardy law is about to undergo some profound changes which could influence the meaning and value of the concept for many years to come. There will be those who will be happy to discard a clause which, to them, appears to be an outworn relic from another day, while there will be others who will see in double jeopardy one potential bulwark of individual rights against an increasingly powerful state. The meaning of this portion of the Bill of Rights has been challenged. The time to respond to the challenge may be at hand.

» «

Bibliography

PRIMARY SOURCES

Constitutions

Arkansas. Constitution (1874).
Colorado. Constitution (1876).
Delaware. Constitution of 1792.
Florida. Constitution (1887).
Georgia. Constitution of 1777.
India. Constitution (1950).
Iowa. Constitution of 1857.
Japan. Constitution (1947).
Kansas. Constitution (1861).
Louisiana. Constitution (1921).
Massachusetts. Constitution of 1780.
Michigan. Constitution (1909).
Mississippi. Constitution (1890).
Missouri. Constitution (1945).
New Hampshire. Constitution of 1784.
———. Constitution of 1842.
New Jersey. Constitution of 1844.
———. Constitution (1947).
New Mexico. Constitution (1912).
New York. Constitution (1895).
Ohio. Constitution (1851).
Pennsylvania. Constitution of 1776.
———. Constitution of 1790.
———. Constitution (1874).

Rhode Island. Constitution (1843).

Texas. Constitution (1876).

United States of America. Constitution (1789).

Vermont. Constitution of 1777.

Wyoming. Constitution (1890).

Cases

Abbate v. *United States,* 359 U.S. 187 (1959).

Adamo v. *Several Justices of Supreme Court,* 280 N.Y.S.2d. 749 (A.D. 1967).

Adamson v. *California,* 332 U.S. 46 (1947).

Adkins v. *Commonwealth,* 175 Va. 590, 9 S.E.2d 349 (1940).

Alarion v. *State,* 2 Tex. Crim. 288, 242 S.W. 1056 (1922).

Albrecht v. *United States,* 273 U.S. 1 (1927).

Altenburg v. *Commonwealth,* 126 Pa. 602, 117 A. 799 (1889).

American Tobacco Company v. *United States,* 328 U.S. 781 (1946).

Ancrim v. *Camden Water, Light & Ice Co.,* 82 S.C. 284, 64 S.E. 151 (1909).

Anderson v. *Bishop,* 304 Mass. 396, 23 N.E.2d 1103 (1939).

Anderson v. *State,* 86 Md. 479, 38 A. 937 (1897).

Application of McNeer, 173 Cal. App. 530, 343 P.2d 304 (1960).

Application of Williams, 85 Ariz. 109, 333 P.2d 280 (1959).

Ashford v. *Thornton,* 1 B. and Ald. 405 (Gr. Brit. 1818).

Badders v. *United States,* 240 U.S. 391, 36 S. Ct. 367 (1916).

Ball v. *United States,* 163 U.S. 662 (1895).

Barnett v. *People,* 53 Ill. 325 (1870).

Barron v. *Baltimore,* 32 U.S. (7 Pet.) 242 (1833).

Bartkus v. *Illinois,* 359 U.S. 121 (1959).

Bartlett v. *United States,* 166 F.2d 928 (10th Cir. 1948).

Barton v. *State,* 58 Ga. App. 354, 199 S.E. 357 (1938).

Bassing v. *Cady,* 208 U.S. 386 (1907).

Bell v. *United Sates,* 349 U.S. 81 (1954).

Blockenburger v. *United States,* 284 U.S. 299 (1932).

Board of Supervisors v. *Simpson,* 36 Cal. 2d 671, 227 P.2d 14 (1951).

Bohanan v. *State,* 18 Neb. 57 (1885).

Bozza v. *United States,* 330 U.S. 160 (1947).

Brack v. *Wells,* 184 Md. 86, 40 A.2d 319 (1944).

Bragan v. *State,* 243 Ala. 102, 8 So.2d 596 (1941).

Brandenburg v. *Steele*, 177 F.2d 279 (8th Cir. 1949).

Brantley v. *Georgia*, 217 U.S. 284 (1910).

Brock v. *North Carolina*, 344 U.S. 424 (1953).

Brown v. *Hallowell*, 197 Iowa 1352, 199 N.W. 257 (1924).

Brown v. *Walker*, 161 U.S. 591 (1896).

Bryan v. *United States*, 338 U.S. 552 (1952).

Buller v. *Windover*, 1 D.L.R. 986 (Can. 1931).

Burdue v. *Commonwealth*, 144 Ky. 428, 138 S.W. 296 (1911).

Burton v. *United States*, 202 U.S. 344 (1906).

Callanan v. *United States*, 364 U.S. 587 (1961).

Calvaresi v. *United States*, 216 F.2d 891 (10th Cir. 1954).

Capone v. *United States*, 51 F.2d 604 (7th Cir. 1931).

Carrizo de Crespo v. *Laserna Pinzon*, 52 Gaceta Judicial 796 (Colom. 1941).

Carroll v. *United States*, 354 U.S. 394 (1957).

Carter v. *McClaughry*, 183 U.S. 365 (1901).

City of Frankfort v. *Aughie*, 114 Ind. 77, 15 N.E. 902 (1888).

City of Macon v. *Massey*, 214 Ga. 589, 106 S.E.2d 23 (1959).

City of Milwaukee v. *Johnson*, 192 Wis. 585, 213 N.E. 335 (1927).

City of Trenton v. *New Jersey*, 262 U.S. 182 (1923).

Ciucci v. *Illinois*, 356 U.S. 571 (1958).

Clawens v. *Rives*, 104 F.2d 240 (D.C. Cir. 1939).

Clem v. *State*, 42 Ind. 420 (1873).

Coleman v. *Tennessee*, 97 U.S. 509 (1878).

Collins v. *Loisel*, 262 U.S. 426 (1922).

Commonwealth v. *Arner*, 149 Pa. 35, 24 A. 83 (1892).

Commonwealth v. *Arnold*, 83 Ky. 1 (1884).

Commonwealth v. *Bressant*, 126 Mass. 246 (1879).

Commonwealth v. *Burk*, 2 Pa. County Ct. 12 (1885).

Commonwealth v. *Cook*, 6 S. & R. 577 (Pa. 1822).

Commonwealth v. *Crecorian*, 264 Mass. 94, 162 A. 7 (1928).

Commonwealth v. *Dietrick*, 221 Pa. 7, 70 A. 275 (1908).

Commonwealth v. *Ellis*, 160 Mass. 165, 135 N.E. 455 (1893).

Commonwealth v. *Fitzpatrick*, 121 Pa. 109, 165 A. 498 (1888).

Commonwealth v. *Kingsbury*, 5 Mass. 106 (1809).

Commonwealth v. *Ladusaw*, 226 Ky. 386, 105 S.W.2d 1089 (1928).

Commonwealth v. *Perrow*, 124 Va. 806, 97 S.E. 280 (1919).

Commonwealth v. *Purchase*, 2 Pick. 521 (Mass. 1824).

Commonwealth v. *Roby,* 14 Pick. 496 (Mass. 1832).

Commonwealth v. *Simpson,* 310 Pa. 310, 165 A. 498 (1932).

Commonwealth v. *Thatcher,* 364 Pa. 326, 69 A.2d 619 (1950).

Commonwealth v. *Wilkerson,* 201 Ky. 729, 258 S.W. 297 (1922).

Cook v. *State,* 60 Ala. 39 (1877).

Cook v. *State,* 43 Tex. Crim. App. 182, 63 S.W. 872 (1901).

Copperthwaite v. *United States,* 37 F.2d 846 (6th Cir. 1930).

Correro v. *United States,* 48 F.2d 69 (9th Cir. 1931).

Dandy v. *State,* 138 Tenn. 364, 13 S.W.2d 794 (1929).

Davis v. *People,* 22 Colo. 1, 125 P. 855 (1895).

Davis v. *State,* 37 Tex. Crim. 359, 38 S.W. 616 (1897).

Denham v. *Robinson,* 72 W. Va. 243, 77 S.E. 970 (1913).

District of Columbia v. *Buckley,* 128 F.2d 17 (D.C. Cir. 1942).

Dreyer v. *Illinois,* 187 U.S. 71 (1902).

Dreyer v. *People,* 188 Ill. 40, 58 N.E.2d 728 (1949).

Dunn v. *United States,* 284 U.S. 390 (1931).

Dykes v. *State,* 232 Miss. 379, 299 So.2d 602 (1957).

Ellis v. *State,* 105 Ala. 72, 17 So. 179 (1894).

Erie R.R. v. *Tompkins,* 304 U.S. 64 (1938).

Estep v. *State,* 11 Okla. Crim. 103, 143 P. 64 (1914).

Everson v. *State,* 66 Neb. 154, 92 N.W. 137 (1902).

Ex parte Bain, 121 U.S. 1 (1887).

Ex parte Duesenberg v. *Rudolph,* 325 Mo. 881, 30 S.W.2d 94 (1930).

Ex parte Gano, 90 Kan. 134, 132 P. 999 (1913).

Ex parte Herren, 191 Cal. 457, 217 P. 728 (1923).

Ex parte Lange, 85 U.S. (18 Wall.) 163 (1873).

Ex parte McLeod, 23 Idaho 257, 128 P. 1106 (1913).

Ex parte Resler, 115 Neb. 335, 212 N.W. 765 (1927).

Ex parte Spencer, 2 Commw. L.R. 250 (Austl. 1905).

Factor v. *Laubenheimer,* 290 U.S. 276 (1933).

Fall v. *State,* 49 F.2d 506 (D.C. Cir. 1931).

Flahaven v. *Allen,* 5 Misc. 2d 1063, 274 N.Y.S.2d 703 (Sup. Ct. 1966).

Fleischer v. *United States,* 91 F.2d 404 (6th Cir. 1939).

Fong Foo v. *United States,* 369 U.S. 141 (1961).

Foran v. *State,* 195 Ind. 55, 144 N.E. 429 (1924).

Forman v. *United States,* 361 U.S. 416 (1960).

Fox v. *Ohio,* 46 U.S. (5 How.) 410 (1847).

Frank v. *Magnum,* 237 U.S. 309 (1915).

French v. *State,* 139 Tenn. 451, 288 S.W. 601 (1929).

Garland v. *State,* 101 Ga. 395, 114 S.E.2d 176 (1960).

Gavieres v. *United States,* 220 U.S. 338 (1911).

Gilbert v. *State,* 19 Ala. App. 104, 95 So. 502 (1923).

Gillespie v. *State,* 168 Ind. 298, 180 N.E. 829 (1907).

Gilpin v. *State,* 142 Md. 464, 121 A. 354 (1923).

Giuseppe v. *Walling,* 144 F.2d 608 (2d Cir. 1944).

Goetz v. *United States,* 39 F.2d 902 (5th Cir. 1930).

Goodall v. *United States,* 180 F.2d 397 (D.C. Cir. 1950).

Goodman v. *McLennan,* 334 Ill. App. 405, 80 N.E.2d 396 (1948).

Gore v. *United States,* 357 U.S. 386 (1958).

Gori v. *United States,* 367 U.S. 364 (1961).

Graff v. *People,* 208 Ill. 321, 70 N.E. 299 (1904).

Grafton v. *United States,* 206 U.S. 333 (1907).

Graham v. *West Virginia,* 224 U.S. 616 (1912).

Gray v. *State,* 14 F.2d 366 (8th Cir. 1926).

Green v. *State,* 147 Tenn. 299, 247 S.W. 84 (1923).

Green v. *United States,* 218 F.2d 856 (D.C. Cir. 1955).

Green v. *United States,* 236 F.2d 708 (D.C. Cir. 1956).

Green v. *United States,* 355 U.S. 184 (1957).

Gunter v. *State,* 111 Ala. 23, 20 So. 632 (1896).

H. M. Advocate v. *Cobb,* 1 Swin. 354 (Scot. 1836).

H. M. Advocate v. *Stewart,* 5 Irv. 310 (Scot 1866).

Hall v. *State,* 134 Ala. 90, 32 S. 750 (1902).

Harris v. *State,* 193 Ga. 109, 17 S.E.2d 573 (1941).

Hartson v. *United States,* 14 F.2d 561 (2d Cir. 1944).

Hawker v. *New York,* 170 U.S. 189 (1898).

Hazlewood v. *State,* 42 Okla. Crim. 38 (1929).

Helvering v. *Mitchell,* 303 U.S. 391 (1937).

Hilands v. *Commonwealth,* 29 Pa. 323 (1857).

Hill v. *Texas,* 316 U.S. 400 (1942).

Himmelfarb v. *United States,* 175 F.2d 924 (9th Cir. 1949).

Hoag v. *New Jersey,* 356 U.S. 464 (1958).

Hobbs v. *Commonwealth,* 156 Ky. 847, 162 S.W. 104 (1914).

Hoffman v. *State,* 20 Md. 434 (1863).

Holiday v. *Johnson,* 313 U.S. 342 (1940).

Holt v. *State,* 160 Tenn. 366, 24 S.W. 824 (1930).

Hoopengarner v. *United States,* 270 F.2d 465 (6th Cir. 1959).

Hourigan v. *State*, 38 Okla. Crim. 11, 258 P. 1057 (1927).

Houston v. *Moore*, 18 U.S. (5 Wheat.) 1 (1820).

Hulton v. *State*, 171 Tex. Crim. 420, 351 S.W.2d 248 (1961).

Hurtado v. *California*, 110 U.S. 516 (1884).

In re Chapman, 166 U.S. 661 (1897).

In re Gottesfeld, 245 Pa. St. 314, 291 A. 494 (1914).

In the matter of Somers, 31 Nev. 531, 103 P. 1073 (1909).

Ingram v. *United States*, 272 F.2d 567 (4th Cir. 1959).

Irvin v. *State*, 7 Tex. App. 78 (1879).

Jarl v. *United States*, 19 F.2d 891 (8th Cir. 1927).

Jay v. *State*, 15 Ala. App. 255, 73 So. 137 (1916).

Jeffries v. *State*, 40 Ala. 381 (1867).

Jerome v. *United States*, 318 U.S. 101 (1943).

Johnson v. *State*, 29 Ark. 31 (1874).

Johnson v. *Zerbst*, 304 U.S. 458 (1938).

Jones v. *Commonwealth*, 124 Ky. 26, 197 S.W. 1118 (1906).

Jones v. *State*, 83 Ariz. 284, 320 S.W.2d 645 (1959).

Kalawati v. *Himichal Pradesh*, 16 India S. Ct. 144 (Ind. 1953).

Keerl v. *Montana*, 213 U.S. 135 (1909).

Kepner v. *United States*, 195 U.S. 100 (1904).

Kessinger v. *State*, 423 P.2d 888 (Okla. 1967).

King v. *Edwards*, 4 Taunt. Rep. 309, 128 Eng. Rep. 348 (Gr. Brit. 1812).

King v. *Mawbey*, 6 Term. R. 619, 101 Eng. Rep. 736 (Gr. Brit. K.B. 1796).

King v. *Scalbert*, 2 Leach. 620 (Gr. Brit. 1794).

King v. Stevenson, 2 Leach. 546 (Gr. Brit. 1791).

King v. *Tonks*, I K.B. 443 (Gr. Brit. 1916).

Ladner v. *United States*, 358 U.S. 169 (1958).

Lewis v. *United States*, 4 F.2d 520 (5th Cir. 1925).

Louisiana ex rel. *Frances* v. *Resweber*, 329 U.S. 459 (1947).

Lovato v. *New Mexico*, 242 U.S. 199 (1916).

Lovern v. *State*, 140 Miss. 635, 105 S. 769 (1925).

Lunsford v. *State*, 187 Ga. 162, 199 S.E. 808 (1939).

McCarn v. *State*, 82 Okla. Crim. 374, 170 P.2d 562 (1949).

McCreary v. *Commonwealth*, 29 Pa. 323 (1857).

McCrosky v. *State*, 17 Ala. App. 523, 87 So. 219 (1920).

McDonald v. *Massachusetts*, 180 U.S. 311 (1901).

McFadden v. *Commonwealth*, 23 Pa. 12 (1853).

McInerny v. *City of Denver*, 17 Colo. 302, 77 P. 862 (1892).

Malloy v. *Hogan*, 378 U.S. 1 (1964).

Marshall v. *State*, 6 Neb. 120 (1877).

Martinis v. *Supreme Court*, 15 N.Y.2d 246, 206 N.E.2d 165 (1965).

Maxwell v. *Dow*, 176 U.S. 581 (1900).

Mayor of Mobile v. *Allaire*, 14 Ala. 400 (1848).

Miranda v. *Arizona*, 384 U.S. 436 (1966).

Mitchell v. *State*, 140 Ala. 118, 37 So. 76 (1904).

Moore v. *Missouri*, 159 U.S. 673 (1895).

Morey v. *Commonwealth*, 108 Mass. 433 (1871).

Morgan v. *Devine*, 237 U.S. 632 (1914).

Morgan v. *State*, 28 Ga. App. 358, 111 S.E. 72 (1922).

Moss v. *State*, 16 Ala. App. 34, 75 So. 179 (1917).

Mount v. *State*, 14 Ohio 295 (1846).

Mullins v. *Commonwealth*, 216 Ky. 182, 286 S.W. 1042 (1926).

Murdock v. *State*, 155 Tex. Crim. 359, 235 S.W.2d 163 (1950).

Murphy v. *Massachusetts*, 177 U.S. 155 (1900).

Murphy v. *United States*, 285 F. 801 (7th Cir. 1923).

Murray & Sorenson, Inc. v. *United States*, 207 F.2d 119 (1st Cir. 1953).

Mutual Benefit Life Insurance Company v. *Tisdale*, 91 U.S. 238 (1876).

Neal v. *State of California*, 55 Cal. 2d 11, 19, 357 P.2d 539, 843–44 (1960)

Nielson v. *Oregon*, 212 U.S. 315 (1909).

Palko v. *Connecticut*, 302 U.S. 319 (1937).

Parks v. *State*, 21 Ga. App. 506, 94 S.E. 581 (1917).

Patton v. *United States*, 281 U.S. 276 (1930).

Peavey v. *State*, 153 Ga. 119, 111 S.E. 420 (1922).

Pennsylvania v. *Nelson*, 350 U.S. 497 (1956).

People v. *Albers*, 137 Mich. 678, 100 N.W. 908 (1904).

People v. *Andrae*, 305 Ill. 530, 137 N.E. 496 (1922).

People v. *Arenstein*, 128 Misc. 176, 218 N.Y.S. 633 (Ct. Gen. Sess. 1926).

People v. *Barrett*, 2 Cai. R. 304 (N.Y. 1805).

People v. *Calloway*, 74 Ill. App. 2d 418, 221 N.E.2d 73 (1966).

People v. *Clensey*, 97 Cal. App. 71, 274 P. 1018 (1929).

People v. *Devlin*, 143 Cal. 128, 76 P. 900 (1904).

People v. *Dowling*, 84 N.Y. 478 (1881).

People v. *Eklof,* 179 Misc. 536, 41 N.Y.S.2d 557 (1942).

People v. *Farrell,* 146 Mich. 264, 109 N.W. 440 (1906).

People v. *Gibson,* 53 Colo. 231, 125 P. 531 (1912).

People v. *Grzesezak,* 77 Misc. 202, 137 N.Y.S. 538 (Nassau County Ct. 1912).

People v. *Head,* 103 Cal. App. 465, 234 P.2d 103 (1951).

People v. *Hickman,* 204 Cal. 470, 268 P. 909 (1928).

People v. *Higgins,* 59 Cal. 357 (1881).

People v. *Johnson,* 81 Mich. 573, 45 N.W. 1119 (1890).

People v. *Keeper,* 65 Cal. 232 (1884).

People v. *Knowles,* 35 Cal. 2d 175, 217 P.2d 1 (1950).

People v. *Laws,* 29 Ill. 2d 221, 193 N.E.2d 806 (1963).

People ex rel. *LeRoy* v. *Hurlbut,* 24 Mich. 44 (1871).

People v. *McDaniel,* 154 Cal. App. 2d 475, 316 P.2d 660 (1957).

People v. *McFarlane,* 138 Cal. 481, 71 P. 568 (1903).

People v. *Majado,* 22 Cal. App. 2d 323, 70 P.2d 1015 (1937).

People v. *Majors,* 55 Cal. 138, 3 P. 597 (1884).

People v. *Marshall,* 48 A.C. 392, 309 P.2d 456 (1957).

People v. *Miller,* 143 App. Div. 251, 128 N.Y.S. 549 (1911).

People v. *Miner,* 144 Ill. 308, 33 N.E. 40 (1893).

People v. *Moore,* 143 Cal. App. 2d 333, 299 P.2d 691 (1956).

People v. *Newcomer,* 284 Ill. 315, 120 N.E. 244 (1918).

People v. *Perry,* 99 Cal. App. 90, 221 P.2d 120 (1950).

People v. *Reynoso,* 50 Cal. Reptr. 46, 412 P.2d 812 (1966).

People v. *Rulloff,* 5 Park. Crim. 77 (N.Y. 1860).

People v. *Savarese,* 201 App. Div. 401, 114 N.Y.S.2d 816 (1952).

People v. *Stephens,* 79 Cal. 428, 21 P. 856 (1889).

People v. *Taylor,* 117 *Mich.* 583, 176 N.W. 158 (1898).

People v. *Webb,* 211 Cal. 143, 323 P.2d 141 (1958).

Perdue v. *State,* 134 Ga. 300, 67 S.E. 810 (1910).

Pereira v. *United States,* 347 U.S. 1 (1953).

Perkins v. *State,* 65 Tex. Crim. 311, 144 S.W. 241 (1912).

Peters v. *Hobby,* 349 U.S. 331 (1955).

Petite v. *United States,* 147 F. Supp. 791 (1959).

Petite v. *United States,* 262 F.2d 788 (D.C. Cir. 1959).

Petite v. *United States,* 361 U.S. 529 (1960).

Pinkerton v. *United States,* 328 U.S. 640 (1946).

Piquett v. *United States,* 81 F.2d 75 (7th Cir. 1936).

Poole v. *Queen,* 3 W.L.R. 770 (Kenya 1960).

Preemam v. *United States,* 244 F.1 (2d Cir. 1917).

Prescott v. *State,* 52 Tex. Crim. 35, 105 S.W. 192 (1907).

Provincial Secy. v. *Egan,* 1 D.L.R. 291 (Can. 1941).

Queen v. *Button,* 11 Q.B. 929, 116 Eng. Rep. 720 (Gr. Brit. 1848).

Queen v. *Chadwick,* II Ad. and El. N.S. 205, 115 Eng. Rep. 201 (Gr. Brit. 1847).

R. v. *Baillee,* 10 State Tr. 647 (Gr. Brit. 1684).

R. v. *Barron,* 2 K.B. 570 (Gr. Brit. 1914).

R. v. *Birdseye,* 4 Ct. P. 386, 172 Eng. Rep. 751 (Gr. Brit. 1830).

R. v. *Bond,* 3 D.L.R. 769 (Can. 1936).

R. v. *Burke,* 47 Ir. L.T.R. 111 (Ire. 1912).

R. v. *Carrier,* 104 Can. Crim. Cas. 75 (Can. 1951).

R. v. *Charlesworth,* 1 B. and S. 460, 121 Eng. Rep. 786 (Gr. Brit. 1861).

R. v. *Chew Deb,* 9 D.L.R. 27 (Can. 1953).

R. v. *Dagnes,* 3 J.P. 293 (Gr. Brit. 1839).

R. v. *Emden,* 9 East. 437, 103 Eng. Rep. 640 (Gr. Brit. 1808).

R. v. *Glenfield,* 1 D.L.R. 37 (Can. 1935).

R. v. *Hennessey,* 2 C.A. 243 (N.Z. 1873).

R. v. *Hill,* 7 Can. Crim. Cas. 38 (Can. 1901).

R. v. *Kelijana,* 30 Nigeria L.R. 437 (S. Afr. 1909).

R. v. *King,* 1 Q.B. 214 (Gr. Brit. 1897).

R. v. *Kissick,* 3 D.L.R. 431, 78 Can. Crim. Cas. 34 (Can. 1942).

R. v. *Lamantagne,* 84 Can. Crim. Cas. 225 (Can. 1941).

R. v. *Lemen,* 6 N.Z.L.R. 329 (N.Z. 1888).

R. v. *Lester,* 27 Crim. App. 8 (Gr. Brit. 1938).

R. v. *Logan,* 81 Can. Crim. Cas. 97 (Can. 1844).

R. v. *Nirmal Kanta Roy,* 1 Indian L.R. 41 (Ind. 1914).

R. v. *Pyne,* 6 J.P. 508 (Gr. Brit. 1842).

R. v. *Quinn,* 10 Can. Crim. Cas. 412 (Can. 1904).

R. v. *Roche,* 1 Leach C.C. 134, 168 Eng. Rep. 169 (Gr. Brit. 1775).

R. v. *Sheen,* 2 C. and P. 634, 172 Eng. Rep. 287 (Gr. Brit. 1827).

R. v. *Sirois,* 27 N.B. 610 (Can. 1887).

R. v. *Sugar,* 90 Eng. Rep. 554 (K.B. 1696).

R. v. *Twalatunga,* 20 S.C. 425 (S. Afr. 1903).

R. v. *Tyrone,* 2 Ir. R. 44, 13 Mews 78 (Ire. 1912).

R. v. *Whitebread,* 7 State Tr. 311 (Gr. Brit. 1679).

Rakes v. *United States,* 169 F.2d 739 (7th Cir. 1946).

Rambo v. *State,* 38 Okla. Crim. 192, 259 P. 602 (1927).

Re Gault, 387 U.S. 1 (1967).

Reid v. *Covert,* 354 U.S. 1 (1957).

Respublica v. *Schaffer,* 1 Dall. 137 (Pa. 1788).

Rex Trailer Co. v. *United States,* 350 U.S. 148 (1956).

Richardson v. *State,* 56 Ark. 367, 19 S.W. 1052 (1892).

Roark v. *United States,* 17 F.2d 570 (8th Cir. 1927).

Robb v. *State,* 190 Md. 641, 60 A.2d 211 (1947).

Roberts v. *State,* 14 Ga. 8 (1853).

Rocha v. *United States,* 288 F.2d 245 (9th Cir. 1961).

Rosser v. *State,* 159 Va. 128, 167 S.E. 257 (1933).

Ruffin v. *State,* 29 Ga. App. 214, 114 S.E. 581 (1922).

Samson v. *Zerbst,* 73 F.2d 670 (10th Cir. 1934).

Sanford v. *Robbins,* 115 F.2d 435 (5th Cir. 1940).

Sapir v. *United States,* 348 U.S. 373 (1955).

Scalf v. *Commonwealth,* 95 Ky. 830, 243 S.W. 1034 (1922).

Settles v. *State,* 403 S.W.2d 417 (Tex. 1966).

Shoerer v. *Pennsylvania,* 207 U.S. 188 (1907).

Short v. *United States,* 91 F.2d 614 (4th Cir. 1937).

Simmons v. *United States,* 142 U.S. 148 (1891).

Slaughter v. *State,* 6 Humph. 410 (Tenn. 1846).

Smith v. *Commonwealth,* 17 Ky. L. Rep. 7, 32 S.W. 137 (1895)

Smith v. *State,* 158 Miss. 355, 128 So. 891 (1930).

Spano v. *New York,* 370 U.S. 315 (1959).

State v. *Ash,* 69 Wash. 194, 122 P. 995 (1912).

State v. *Banter,* 80 Idaho 552, 335 P.2d 887 (1960).

State v. *Battle,* 148 S.E.2d 599 (N.C. 1966).

State v. *Benham,* 7 Conn. 414 (1829).

State v. *Billete,* 104 Ohio St. 13, 135 N.E. 285 (1922).

State v. *Blackledge,* 216 Iowa 199, 243 N.W. 534 (1932).

State v. *Blackman,* 35 La. 403 (1883).

State v. *Bradley,* 67 Vt. 465, 32 A. 238 (1894).

State v. *Brownrigg,* 87 Me. 500, 33 A. 11 (1895).

State v. *Brunn,* 22 Wash. 2d 120, 154 P.2d 826 (1945).

State v. *Calendine,* 8 Iowa 288 (1859).

State v. *Carabetta,* 106 Conn. 114, 137 A. 394 (1927).

State v. *Coblentz,* 169 Md. 159, 180 A. 266 (1935).

State v. *Colgate*, 31 Kan. 511, 3 P. 346 (1884).

State v. *Corbett*, 117 S.C. 356, 109 S.E. 133 (1921).

State v. *Corimer*, 46 N.J. 494, 218 A. 2d 138 (1966).

State v. *Cosgrove*, 103 N.J.L. 412, 131 A. 402 (1927).

State v. *Crook*, 16 Utah 212, 51 P. 1091 (1898).

State v. *Cross*, 44 W. Va. 315, 29 S.E. 527 (1897).

State ex rel. *Dato* v. *Himes*, 134 Fla. 675, 184 So. 244 (1938).

State v. *DeGraffenreid*, 9 Baxt. 287 (Tenn. 1878).

State v. *Deso*, 110 Vt. 1, 1 A.2d 710 (1938).

State v. *Dickson*, 200 Iowa 17, 202 N.W. 225 (1925).

State v. *Duvall*, 135 La. 710, 165 So. 104 (1914).

State v. *Elder*, 41 Me. 165 (1865).

State v. *Emery*, 59 Vt. 84, 7 A. 129 (1886).

State v. *Empey*, 65 Utah 609, 239 P. 25 (1925).

State v. *Farmer*, 48 N.J. 145, 224 A.2d 481 (1966).

State v. *Felch*, 92 Vt. 477, 105 A. 23 (1918).

State v. *Findling*, 123 Minn. 413, 144 N.W. 142 (1913).

State v. *Fitzsimmons*, 59 N.J. Super. 478, 158 A.2d 73 (1960).

State v. *Friedlund*, 200 Minn. 44, 273 N.W. 353 (1935).

State v. *Gillis*, 73 S.C. 318, 53 S.E. 487 (1905).

State v. *Green*, 111 Mo. 585, 20 S.W. 304 (1892).

State v. *Horville*, 171 La. 258, 130 So. 348 (1930).

State v. *Hoag*, 21 N.J. 496, 87 A.2d 79 (1955).

State v. *Houchins*, 102 W. Va. 169, 134 S.E. 790 (1926).

State v. *I.S.S.*, Tyler's Rep., Case No. 178 (Vt. 1801).

State v. *Johnson*, 212 N.C. 566, 194 S.E. 319 (1937).

State ex rel. *Johnston* v. *Foster*, 32 Kan. 14, 3 P. 534 (1883).

State v. *Jones*, 7 Ga. 422 (1849).

State v. *Kennedy*, 96 Miss. 624, 50 So. 978 (1910).

State v. *Kessler*, 15 Utah 142, 49 P. 293 (1897).

State v. *Labato*, 7 N.J. 137, 80 A.2d 617 (1951).

State v. *Learned*, 73 Kan. 328, 85 P. 293 (1906).

State v. *LeBlanc*, 160 La. 1053, 108 So. 87 (1926).

State v. *Lee*, 65 Conn. 265, 30 A. 1110 (1894).

State v. *Lewis*, 226 N.C. 249, 37 S.E. 691 (1946).

State v. *McCord*, 8 Kan. 232 (1871).

State v. *McCrary*, 365 Mo. 799, 287 S.W.2d 785 (1956).

State v. *McGarrity*, 140 La. 436, 73 So. 259 (1916).

239

State v. *M'Kee*, 17 S.C.L. 651 (1830).

State v. *Mark*, 23 N.J. 162, 128 A.2d 487 (1957).

State v. *Matthews*, 142 N.C. 621, 55 S.E. 342 (1906).

State v. *Mayberry*, 48 Me. 218 (1839).

State v. *Midgely*, 28 N.J. Super. 474, 101 A.2d 51 (1953).

State v. *Moor*, 1 Miss. 134 (1823).

State v. *Morse*, 229 A.2d 232 (Vt. 1967).

State v. *Mowser*, 92 N.J.L. 474, 106 A. 416 (1919).

State v. *Nash*, 86 N.C. 650 (1882).

State v. *Naylor*, 28 Del. 99, 90 A. 880 (1914).

State v. *Nolon*, 129 Wash. 284, 224 P. 932 (1924).

State v. *Norvell*, 2 Yerg. 24 (Tenn. 1820).

State v. *O'Brien*, 106 Vt. 97, 170 A. 98 (1934).

State v. *Osborne*, 413 S.W.2d 571 (Mo. 1967).

State v. *Pace*, 210 Miss. 448, 49 So. 2d 710 (1950).

State v. *Panchuck*, 53 N.D. 669, 207 N.W. 991 (1926).

State v. *Parish*, 43 Wis. 395 (1877).

State v. *Parman*, 101 Ken. 115, 165 P. 663 (1919).

State v. *Pa. R.R. Co.*, 9 N.J. 194, 87 A.2d 709 (1952).

State v. *Phillips*, 27 Ariz. 349, 223 P. 568 (1925).

State v. *Pianfetti*, 79 Vt. 236, 65 A. 84 (1906).

State v. *Poe*, 214 La. 606, 38 So.2d 359 (1948).

State v. *Preto*, 51 N.J. Super. 175, 144 A. 919 (1958).

State v. *Price*, 127 Iowa 301, 103 N.W. 195 (1905).

State v. *Ragan*, 123 Kan. 399, 256 P. 169 (1927).

State v. *Reinhard*, 202 Iowa 168, 209 N.W. 419 (1926).

State v. *Richardson*, 47 S.C. 106, 25 S.E. 220 (1896).

State v. *Roberts*, 152 La. 283, 93 So. 95 (1922).

State v. *Rose*, 72 N.J.L. 462, 62 A. 695 (1905).

State v. *Seingood*, 80 Vt. 412, 68 A. 51 (1907).

State v. *Shimmon*, 122 Ohio St. 522, 172 N.E. 367 (1930).

State v. *Simpson*, 78 N.D. 360, 49 N.W.2d 777 (1951).

State v. *Soloman*, 93 Utah 70, 71 P.2d 104 (1937).

State v. *Stanker*, 3 Conn. Cir. 580, 222 A.2d 356 (1966).

State v. *Steeves*, 29 Ore. 85, 43 P. 947 (1896).

State v. *Swain*, 147 Ore. 207, 36 P.2d 211 (1934).

State v. *Thierfelder*, 114 Mont. 104, 132 P.2d 1035 (1942).

State v. *Thompson*, 241 Minn. 59, 62 N.W.2d 512 (1954).

State v. *Vandemark*, 77 Conn. 201, 58 A. 715 (1904).

State v. *Van Horton*, 26 Iowa 402 (1868).

State v. *Van Ness*, 82 N.J.L. 181, 83 A. 195 (1912).

State v. *Vines*, 34 La. App. 1079 (1882).

State v. *Vornado*, 124 La. 711, 50 A. 661 (1909).

State v. *Walker*, 133 Iowa 489, 110 N.W. 125 (1907).

State v. *Ward*, 422 P.2d 961 (Kan. 1967).

State v. *Waterman*, 87 Iowa 255, 54 N.W. 359 (1893).

State v. *Way*, 76 Kan. 928, 93 P. 159 (1907).

State v. *Winne*, 12 N.J. 152, 96 A.2d 63 (1953).

State v. *Witte*. 243 Wis. 423, 10 N.W.2d 117 (1943).

State v. *Wyse*, 33 S.C. 582, 10 S.E. 827 (1890).

Steen v. *State*, 92 Tex. Crim. 99, 242 S.W. 1047 (1922).

Steinberg v. *United States*, 14 F.2d 564 (2d Cir. 1926).

Stewart v. *State*, 35 Tex. Crim. 174, 32 S.W. 766 (1895).

Stone v. *United States*, 167 U.S. 178 (1897).

Strobhan v. *State*, 55 Fla. 167, 47 So. 4 (1908).

Stroud v. *United States*, 251 U.S. 15 (1919).

Strout v. *State*, 36 Okla. 744, 78 P. 553 (1913).

Taylor v. *Curry*, 215 Ga. 734, 113 S.E.2d 398 (1960).

Taylor v. *State*, 4 Tex. Crim. 29 (1898).

Thomas v. *State*, 76 Ga. App. 637, 67 S.E. 894 (1910).

Thompson v. *United States*, 155 U.S. 271 (1894).

Tomlin v. *State*, 155 Tex. Crim. 207, 233 S.W.2d 333 (1950).

Toth v. *Quarles*, 350 U.S. 11 (1955).

Trono v. *United States*, 199 U.S. 521 (1905).

Trop v. *Dulles*, 356 U.S. 86 (1958).

Turner v. *Territory*, 16 Okla. Crim. 557, 82 P. 650 (1905).

Twining v. *New Jersey*, 211 U.S. 78 (1908).

Tyler v. *People*, 8 Mich. 320 (1860).

Ullman v. *United States*, 350 U.S. 422 (1956).

United States v. *Accardo*, 113 F. Supp. 783 (D.N.J. 1953).

United States v. *Aurandt*, 15 N.M. 292, 107 P. 1064 (1909).

United States v. *Baker*, 61 F.2d 469 (2d Cir. 1932).

United States v. *Ball*, 163 U.S. 662 (1896).

United States v. *Bayer*, 331 U.S. 532 (1947).

United States v. *Ben Grunstein & Sons,* 127 F. Supp. 907 (D.N.J. 1955).

United States v. *Benz,* 282 U.S. 304 (1931).

United States v. *Bitty,* 208 U.S. 393 (1907).

United States v. *Block,* 262 F. 205 (7th Cir. 1920).

United States v. *Brokan et al.,* 60 F. Supp. 100 (S.D. Ill. 1945).

United States v. *Candalaria,* 131 F. Supp. 797 (S.D. Cal. 1955).

United States v. *Carlisi,* 32 F. Supp. 479 (E.D.N.Y. 1940).

United States v. *Coolidge,* 25 F. Cas. 622 (No. 14,858) (C.C.D. Mass. 1815).

United States v. *Costello,* 350 U.S. 359 (1956).

United States v. *Curtiss-Wright Export Corp.,* 299 U.S. 304 (1936).

United States v. *Dickerson,* 168 F. Supp. 899 (D.C.D.C. 1959).

United States v. *42 Jars . . . Bee Royal Capsules,* 160 F. Supp. 818 (D.N.J. 1958).

United States v. *Furlong,* 18 U.S. (5 Wheat.) 184 (1820).

United States v. *Gilbert,* 25 F. Cas. 1287 (No. 15,204) (C.C.D. Mass 1834).

United States v. *Guest,* 383 U.S. 745 (1966).

United States v. *Heinze,* 218 U.S. 532 (1910).

United States v. *Janitz,* 161 F.2d 19 (3d Cir. 1947).

United States v. *Keen,* 27 F. Cas. 510, 686 (No. 15) (1939).

United States v. *Kissel,* 173 F. 823 (C.C.N.Y. 1909).

United States v. *LaFranca,* 282 U.S. 568 (1931).

United States v. *Lanza,* 260 U.S. 377 (1922).

United States ex rel. *Marcus* v. *Hess,* 317 U.S. 537 (1942).

United States v. *Michener,* 332 U.S. 784 (1947).

United States v. *Oppenheimer,* 242 U.S. 85 (1916).

United States v. *Parcon,* 6 Phil. 632 (1906).

United States ex rel. *Pasella* v. *Fenno,* 76 F. Supp. 203 (D. Conn. 1947).

United States v. *Perez,* 22 U.S. (9 Wheat.) 379 (1824).

United States v. *Potash,* 118 F.2d 54 (2d Cir. 1941).

United States v. *Rodgers,* 150 U.S. 259 (1893).

United States v. *Rosenwasser,* 145 F.2d 1015 (9th Cir. 1944).

United States v. *Sanges,* 144 U.S. 310 (1892).

United States v. *San Jacinto Tin Co.,* 125 U.S. 278 (1888).

United States v. *Segelman,* 86 F. Supp. 144 (D.C. Pa. 1949).

United States v. *Sherman,* 84 F. Supp. 130 (D.E.N.Y. 1947).

United States v. *Sinigar*, 6 U.S.C.M.A. 330, 20 C.M.R. 46 (U.S.Ct.M.A. 1955).

United States v. *Speed*, 78 F. Supp. 366 (D.C.D.C. 1948).

United States v. *Tateo*, 377 U.S. 463 (1964).

United States v. *Thompson*, 251 U.S. 407 (1920).

United States v. *Ulrici*, 102 U.S. 612 (1881).

United States v. *Whitlow*, 110 F. Supp. 871 (D.C. Cir. 1953).

United States v. *Williams*, 341 U.S. 58 (1951).

United States v. *Wilson*, 32 U.S. (7 Pet.) 150 (1883).

United States v. *Zimmerman*, 2 C.M.R. 66 (1952).

Vandercomb's Case, 2 Leach C.C. 780 (Gr. Brit. 1796).

Various Items of Personal Property v. *United States*, 282 U.S. 577 (1931).

Wade v. *Hunter*, 336 U.S. 684 (1949).

Waterloo Distilling Corp. v. *United States*, 282 U.S. 577 (1931).

Wetherel v. *Dary*, 76 Eng. Rep. 982 (Gr. Brit. K.B. 1588).

West v. *State*, 55 Fla. 200, 46 So. 93 (1908).

Westfall v. *United States*, 20 F.2d 604 (6th Cir. 1927).

Whaley v. *North Carolina*, 379 F.2d 22 (Ct. App. N.C. 1967).

White v. *R.*, 2 W.I.R. 268 (W. Indies Fed. Sup. Ct. 1960).

Williams v. *Commonwealth*, 78 Ky. 93 (1879).

Williams v. *Mayor and City Council of Baltimore*, 289 U.S. 36 (1928).

Williams v. *Oklahoma*, 358 U.S. 576 (1959).

Winn v. *State*, 82 Wis. 571, 52 N.W. 775 (1892).

Winsor v. *Queen*, L.R. 1 Q.B. 289, 122 Eng. Rep. 1150 (Gr. Brit. 1866).

Woodbury Corp. v. *Pick*, 41 F.2d 148 (1st Cir. 1930).

Wright v. *State*, 7 Tex. App. 152 (1884).

Wrublewski v. *McInerney*, 166 F.2d 243 (9th Cir. 1948).

Wurt v. *United States*, 240 U.S. 111 (1915).

Yates v. *United States*, 355 U.S. 66 (1957).

Young v. *People*, 54 Colo. 293, 130 P. 1011 (1913).

Young v. *Slaughterford*, 1 Queen Anne's Cases 217, 88 Eng. Rep. 999, 1007 (Gr. Brit. 1709).

Other Public Documents

Alabama. Code (1940).

——. Code (1954).

Arizona. Code (1939).

———. Revised Statutes (1941).

Arkansas. Statutes Annotated (1947).

California. Penal Code (1931).

Connecticut. General Statutes Revised (1958).

France. Code d'instruction criminelle (1958).

Georgia. Code Annotated (1948).

Idaho. Compiled Statutes (1919).

———. Code Annotated (1948).

Illinois. Revised Statutes (1959).

Indiana. Statutes Annotated (1933).

Iowa. Code Annotated (1949).

Kenya. Code of Criminal Procedure (1952).

Louisiana. Code of Criminal Procedure (1929).

Massachusetts Bay Colony. Habeas Corpus Act (1681).

Michigan. Statutes Annotated (1952).

Montana. Revised Code (1921).

Nevada. Compiled Laws (1929).

New Jersey. Statutes Annotated (1952).

New York. Penal Code (1919).

———. Criminal Code (1930).

North Atlantic Treaty Organization. Status of Forces Agreement (1950).

Oklahoma. Compiled Statutes (1921).

Pennsylvania. Statutes Annotated (1860).

Somalialand. The Laws of the Somalialand Protectorate (1950).

South Dakota. Code (1939).

Texas. Revised Criminal Statutes (1925).

———. Code of Criminal Procedure (1954).

United Kingdom (Great Britain). Statutes at Large: 44 Edward III (1369), 7 Henry IV (1406), 9 Henry V (1421), 33–34 Henry VI (1455), 16–22 Edward IV (1477–1482), 9 Henry VII (1504), 18 George II (1744), 37 George III (1797), 52–53 Victoria (1851), 20–21 George V (1930).

United States. Rules of Criminal Procedure.

———. Statutes at Large: Vol. XXX (1792), Vol. XXXIV (1907), Vol. LIV (1940), Vol. LXVI (1952), Vol. LXVIII (1954).

———. Uniform Code of Military Justice.

United States House of Representatives, Judiciary Committee. *Revision of Title 18, U.S. Code*, Report No. 304, 80th Cong., 1st Sess., 1947.

United States Senate, Judiciary Committee. *Revision of Title 18, U.S. Code,* Report No. 1620, 80th Cong. 2d Sess., 1948.

Utah. Code Annotated (1953).

Virginia. Code (1955).

Wisconsin. Statutes Annotated (1955).

——. Statutes Annotated (1958).

SECONDARY SOURCES

Books

Alexander, Franz. *The Criminal, the Judge and the Public.* Glencoe, Ill.: Free Press, 1956.

American Bar Association, Section on Criminal Law. *Proceedings.* Ed. W. Hickman. Chicago: American Bar Center, 1959.

American Bar Foundation. *The Administration of Criminal Justice.* Chicago: The Foundation, 1959.

American Law Institute. *Administration of the Criminal Law, Draft No. 1.* Chicago: The Institute, 1935.

——. *Model Penal Code, Tentative Draft No. 5.* Chicago: The Institute, 1956.

——. *Proceedings.* Chicago: The Institute, 1956.

Ancel, Marc, and Yvonne Marx. *Les codes pénaux européens.* 4 vols. Paris: Le Centre Français de Droit Comparé, 1957–60.

Balldon, William Paley (ed.). *Les reportes del cases in camera stellata.* London: Private printing, 1894.

Baker, Benjamin. *Urban Goverment.* Princeton: D. Van Nostrand, 1957.

Barnes, Harry Elmer, and Negley K. Teeters. *New Horizons in Criminology.* Englewood Cliffs, N.J.: Prentice-Hall, 1951.

Barton, R. T. (ed.). *Virginia Colonial Decisions: The Reports by Sir John Randolph and by Edward Barradall of Decisions of the General Court of Virginia 1728–1741.* Boston: N.pub., 1909.

Bell, Daniel. *The End of Ideology.* Glencoe, Ill.: Free Press, 1960.

Beutel, Frederick K. *Some Potentialities of Experimental Jurisprudence as a New Branch of Social Science.* Lincoln, Neb.: University of Nebraska Press, 1957.

Bigelow, Melville Madison. *History of Procedure in England.* Boston: Little, Brown, 1880.

Bishop, Joel P. *Commentaries on the Criminal Law.* 6th ed. Boston: Little, Brown, 1923.

Blackstone, William. *Commentaries on the Laws of England.* Worcester, Mass.: Isaiah Thomas, 1790.

Bonner, Robert J. *Lawyers and Litigants in Ancient Athens.* Chicago: University of Chicago Press, 1927.

Bouscaren, T. Lincoln, and Adam C. Ellis. *Canon Law.* Milwaukee: Bruce, 1955.

Bouton, Nathaniel (ed.). *Documents and Records Relating to Towns in New Hampshire.* Concord: State of New Hampshire, 1874.

Bowen, Catherine Drinker. *The Lion and the Throne.* Boston: Little, Brown, 1957.

Bracton, Henry de. *Bracton's Note Book.* Ed. F. W. Maitland. 2 vols. London: C. J. Clay, 1887.

Brant, Irving. *James Madison, Father of the Constitution, 1787–1800.* Indianapolis: Bobbs-Merrill, 1950.

Britton. *De Legibus Anglicanes.* Trans. Francis M. Nichols. Oxford: Clarendon Press, 1865.

Broom, Herbert. *A Selection of Legal Maxims.* Philadelphia: T. and J. W. Johnson, 1845.

Browne, William H., *et al.* (eds.). *Archives of Maryland.* 8 vols. Baltimore: State of Maryland, 1883.

Callison, I. P. *Courts of Injustice.* New York: Twayne, 1956.

Care, Henry. *English Liberties, or the Free-Born Subject's Inheritance.* Boston: N.pub., 1721.

Chitty, Joseph. *A Practical Treatise on the Criminal Law.* 2 vols. Philadelphia: Issac Riley, 1819.

Coke, Sir Edward. *The Third Part of the Institutes of the Laws of England.* 4th ed. London: Croone *et al.*, 1669.

Commissioners of the Public Records of the Kingdom. *Ancient Laws and Institutes of England.* London: The Commissioners, 1840.

Corbett, P. E. *Law and Society in the Relations of States.* New York: Harcourt, Brace, 1951.

Corwin, Edward S. *The Constitution and What It Means Today.* Princeton: Princeton University Press, 1958.

Criminal Code of Japan. Trans. Thomas L. Blakemore. Rutland, Vt.: Charles E. Tuttle, 1954.

Dagge, H. *Considerations on Criminal Law*. London: N.pub., 1772.

De Vabres, Donnedieu. *Traité de droit criminel*. 3d ed. Paris: University of Paris, 1947.

Devlin, Patrick. *The Criminal Prosecution in England*. New Haven: Yale University Press, 1958.

Documentary History of the United States. Washington: Government Printing Office, 1894.

Douglas, William O. *An Almanac of Liberty*. Garden City, N.Y.: Doubleday, 1954.

Eder, Phanor J. *A Comparative Study of Anglo-American and Latin-American Law*. New York: New York University Press, 1950.

Elliott, Jonathan. *The Debates on the Adoption of the Federal Constitution*. 2d ed. Washington: Government Printing Office, 1881.

Elstrodt, Johanna Hillegonda. *Das Anrechnungs und Erleidigungsprinzip (ne bis in idem) im internationalem Strafrecht der Schweiz*. Zurich: N.pub., 1932.

Esmein, A. *A History of Continental Criminal Procedure*. Boston: Little, Brown, 1913.

Farrand, Max (ed.). *The Laws and Liberties of Massachusetts*. Cambridge: Harvard University Press, 1929.

Federal Bureau of Investigation. *Uniform Crime Reports for the United States*. Washington: Government Printing Office, 1960.

Fellman, David. *The Defendant's Rights*. New York: Rinehart, 1958.

Finlason, W. F. (ed.). *Reeve's History of the English Law*. 6 vols. London: Reeve's and Turner, 1869.

Fleta. Trans. H. C. Richardson. Selden Society; London: Bernard Quarich, 1955.

Frank, Martin M. *Diary of a D.A.* New York: Henry Holt, 1957.

Fuller, Hugh N. *Criminal Justice in Virginia*. New York: Century, 1931.

Glanville, Ranulph de. *A Treatise on the Laws and Customs of the Kingdom of England in the Time of King Henry the Second*. Trans. John Beames. Washington: John Byrne, 1900.

Glueck, Sheldon. *Crime and Correction: Selected Papers*. Cambridge: Addison-Wells, 1952.

Goebel, Julius Jr. *Law Enforcement in Colonial New York*. New York: Commonwealth Fund, 1944.

Gsovski, Vladimir, and Kazimierz Grzybowski (eds.). *The Laws and Courts in the Soviet Union and Eastern Europe.* 2 vols. London: Stevens, 1959.

Greenidge, A. H. J. *The Legal Procedure of Cicero's Time.* Oxford: Clarendon Press, 1901.

Gutteridge, H. C. *Comparative Law.* Cambridge: Cambridge University Press, 1946.

Hale, Sir Matthew. *The History of the Pleas of the Crown.* 3 vols. Philadelphia: Robert H. Small, 1847.

Hall, Jerome. *Theft, Law and Society.* 2d ed. Indianapolis: Bobbs-Merrill, 1952.

Hamilton, William Baskerville. *Anglo-American Law on the Frontier.* Durham, N.C.: Duke University Press, 1953.

Haskins, George Lee. *Law and Authority in Early Massachusetts.* New York: Macmillan, 1960.

Hawkins, William. *A Treatise of the Pleas of the Crown.* London: N.pub., 1716.

Holdsworth, W. S. *A History of English Law.* 21 vols. London: Methuen, 1903.

Lunden, Walter A. *A Quarter Century of Criminal Justice in Iowa.* Des Moines: Iowa State University Press, 1960.

McMaster, John Bach, and Frederick D. Stone. *Pennsylvania and the Federal Convention.* Lancaster: Historical Society of Pennsylvania, 1888.

McWhinney, Edward (ed.). *Canadian Jurisprudence.* Toronto: Carswell, 1958.

—— (ed.). *Select Pleas of the Crown.* Selden Society; London: Bernard Quaritch, 1888.

—— (ed.). *Yearbook of Edward II.* 2 vols. Selden Society; London: Bernard Quaritch, 1904.

—— (ed.). *Yearbook of Edward III.* 4 vols. Selden Society; London: Bernard Quaritch, 1904.

Marcus, Phillip. *Proceedings of the Governor's Conference on Crime, the Criminal and Society.* Albany: State of New York, 1935.

Mason, A. T., and W. M. Beaney. *American Constitutional Law.* 2d ed. Englewood Cliffs, N.J.: Prentice-Hall, 1959.

Missouri Association for Criminal Justice. *The Missouri Crime Survey.* New York: Macmillan, 1920.

Mueller, Gerhard O. W. *Annual Survey of American Law—1958.* New York: New York University School of Law, 1959.

Murray, James A. H. (ed.). *A New English Dictionary on Historical Principles.* Oxford: Clarendon Press, 1901.

O'Conner, Austin. *An Analysis of and a Guide to the New Criminal Code of Canada.* Toronto: Carswell, 1955.

Oppenheim, Lassa F. L. *International Law.* 7th ed. London: Longman's Green, 1948.

Padover, Saul K. *The Complete Madison.* New York: Harper, 1953.

Palmer, H. A., and Henry Palmer. *Wilshere's Criminal Procedure.* London: Sweet and Maxwell, 1954.

Perry, Richard L., and John C. Cooper. *Sources of Our Liberties.* New York: Associated College Presses, 1959.

Pollock, Sir Frederick, and Frederick W. Maitland. *A History of English Law.* 2d ed. Cambridge: Cambridge University Press, 1899.

Poore, Benjamin P. (comp.). *The Federal and State Constitutions, Colonial Charters, and Other Organic Laws of the United States.* 8 vols. Washington: Government Printing Office, 1878.

Pound, Roscoe. *Criminal Justice in America.* New York: Henry Holt, 1930.

—— and Felix Frankfurter (eds.). *Criminal Justice in Cleveland.* Cleveland: Cleveland Foundation, 1922.

Pritchett, C. Herman. *The Roosevelt Court: A Study in Judicial Politics and Values.* New York: Macmillan, 1948.

Puttkammer, Ernst W. *Administration of Criminal Law.* Chicago: University of Chicago Press, 1953.

Radin, Max. *Handbook of Anglo-American Legal History.* St. Paul, Minn.: West, 1936.

Radzinowicz, Leon. *A History of English Criminal Law and Its Administration since 1850.* 3 vols. New York: Macmillan, 1948.

—— and J. W. C. Turner (eds.). *The Modern Approach to Criminal Law.* London: Macmillan, 1941.

Rutland, Robert Allen. *The Birth of the Bill of Rights.* Chapel Hill: University of North Carolina Press, 1955.

Schubert, Glendon A. *Quantitative Analysis of Judicial Behavior.* Glencoe, Ill.: Free Press, 1959.

——. *Constitutional Politics.* New York: Holt, Rinehart and Winston, 1960.

Scott, Arthur P. *Criminal Law in Colonial Virginia.* Chicago: University of Chicago Press, 1930.

Scott, S. P. (trans.). *Digest of Justinian.* 20 vols. Cincinnati: Law Forum, 1932.

Seale, William. *Law, the Science of Inefficiency.* New York: Macmillan, 1952.

Sirey, I. *Code d'instruction criminelle.* 4th ed. Paris: University of Paris, 1903.

Stephen, Sir James Fitzjames. *A History of the Criminal Law of England.* 12 vols. London: Macmillan, 1883.

Stubbs, William. *The Constitutional History of England.* Oxford: Clarendon Press, 1880.

Sutherland, Edwin H., and Donald R. Cressey. *Principles of Criminology.* New York: J. B. Lippincott, 1955.

Szirmal, Z. (ed.). *The Federal Criminal Law in the Soviet Union.* Leyden, Neth.: A. W. Sythoff, 1959.

Taft, Donald R. *Criminology, a Cultural Interpretation.* New York: Macmillan, 1942.

Thomas, J. H. *A Systematic Arrangement of Lord Coke's First Institute on the Plan of Sir Matthew Hale's Analysis.* 4 vols. Philadelphia: Robert H. Small, 1826.

Thurstone, L. L., and J. W. Degan. *A Factorial Study of the Supreme Court.* (Psychometric Laboratory Report No. 64.) Chicago: University of Chicago Press, 1951.

Upton, Richard F. *Revolutionary New Hampshire.* Hanover: State of New Hampshire, 1936.

Viner, Charles. *A General Abridgement of Law and Equity.* 20 vols.; 2d ed. London: G.G.J. & J. Robinson, 1793.

Von Bar, Carl Ludwig. *A History of Continental Criminal Law.* Boston: Little, Brown, 1916.

Wagner, W. J. *The Federal States and Their Judiciary.* 's-Gravenhage, Neth.: Mouton, 1959.

Whitmore, W. H. (ed.). *The Colonial Laws of Massachusetts.* Boston: State of Massachusetts, 1889.

Whittaker, William J. (ed.). *The Mirror of Justices.* Selden Society; London: Bernard Quaritch, 1895.

Wood, Arthur Evans, and John Barker Waite. *Crime and Its Treatment.* New York: American Book Co., 1941.

Articles

Abe, Harue. "Criminal Procedure in Japan," 48 *Journal of Criminal Law and Criminology* 365 (1957).

Allen, Frances A. "The Supreme Court, Federalism, and State Systems of Criminal Justice," 8 *DePaul Law Review* 213 (1958).

Ancel, Marc. "Observations on the International Comparison of Criminal Statistics," 2 *International Review of Criminal Policy* 43 (United Nations, 1952)

Appleton, Richard B. "Reforms in Japanese Criminal Procedure under Allied Occupation," 24 *Washington Law Review* 401 (1949).

Baker, Newman F., and Earl H. De Long. "The Prosecuting Attorney: Powers and Duties in Criminal Prosecution," 24 *Journal of Criminal Law and Criminology* 1025 (1934).

Batchelder, Charles E. "Former Jeopardy," 17 *American Law Review* 748 (1883).

Beattie, Ronald H. "Criminal Statistics in the United States—1960," 51 *Journal of Criminal Law, Criminology and Police Science* 65 (1960).

Berg, Raymond K. "Criminal Procedure: France, England, and the United States," 8 *DePaul Law Review* 256 (1958).

Bigelow, John O. "Former Conviction and Former Acquittal," 11 *Rutgers Law Review* 490 (1957)

Binkley, W. "The Prosecuting Attorney in Ohio—An Obsolete Office," 18 *National Municipal Review* 572 (1929).

Byrant, John D. "Note," 45 *Cornell Law Quarterly* 579 (1960).

Cahn, Edmond. "The Consumers of Injustice," 34 *New York University Law Review* 1166 (1959).

Calvert, Harry. "The Vitality of Case-Law under a Criminal Code," 22 *Modern Law Review* 638 (1959).

Comley, William H. "Former Jeopardy," 35 *Yale Law Journal* 678 (1926).

"A Comparative Study of Criminal Law Administration in the United States and Great Britain," 50 *Journal of Criminal Law and Criminology* 67 (1959).

"Conflicts between State Statutes and Municipal Ordinances," 72 *Harvard Law Review* 747 (1958).

Crowe, Judson A. "Double Jeopardy and Courts-Martial," 3 *Minnesota Law Review* 181 (1919).

Dangel, Edward M. "Double Jeopardy in Massachusetts," 16 *Boston University Law Review* 384 (1936).

Dession, George H., and Harold D. Lasswell. "Public Order under Law: The Role of the Advisor-Draftsmen in the Formation of the Code or Constitution," 65 *Yale Law Journal* 192 (1955).

"Double Jeopardy," 24 *Minnesota Law Review* 561 (1940).

"Double Jeopardy and the Concept of Identity of Offenses," 7 *Brooklyn Law Review* 80 (1937).

Einstein, Joseph H. "Allowable Unit of Criminal Prosecution," 16 *Intramural Law Review* 139 (1961).

Ewing, Samuel E., III, and George Lee Haskins. "The Spread of Massachusetts Law in the Seventeenth Century," 106 *University of Pennsylvania Law Review* 413 (1958).

Ferguson, Clarence C., Jr. "Formulation of Enforcement Policy: An Anatomy of the Prosecutor's Discretion Prior to Accusation," 11 *Rutgers Law Review* 511 (1957).

Fischer, Walter T. "Double Jeopardy," 28 *University of Chicago Law Review* 592 (1961).

Fox, Sanford J. "Statutory Criminal Law," 52 *Journal of Criminal Law and Criminology and Police Science* 392 (1961).

Franck, Thomas. "An International Lawyer Looks at the Bartkus Case," 34 *New York University Law Review* 1103 (1959).

Frank, Jerome. "A Plea for Lawyer-Schools," 56 *Yale Law Journal* 1303 (1947).

———. "Civil Law Influences in the Common Law—Some Reflections on 'Comparative' and 'Contrastive' Law," 104 *University of Pennsylvania Law Review* 887 (1956).

Goldstein, Abraham S. "The State and the Accused: Balance of Advantage in Criminal Procedure," 69 *Yale Law Journal* 1173 (1960).

Goodhart, A. L. "Acquitting the Guilty," 70 *Law Quarterly Review* 514 (1954).

Grant, J. A. C. "The Lanza Rule of Successive Prosecution," 32 *Columbia Law Review* 1309 (1932).

———. "Penal Ordinances and the Guarantee against Double Jeopardy," 25 *Georgetown Law Journal* 294 (1937).

———. "Successive Prosecutions by State and Nation: Common Law and British Empire Comparison," 4 *U.C.L.A. Law Review* 1 (1956).

Greaves, H. R. G. "Bentham on Legislative Procedure," 33 *Economica,* No. 35, 308 (1931).

Gross, Alan D. "Successive Prosecution by City and State," 43 *Oregon Law Review* 251 (1964).

Grzybowski, Kazimierz. "Soviet Criminal Law Reform of 1958," 35 *Indiana Law Journal* 129 (1960).

Hall, Jerome. "Objectives of Federal Criminal Procedural Revision," 51 *Yale Law Journal* 728 (1942).

Hanus, Jerome J. "Denial of Certiorari and Supreme Court Policy-Making," 17 *American University Law Review* 41 (1967).

20 *Harvard Law Review* 643 n. (1907).

Harvey, O. B. "Former Jeopardy," 10 *Virginia Law Review* 411 (1904).

Haskins, George Lee. "Codification of the Law in Colonial Massachusetts: A Study in Comparative Law," 30 *Indiana Law Journal* 1 (1954).

Hobbs, Sam Earle. "Prosecutor's Bias, an Occupational Disease," 2 *Alabama Law Review* 51 (1949).

Horack, Frank. "The Multiple Consequences of a Single Criminal Act," 21 *Minnesota Law Review* 805 (1937).

35 *Indiana Law Journal* 445 n. (1960).

Ireland, Gordon. "Double Jeopardy annd Conspiracy in the Federal Courts," 40 *Journal of Criminal Law, Criminology and Political Science* 447 (1949).

Jackson, Robert H. "The Federal Prosecutor," 31 *Journal of Criminal Law and Criminology* 3 (1940).

Jacob, Herbert. "Politics and Criminal Prosecution in New Orleans," 8 *Tulane Studies in Political Science* 77 (1963).

Jones, Margaret. "What Constitutes Double Jeopardy?" 38 *Journal of Criminal Law, Criminology and Police Science* 383 (1947).

Kirchheimer, Otto. "The Act, the Offense, and Double Jeopardy," 58 *Yale Law Journal* 513 (1949).

Kirk, Marion S. "Jeopardy during the Period of the Yearbooks," 82 *University of Pennsylvania Law Review* 602 (1934).

Kline, A. M. "New Principles of Criminal Law in the U.S.S.R.," 7 *Review of Contemporary Law* 114 (1959).

Kneier, Charles M. "Prosecution under State Law and Municipal Ordinance as Double Jeopardy," 16 *Cornell Law Quarterly* 208 (1931).

Knowlton, Robert E. "Criminal Law and Procedure," 11 *Rutgers Law Review* 94 (1957).

Laws, Bolitha J. "Criminal Courts annd Adult Probation," 3 *National Parole & Probation Association Journal* 354 (1957).

Lipson, Leon. "The New Face of 'Socialist Legality,'" 7 *Problems of Communism* 25 (1959).

Love, Murray S., and Raymond A. Thistle. "Double Jeopardy and the Necessity Rule," 14 *University of Pittsburgh Law Review*, 588 (1953).

McDougal, Myres S. "The Comparative Study of Law for Policy Purposes: Value Clarification as an Instrument of Democratic World Order," 1 *American Journal of Comparative Law* 24 (1952).

——. "Law as a Process of Decision: A Policy-Oriented Approach to Legal Study," 1 *National Law Forum* 53 (1956).

McLaren, I. "The Doctrine of Res Judicata as Applied to the Trial of Criminal Cases," 10 *Washington Law Review* 198 (1935).

Mannheim, Herman. "Developments in Criminal Law and Criminology in Post-War Britain," 51 *Journal of Criminal Law, Criminology and Police Science* 600 (1961).

Mayers, Daniel K., and Fletcher L. Yarbrough. "*Bis Vexari:* New Trials and Successive Prosecutions," 74 *Harvard Law Review* 37 (1960).

Miller, Justin. "Appeal by the State in Criminal Cases," 36 *Yale Law Journal* 493 (1927).

——. "The Historical Relation of Estoppel by Record to Res Judicata," 35 *Illinois Law Review* 41 (1940).

Moran, Gerard R. "The Future of the Criminal Law: Criminal Law in Its Modern Public Law Context," 11 *Rutgers Law Review* 587 (1957).

Mueller, Gerhard O. W. "Teaching Comparative Law," 49 *Journal of Criminal Law, Criminology and Police Science* 103 (1958).

National Association of County and Prosecuting Attorneys. "Report," 50 *Journal of Criminal Law, Criminology and Police Science* 67 (1959).

Nedrud, Duane R. "The Career Prosecutor, Part 111," 51 *Journal of Criminal Law, Criminology and Police Science* 649 (1961).

61 *Northwestern University Law Review* 521 n. (1953).

Parker, Frank J. "Some Aspects of Double Jeopardy," 25 *St. Johns Law Review* 188 (1951).

Payne, H. "The Doctrine of Previous Jeopardy," 62 *Century Law Journal* 295 (1906).

Platz, William A. "The Criminal Code," *Wisconsin Law Review* 353 (1956).

Pound, Roscoe. "Cooperation in Enforcement of Law," 17 *American Bar Association Journal* 9 (1931).

——. "A Comparison of Ideals of Law," *Mémoires de l'Académie Internationale de Droit Comparé*, II (Paris: The Academy, 1935), 209.

"Prosecutor's Discretion," 103 *University of Pennsylvania Law Review* 1057 (1955).

Remington, Frank J. "Criminal Law Revision: Codification vs. Piecemeal Appeal," 33 *Nebraska Law Review* 400 (1954).

——. "Criminal Justice Research," 51 *Journal of Criminal Law and Criminology and Police Science* 12 (1960).

Rogge, O. John. "Immunity from Self-Incrimination under the Federal Compulsory Testimony Act," 46 *Journal of Criminal Law and Criminology and Police Science* 680 (1956).

Rose, Arnold M., and Arthur E. Prell. "Does the Punishment Fit the Crime?" 61 *American Journal of Sociology* 259 (1955).

Saxbe, William A. "Functions of the Office of Attorney General of Ohio," 6 *Cleveland-Marshall Law Review* 323 (1957).

Schafer, Stephen. "Hungarian Criminal Law," 22 *Modern Law Review* 172 (1959).

Schmideberg, Melitta. "The Offender's Attitude toward Punishment," 51 *Journal of Criminal Law, Criminology and Police Science* 332 (1960).

Schwartz, L. B. "Federal Criminal Jurisdiction and Prosecutor's Discretion," 13 *Law and Contemporary Problems* 73 (1948).

Schwenk, L. "Criminal Law in Germany," 15 *Tulane Law Review* 541 (1941).

Sears, Roy W. "The Illinois Double Jeopardy Act: An Empty Gesture," 51 *Journal of Criminal Law, Criminology and Police Science* 236 (1960).

Slovenko, Ralph. "The Law on Double Jeopardy," 30 *Tulane Law Review* 428 (1955).

Smith, J. Denson. "How Louisiana Prepared and Adopted a Criminal Code," 41 *Journal of Criminal Law, Criminology and Police Science* 126 (1950).

Snee, Joseph M., and A. Kenneth Pye. "Due Process in Criminal Procedure: A Comparison of Two Systems," 21 *Ohio State Law Journal* 467 (1960).

"Statutory Implementation of Double Jeopardy Clauses: New Life for a Moribund Constitutional Guarantee," 65 *Yale Law Journal* 344 (1956).

Steffen, Roscoe T. "Concerning Double Jeopardy and the New Rules," 7 *Federal Bar Journal* 92 (1945).

Stone, Ferdinand Fairfax. "A Primer on Codification," 29 *Tulane Law Review* 304 (1955).

Sunderland, Louis. "Circumventing the Corrupt Prosecutor," 48 *Journal of Criminal Law, Criminology and Police Science* 537 (1958).

"Trial by Persistence," 4 *Stanford Law Review* 537 (1952).

14 *University of Pittsburgh Law Review* 583 n. (1953).

U.S. News and World Report, Sept. 26, 1960, 64.

Van Alstyne, W. Scott. "The District Attorney—a Historical Puzzle," *Wisconsin Law Review* (1952), p. 126.

Van Vechten, C. C. "The Reliability of Criminal Statistics," 26 *Journal of Criminal Law, Criminology and Police Science* 10 (1954).

Vouin, Robert. "The Protection of the Accused in French Criminal Procedure," 5 *International and Comparative Law Quarterly* 173 (1956).

Wagner, Wienczyslaw J. "Codification in Europe and the Codification Movement in the Middle of the 19 Century in the United States," 2 *St. Louis University Law Journal* 359 (1953).

Wang, Huai Ming. "Chinese and American Criminal Law: Some Comparisons," 46 *Journal of Criminal Law, Criminology and Police Science* 798 (1955).

Warren, A. "A State Department of Justice," 21 *American Bar Association Journal* 495 (1935).

Wechsler, Herbert. "The Challenge of a Model Penal Code," 65 *Harvard Law Review* 1097 (1952).

Williams, Paul W. "Through the Looking Glass: The Office of the United States Attorney," 3 *Practical Lawyer* 49 (1957).

——. "The Prosecutor and Civil Rights," 13 *Record of the Bar Association of the City of New York* 129 (1958).

Wolff, Hans Joseph. "German Criminal Justice," 43 *Michigan Law Review* 171 (1944).

Wood, Arthur Lewis. "Informal Relations in the Practice of Criminal Law," 62 *American Journal of Sociology* 54 (1956).

40 *Yale Law Journal* 469 n. (1931).

57 *Yale Law Journal* 133 n. (1947).

Zinn, Charles S. "Revision of the United States Criminal Code," 51 *Law Library Journal* 394 (1958).

Newspapers

New Jersey Law Journal, April 25, 1957.

New York Times, April 6, 1959; Dec. 3, 1959; June 13, 1961.

Draft Documents

American Law Institute. "Double Jeopardy," *Commentaries on the Administration of the Criminal Law—Official Draft* (Chicago: The Institute, 1935).

——. *Model Penal Code, Tentative Draft* (Chicago: The Institute, 1956).

——. *Model Penal Code, Proposed Official Draft* (Philadelphia: The Institute, 1962).

Unpublished Materials

Anonymous. "Constitutional Rights in the United States and the Criminal Laws of Turkey." Mimeographed article, Library of Congress, 1950.

Cole, George F. "The Decision to Prosecute." Mimeographed article, American Political Science Association, 1968.

Dession, George H. "Code of Correction." Unpub. MS, Yale Law School, 1955.

Eisenstein, James. "The Federal Prosecutor and His Environment." Mimeographed article, American Political Science Association, 1968.

Index

DATE DUE

GAYLORD

PRINTED IN U.S.A.